Safety and Rescue

www ... om

First published in Great Britain 1998
by Pesda Press
'Elidir'
Ffordd Llanllechid
Rachub
Bangor
Gwynedd
LL57 3EE

Reprinted 2000

ISBN 0 - 9531956 - 0 - 0

Printed by Technographic, Colchester Essex

Acknowledgements

When I first started this project I never realised just how many people would be involved in one way or another. I just pray that I don't forget to thank anyone!

My wife Joan and our daughters Lisa and Anna for putting up with me spending so much precious time that could have been spent in their company.

The too many to list people who have influenced my knowledge of, and approach to, white water safety and rescue over the years. In particular Ray Rowe who first introduced me to 'serious' (but fun) white water paddling.

Loel Collins, Kevin Danforth, Joan Ferrero, Tony Ferrero, Ray Goodwin, Tim Harvey, Dave Luke, Graham Mackereth, Paul O'Sullivan, Chris Sladden and Bob Timms, for proof reading and/or technical advice of one sort or another.

Colin Broadway, Dave Cheetham, Iain Peter, and Ken Vickers for valuable advice on publishing and marketing matters.

Dave Siviter for helping out with any computer related problems.

Plas y Brenin and Canolfan Tryweryn for their encouragement and unrestricted use of their facilities. In particular Martin Doyle for accepting ridiculous requests for time off at short notice when those deadlines were looming, without a murmur!

Loel Collins, Ray Goodwin, Lara Tipper, Paul O'Sullivan, John Moxham, Chris Sladden, Palm and Pyranha for the use of their photographs, and Bob Timms who took most of the technical shots.

Danny Jones for his cartoons and Barney Caulfield of Palm for the drawings which formed the basis of the drawings and diagrams I put together in Photoshop.

Becky Goodsell, Rachel Gregory, Mitesh Makanjee, Andy Morris, Sarah Phillips and Richard Townsend for being 'models' for the photo sessions.

Last but by no means least, Andy Knight of Palm Equipment International, without whose moral and financial support, this book would not have been feasible.

Dedication

To the memory of 'Ack' Hairon. Without his encouragement and practical support, neither I, nor his son Derek, would have been able to take up kayaking and get into so many scrapes at such a young age.

Contents

Introduction

The writing of this book started when I tried to put some notes together as course notes for the safety and rescue courses I was running at Plas y Brenin. It soon became clear what a huge topic it is and in sheer frustration I explained to a friend that I would have to write a book to cover it properly. His answer was, "Why don't you?"

This is the result. I hope you find it enjoyable and informative.

Learning About Safety and Rescue

The point of safety and rescue training is that there is rarely the time to develop a technique during a life threatening emergency. Paddlers must already be in possession of a range of techniques that will allow them to solve the problem quickly. There isn't the time to re-invent the wheel. New techniques are often developed in training and practise situations.

There are three parts to becoming a safe and effective paddler and rescuer:

- knowledge
- training
- experience

This book can only provide the knowledge. It is important that the reader should consider attending practical safety and rescue courses in order to evaluate a range of techniques under controlled conditions. This will also ensure that the techniques are fully and correctly understood.

For those who already have a good deal of training and experience the book will be useful as an 'aide-memoire', and probably cover some areas that are new to the reader.

Practise

Like all skills, safety and rescue skills need to be practised; initially to become competent and thereafter to maintain competence. Great care should be taken in selecting suitable sites, where the skills can be practised in controlled conditions. Nothing could be worse than to be, or see a friend, injured whilst practising how to stay safe! It is also important to try and practise as a team with the people you normally paddle with.

Structure

This book is in four parts. The order they are in reflects the importance that I attach to them.

Part One deals with safety, which is about staying out of trouble in the first place.

Part Two is about rescuing **people.** This is what we do when our safety has failed.

Part Three is about caring for and evacuating people who are physically or emotionally injured.

Part Four is primarily about recovering equipment.

Terminology

The following words are given specific meanings for the purposes of this book:

Paddler means anyone who paddles on white water.

Boater means kayakers and canoeists.

Where there is a Standard American English word in 'paddle speak' that is different from Standard English, it is indicated by italics and single quotation marks, i.e. weir, *'low head dam'.*

Gender

Despite being rich in words, English has a simple grammar which can't cope with the equal opportunities world we live in. Unless the context implies otherwise, 'he', 'him' and 'his' are used as neuter words, and could refer to a male or female person.

Disclaimer

Many of the safety and rescue techniques described in this book are intended for use in specific circumstances, and may be hazardous if applied inappropriately by unskilled or insufficiently trained paddlers. The onus is on the reader to apply the techniques described appropriately and correctly. These techniques are best learned and practised under the guidance of a qualified instructor.

PART

WHITE WATER SAFETY

I

"Safety is the art of staying out of trouble."

Chapter 1
Principles of Safety

White water safety can appear a complex subject. However, it can be distilled into a few basic principles. These should be constantly borne in mind when reading the rest of this section.

Principle of Mutual Support

"Boaters should paddle as a mutually supportive team."

This involves safeguarding each other physically, and supporting each other psychologically.

Principle of Line of Sight

"Never run anything blind."

Paddlers can only choose a line and assess the level of risk if they are in a position to see what is coming. All members of the group should remain in the line of sight of at least one other member of the group.

Principle of Calculated Risk

"Every paddler should assess the risks involved in paddling a section of white water."

Individuals should decide how high a risk they can justify taking and assess what risk any given section of water poses for them. This is more likely to occur in the positive environment created by a supportive team.

Principle of Clear Communication

"Misunderstandings must be avoided at all costs."

Signals, instructions and briefings must be simple, clear and concise. Do not make assumptions. If necessary, question to check understanding.

When using signals:

- Point at where to go, rather than at the hazard
- Confirm understanding by repeating the same signal

Principle of Prevention

"Prevention is better than cure."

Enough said!

Chapter 2
Reading White Water

Knowledge is power. Only by understanding how moving water behaves can we use it, and by so doing avoid unnecessary or unacceptable levels of danger.

Directions

When giving directions or describing a feature on a river it is important to use the same language so as to avoid misunderstandings. The terms we use are:

- Upstream
- Downstream
- River Left
- River Right

Upstream is where the water is flowing from and downstream is where it is flowing to. River right and left are simply right and left when facing downstream. (Fig. 2.1).

Straight Section of River

As a general rule, when a river is running in a straight line the current is strongest in the middle and weakest near the banks. (Fig. 2.1).

Main Flow

Away from the friction caused by contact with the banks, the current flows at its fastest. The layer nearest the river bed is the slowest and the layer just beneath the surface is the fastest. This is because the surface layer is slowed down a little by the friction caused by contact with the air.

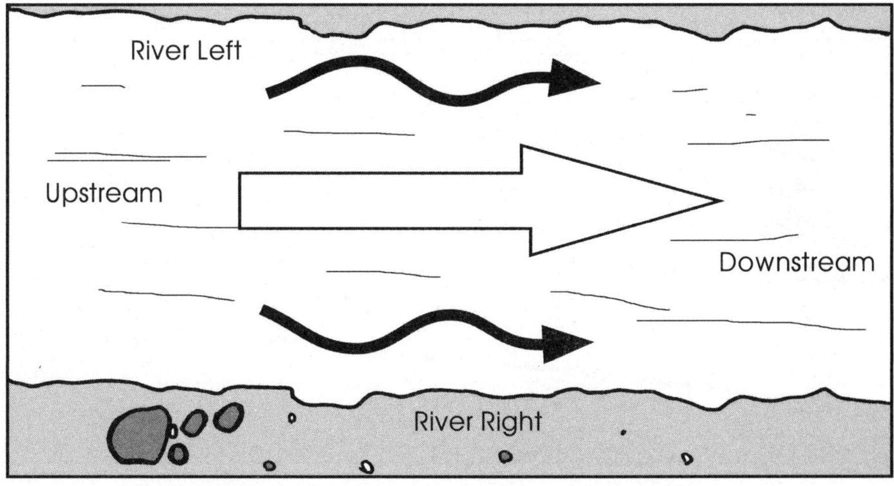

Fig. 2.1 The water flow on a straight section of river.

Fig. 2.2 The current caused by the Helical Flow, (cross-section).

Helical Flow

The friction provided by the banks slows the current down and causes it to spiral in such a way that the surface water near the edges of a fast flowing, straight sided river can push a swimmer away from the bank. (Fig. 2.2) Therefore one should never assume that swimmers are safe, even if they are swimming strongly, until they are actually out of the water and on the bank. Despite this, it is far easier to get ashore against the relatively slow helical flow than where the powerful main flow sets into the bank.

There may be a shallow counter current very close in to the bank. These create minute eddies that can be exploited by the boater. However, because they are relatively shallow, they are of little help to a swimmer.

Flood Channels

Where the banks of a watercourse are smooth sided there may be no helical flow and the main flow runs right up to the bank. This usually happens in man made structures such as flood relief channels and canalised rivers.

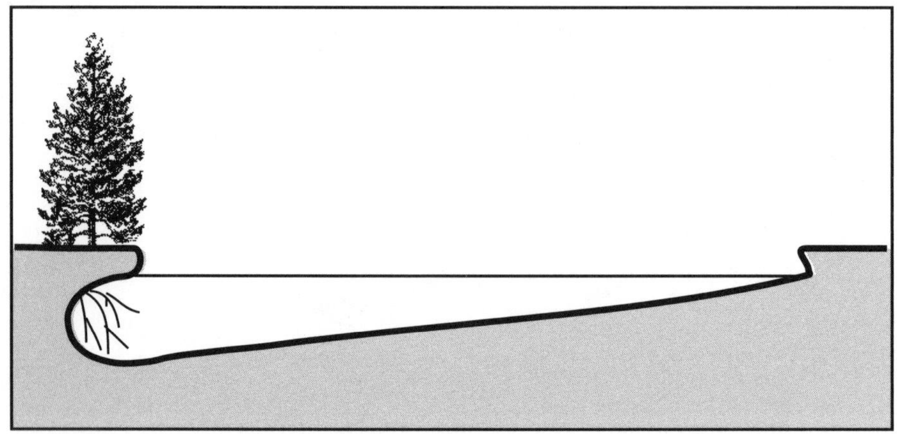

Fig. 2.3 Erosion of bank caused by water flowing around the outside of a bend.

Bends

The main current will always go towards the outside of a bend. (Fig. 2.4). On the outside of a bend the water is deep and fast where the main flow sets right into the bank. On the inside it is slow and shallow. Because of the erosion thus caused, undercut banks and overhanging trees are often a hazard. Undercut banks can be doubly dangerous, as there may be tree roots or debris, which can act as a 'strainer' and trap a swimmer. (Fig. 2.3).

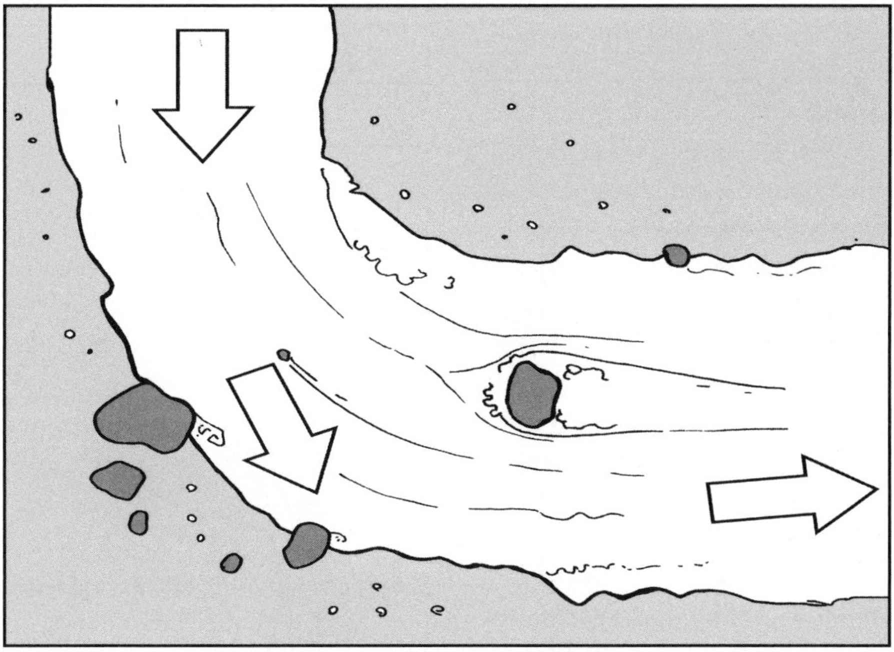

Fig. 2.4 The main flow being forced to the outside of the bend.

Upstream and Downstream 'V's

Rocks that are just above or just below the surface are usually indicated by a 'V' shape on the surface of the water. The point of the letter 'V' is pointing upstream.

Conversely, the route taken by the main flow of water is indicated by a letter 'V' shape whose point is pointing downstream. (Fig. 2.5). This 'tongue' of clear water usually indicates the best route.

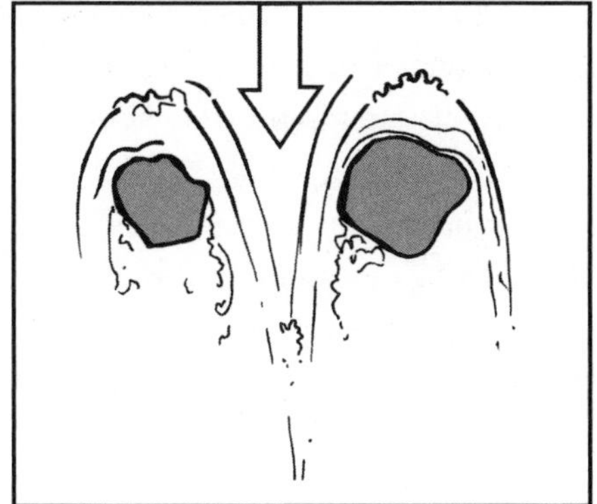

Fig 2.5 Upstream and downstream 'V's, viewed from above.

Rooster Tails

In a fast flowing river which has a steep gradient, a rock that is only just covered may be indicated by a 'rooster tail', a plume of white frothy water. (Fig. 2.6)

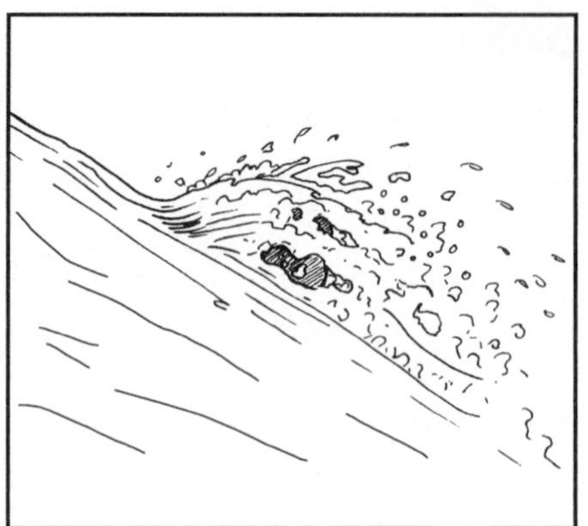

Fig. 2.6 A rooster tail.

Eddies

Wherever flowing water is forced around an obstruction, an 'eddy' is formed. This is caused by a counter current flowing in the opposite direction to the main flow, to fill what would otherwise be a hole! (Fig. 2.7).

Eddies are usually places of relative calm in which we can rest, or pause to read the next section of rapid, before we commit ourselves to paddling it. We often paddle a river by hopping from one safe eddy to another. This can be visualised by imagining the main flow of the river as a fast moving conveyor belt and the eddies as a series of stable platforms which we can hop on to, in order to rest and get our bearings.

In slow flowing or low volume technical rivers, eddies are usually calm places. In fast flowing, high volume rivers, the counter current can be fast flowing and the water in the eddy fairly turbulent.

In the worst case scenario the recirculating current in an eddy can feed you straight back into the main current, or into a hazard you were trying to avoid.

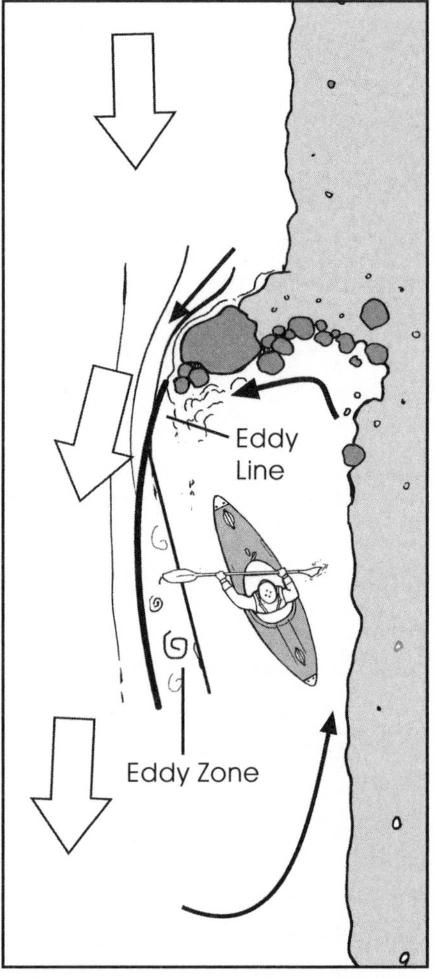

Fig 2.7 An eddy with a kayaker paddling across the eddy-line at a 45° angle.

Eddy Lines

The eddy-line or *'eddy fence'* is a visible line on the surface of the water that marks the border between the main flow and the counter current. Think of it as the point where the edge of the conveyor belt meets the platform. When one aims to break-in, *('eddy-out')*, or break-out, *(eddy-in)*, at an angle of, say 45 degrees, the angle is between the direction of travel and the main flow, which is not necessarily the same as the general direction that the river is heading in.

Eddy Zones

On less powerful rivers the line between the eddy and the main current will be quite distinct at the top of the eddy. However, the line will gradually become less distinct and broaden so that it becomes a zone rather than a line.

In powerful flows this zone may be full of swirls and boils. For this reason it is generally a good idea to cross an eddy line as high up the eddy as possible. If a boater has to cross lower down he will need to get his boat moving as fast as possible to have enough momentum to carry him clear across the zone.

Standing Waves

Standing waves are formed when fast flowing water hits a layer of relatively still water. The waves that are formed are of 'green' water, i.e. water that isn't full of air bubbles, although the very top of the wave may curl over and therefore be a little frothy. (Fig. 2.8 and 2.9).

The waves produced appear to be jogging on the spot. Paddling downstream straight over them is like riding a roller-coaster.

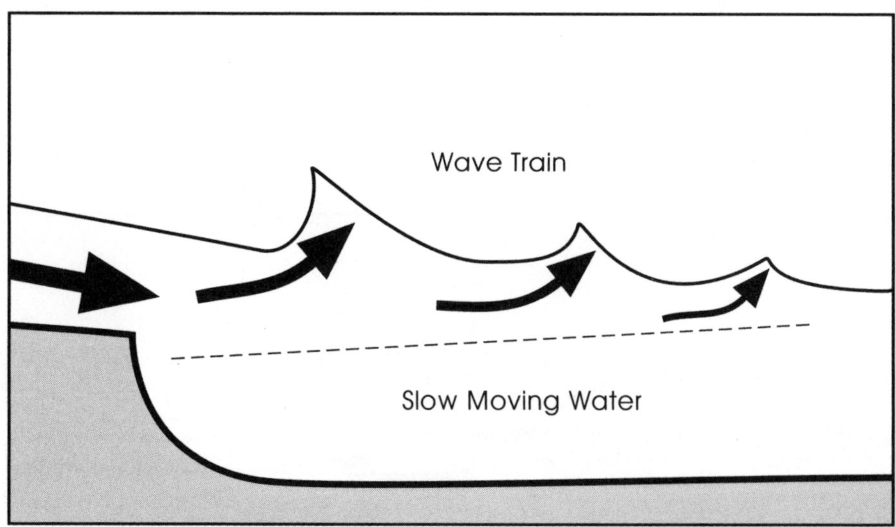

Fig. 2.8 Cross-sectional view of standing waves seen from the side.

On most rivers they make great play-spots, where boaters can practice their surfing skills. When paddling on volume rivers, we can use them to surf from one side of the river to the other, thereby saving energy. Boaters can also use them to turn more easily by timing the turn so that it is executed at the top of the wave, when only the centre section of the boat is in the water. A bit like skiing a 'mogul'.

Last but not least, the top of a standing wave can be a great place from which to get a view of the river to come.

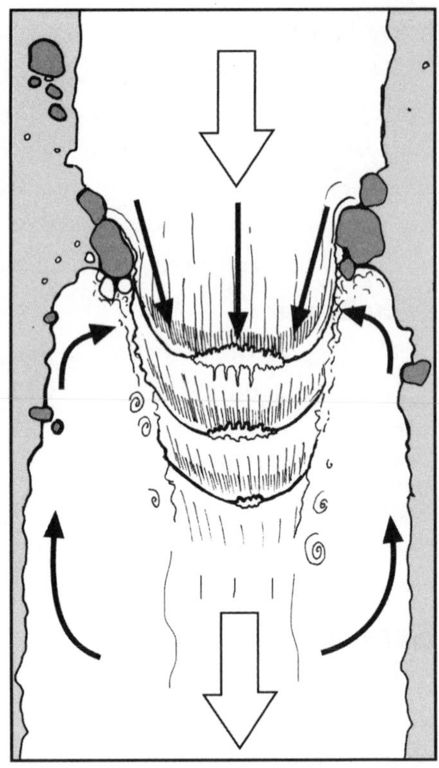

Fig. 2.9 Standing waves viewed from above.

Stoppers

Stoppers are formed when water that has speeded up as a result of flowing over a drop, needs to get rid of the extra energy that has thus been created. It does this by sending the water that can't flow away normally, rushing to the surface. Some of this water is then forced to recirculate back into the stopper. The technical term for a stopper is a 'hydraulic jump'.

Surface Stopper (Noisy)

There are different types of stopper and at one end of the scale is the **surface stopper or *'hole'*,** (fig. 2.10). In this kind of stopper all the action takes place on the surface. Therefore, although it will hold a buoyant object such as a kayak, a

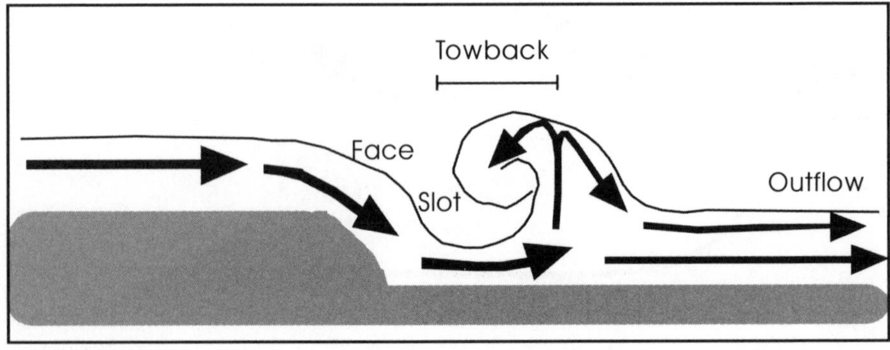

Fig. 2.10 Surface Stopper, (cross-section)

swimmer would normally be flushed through the stopper in the green slab of water that is below the surface. The fact that the action is on the surface also means that they are visually very obvious and tend to be quite noisy.

'Friendly' surface stoppers make great 'play-holes', in which to learn the skills needed to get out of the not so friendly ones. Small surface stoppers can be deliberately 'side-surfed' and used to stop and get a good look at the way ahead.

The angle of the **face** of a surface stopper is usually relatively shallow. Small stoppers with steep faces that make 'side surfing' difficult, if not impossible, are sometimes referred to as 'pour-overs'.

Deep Re-Circulating (Quiet)

At the other end of the scale is the **deep recirculating stopper or *'hydraulic'*.** (Fig. 2.11). As the name implies, most of the action is happening below the surface. When the volume of water involved is taken into consideration, these stoppers are relatively quiet.

This is a dangerous type of stopper because the tow back will often hold a swimmer. They are also dangerously deceptive because the water isn't very aerated. This means that to the untutored eye it may appear as if the water is fairly calm.

The angle of the **face** of these stoppers is usually steep.

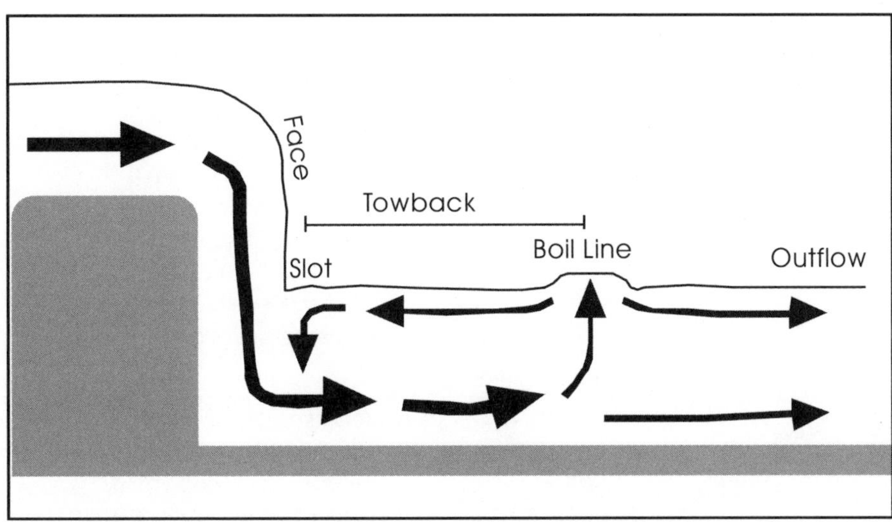

Fig. 2.11 Deep re-circulating stopper (cross-section).

The critical factor is the distance between the **slot** and the **boil line,** in other words, the length of the **towback.** As a rough guideline, anything over half a boat length is probably worth walking around.

Natural stoppers are rarely 100% surface or 100% deep recirculating. Due to the uneven nature of the river bed they are normally a blend, and often exhibit different characteristics throughout their length. So you may find that one end of a stopper is very 'grabby', while the other end is very forgiving.

Open versus Closed

More importantly, most, though by no means all, natural stoppers will have one or more weaknesses where the re-circulation is broken and the water flows through. These may be caused by a break in the underwater feature that is causing the stopper or by the fact that the stopper is not at 90 degrees to the main flow. In the case of the latter, some of the recirculating water flows towards the down stream end of the stopper. (Fig. 2.12).

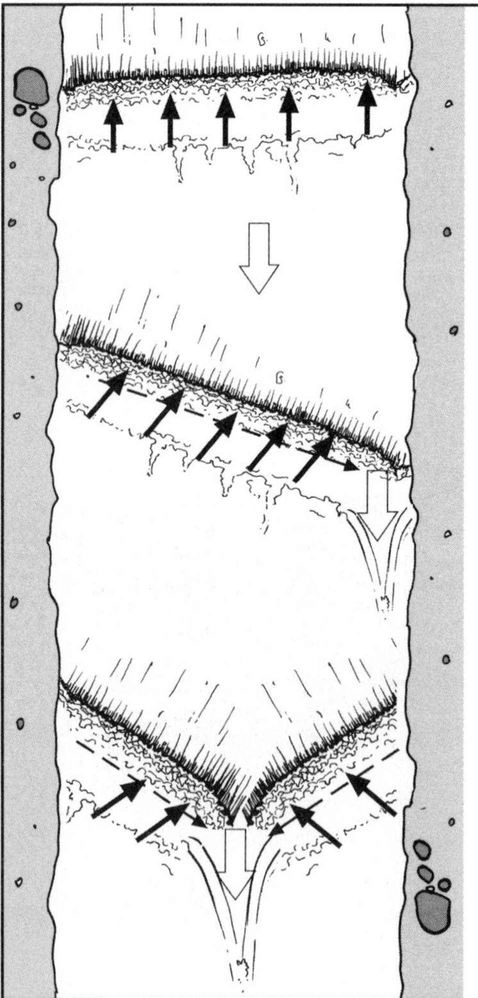

Deep re-circulating stopper produced by a full length ledge.
The towback is regular and there is no means of escape.
This stopper is closed.

This ledge produces a diagonal deep re-circulating stopper.
The towback feeds water to the down-stream end of the stopper. This usually produces an outflow and a means of escape.
This stopper is open.

A 'V' shaped stopper.
The towback feeds water into the centre and usually produces an outflow.
This stopper is open.
If the 'V; faces the other way it often produces a very turbulent stopper.

Fig. 2.12 A selection of stopper profiles.

Unless you are **100%** certain that you can power through, or in certain cases jump over, a stopper, you should keep well clear of any stopper that does not have a weakness that will allow you to escape its clutches. Americans call these undesirables *'keepers'*.

'Smiling' or 'Frowning'

Many 'surface' and 'pour-over' stoppers occur when water flows over an isolated boulder in midstream. If, ***when facing downstream,*** the resulting stopper makes the same shape as a child's drawing of a smile, the towback will be recirculating in such a way as to feed boats or people into the outflow and out of the stopper. If the stopper appears to be frowning, the towback is recirculating back into the stopper, and is best avoided.

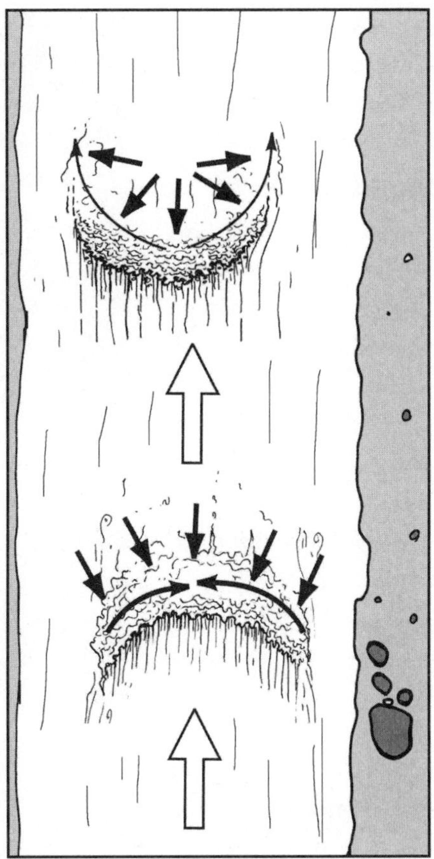

Fig. 2.13 'Frowning' stopper (bottom), and 'Smiling' stopper (top).

Water Levels

Be aware that rivers and their hazards change dramatically as their water levels change. Most guide books describe rivers as they will be found in medium levels.

Low Water

As water levels drop, rivers usually become more technical but more forgiving. This means that it is harder to make the line because there are more obstacles but due to the fact that the current is less powerful mistakes are less costly.

There are some notable exceptions, where even in low levels the current is powerful enough to make entrapment lethal. Due to the fact that entrapments

Fig. 2.14 Side surfing a 'smiling' stopper. Photo: Bob Timms.

are more likely in lower water levels, these rivers are **more** dangerous in low water.

High Water

As water levels rise, some rapids will become simpler or even wash out altogether. Others will become much harder and weirs or *'low head dams'* that don't wash out will probably become killers.

The current will become much faster, giving you little time to react, and more powerful leaving little scope for errors. Trees that were just a nuisance become massive strainers.

Fig. 2.15 Cobdens Falls in low but paddleable water levels, a 'soft touch' grade IV. Afon Llygwy, North Wales.

Fig. 2.16 Cobdens Falls at 'bank full' water levels, a 'stiff' grade IV.

Fig. 2.17. Cobdens Falls, just reaching flood level, grade V. Photos: Franco Ferrero

Flood

You should only run flood stage rivers when you are very competent and know the river well. Everything now happens so fast that if you go for a swim **you are on your own.** On all but the easiest rivers any other boaters will probably be too busy surviving to come to your rescue. You will be moving so fast that any bank based rescuers will be unable to keep up on foot. Should

River Ogwen, North Wales.
Five of us stood on the bridge above the village of Bethesda, looking at the distinctive boulder that served the locals as a water gauge. We all agreed that it was going to be high/exciting rather than high/terrifying, more an easy grade V than its normal grade IV.
We set off and enjoyed the exhilarating ride, until we arrived at the confluence of the Caseg. This tributary drains off the Carneddau mountains. Normally it carries far less water than the Ogwen itself, but today was different. A huge mass of grey snow melt water thundered in, swelling the already high Ogwen. It was like being hit by an express train. It didn't take long to work out that our estimates of water level and difficulty were going to have to be altered radically. By the time we got to the hard bit all bar two of us decided to walk. I got such a spanking that when I finally managed to break out, (Eddy in), I decided to walk the last hard rapid, even though I only had a hundred metres to go. After all, how much adrenaline do you need?

they manage to get a line to you, the current will be so powerful that you may well be unable to hold on.

William Neally in his book 'Kayak', states that there are three reasons for running a river in flood: Accident (flash flood), misadventure (ignorance of river level), or choice (defective genetic programming). He goes on to say that lots of paddlers do run flood-stage rivers, because it's exciting. You must, however, have first class river reading skills, a bombproof roll, a cool head and a cavalier attitude.

Flood-stage rivers are extremely high risk. If you need to ask another paddler if they think you are ready for it, **you aren't!** If you think you are, you had better be right!

Big Drops and Waterfalls

From a safety point of view, any drop over 3 metres is the same as a waterfall, so from now on I will use the term 'drop' for anything over 3 metres and 'small drop' for anything smaller. The good news is that remarkably few people have been killed paddling drops. The bad news is that quite a number of people have been badly injured. The reason I use 3 metres as my definition of a big drop is that it has been proven in research with crash test dummies that, if you land bow first onto a hard surface from that height, you will fracture your lower legs. A flat landing onto non-aerated water from that height could result in spinal damage.

Having said that, drops of 40 metres have been paddled; so what's the difference between a good drop and a bad drop?

In my way of thinking there are three types of drops: Easy drops, hard drops, and drops that will probably hurt you.

Easy Drops

Easy drops demand only raw courage or a lack of imagination; skill doesn't really come into it. They have deep plunge pools full of **aerated** water to provide you with a soft landing. They also have an easy approach that requires little or no technical skill to set yourself up so that you go over the lip pointing in the right direction. Runnable drops of over 7 or 8 metres usually consist of very steep slabs rather than vertical drops. This is because if you free-fall for a considerable distance it becomes difficult to ensure that your boat hits the water at a safe angle. If the boat lands too flat there is the risk of spinal compression. Another requirement is that, if there is a stopper at the base of the drop, it isn't a hazard in itself.

Hard Drops

Hard drops require technical skill and a cool head. These are essentially the same as easy drops in terms of the landing. The difference is that the approach to the lip of the drop is technically difficult and may be close to the limit of your paddling skill. Failure to get the entry right may result in landing at a bad angle or missing the plunge pool altogether. The most technically difficult drops of all are complex falls that require the paddler to manoeuvre during the descent. To a degree, the difference between a hard drop and an easy drop is subjective, as it depends on each individual's skill level.

Drops That Will Hurt You

I don't run these! Into this category go any drop where the landing is so poor that, no matter how perfectly you run the drop, there is a reasonable chance of ending up in hospital. Landings that come into this category include: bare rock, barely covered rock, shallow or obstructed plunge pools, non aerated water and killer stoppers. Hitting water that has not had its surface tension disturbed can be like landing on concrete!

Remember that unlike weirs there may be no warning change in the nature or the flow of the river upstream of the drop. You will have to rely on good scouting technique and signs such as noise to forewarn you.

Chapter 3
Hazards

This section looks at hazards that, as paddlers, we need to identify and in most cases avoid. The mere presence of these hazards on a section of river does not automatically mean a portage. Providing we identify the hazard in good time, it is usually easy to choose a line down the river that keeps well clear of them. However, if the degree of technical difficulty involved in avoiding one of these features exceeds, or even comes close to, the limits of our paddling ability, it's time to get out and walk!

...'time to get out and walk!'...

Overhanging Branches

These are usually found on the outside of bends where the current tries to set you into the bank. They are usually easily avoided, although novices seem to have a morbid fascination for them.

Emergency Action

If unable to avoid overhanging branches, and they are **only thin ones,** one should not hold on to them as this will capsize boaters and pull rafters into the water. Paddlers in this situation should lean forward, make themselves as small as possible and allow the current to push them through. For thick branches see below.

Strainers

A strainer is any obstruction that leaves gaps that are large enough for the current to flow but not big enough for a boat or swimmer to pass through. Examples are: tree branches or roots, fences, eroded and exposed steel reinforcing rods and virtually any junk you can think of that has been thrown into the river. (Fig. 3.1). Avoidance really is the name of the game here.

...'paddling away from the strainer and avoiding it is the best bet.'...

Emergency Action

If swept into a strainer whilst boating or rafting, the only hope is to jump or climb over the obstacle rather than be swept under it. Open boaters have a definite advantage here as it is much easier to ...."Get out of the kitchen if you don't like what's cooking"! That said, the chances of success are slim and paddling away from the strainer and avoiding it is the best bet.

What to do as a swimmer is covered in Chapter 15: Swimmers, Boats and Paddles.

Boulder Sieve

This is essentially the 'mother of all strainers', where the whole or a large portion of the river is strained through the gaps in a mass of boulders.

Broaches

Broaches usually happen on boulders but can involve other obstacles. It involves being swept sideways onto and being held against one or more obstacles. On easier rivers this is a common occurrence with novices who lack the skill to take evasive action. In gentler waters it is not usually too much of a problem, but if the current involved is very powerful, it may cause serious damage to the boat or raft, or even trap the boater.

Emergency Action - Kayaks

If avoiding action has been unsuccessful and being pushed sideways onto a rock is inevitable, immediately lift the upstream edge of your boat by snapping up the appropriate knee and lean onto the offending obstacle. This will allow the water to pass under the boat and leave you in a stable, if unenviable, position, (fig. 3.2) Unless getting off the rock will put you in a worse position than you are already in, work your way off the rock by pushing or pulling your way along the obstacle, while at the same time keeping your edge up.

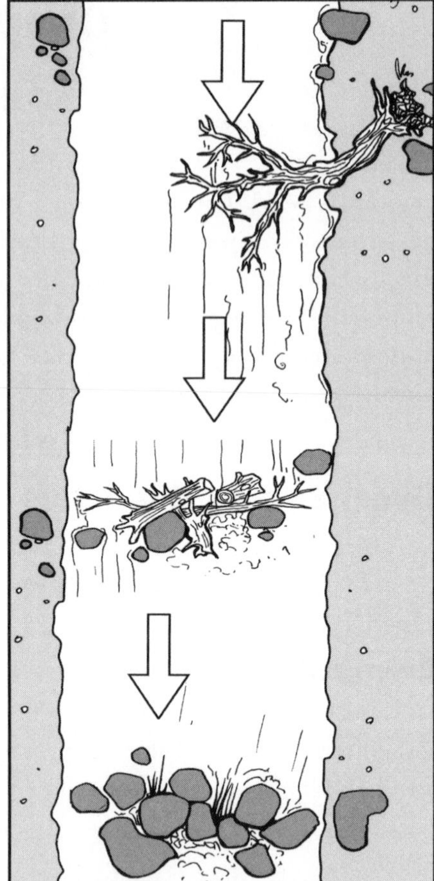

Fig. 3.1 A selection of strainers.

Fig. 3.2 Emergency action on broach. Photo: Bob Timms.

If you don't react quickly enough and the current catches your upstream edge, the boat will rotate towards the current and the pressure rapidly builds up on the spray deck and deck as the pressure wave transfers from the rock to the deck of your boat. Your best bet is to get out of the boat as quickly as possible, before the deck collapses. This is one of the situations where a 'keyhole' cockpit is a very desirable design feature as it will make it much easier to get out quickly and reduce the likelihood of your legs being trapped. (See Chapter 12).

Emergency Action - Open Boat

In an open boat you will have to throw your weight hard towards the offending object and weight the downstream side of the boat.

In an open boat it is easier to bale out. On the other hand, because of the extra surface area involved, a 'wrap', even in a relatively slow current, can result in a complete write off. Even worse, it is possible for the ends of the boat to fold right around the rock and trap the paddler. This is known as being 'bear trapped'.

Emergency Action - Rafts

When a raft is broached the pressure wave moves from the rock to the outside edge of the raft. The pressure rapidly builds up and can push the upstream air tank under the water and wrap the raft around the obstruction. If the crew is experienced or well briefed they can counter this by 'high siding'. This involves moving their weight to the 'high' side of the raft. In the case of a raft this is the downstream side. The raft guide will usually shout, "High side left", or right depending on the circumstances.

Should the raft go on to wrap the crew should climb up over the high side of the raft and onto the obstacle or into the eddy that will have formed behind it.

Fig. 3.3 Emergency action if the raft wraps.

Vertical Pins

This is where water flows over a vertical drop that has obstacles and shallow water at its base rather than a deep plunge pool. If the bow of a boat gets lodged, the boater ends up pinned vertically, rather than broached horizontally. If a vertical pin looks like a possibility you should not run the drop unless you are sure that you have the technique required to 'ski-jump' the drop, keeping the bow up. Even then, as a precaution you should ensure that other members of the team could get in a position to help should there be a case of 'pilot error'. What to do in this situation is covered in Chapter 17: Pins and Entrapments.

Undercuts

An undercut is wherever a current flows under some form of overhanging obstacle, such as an eroded bank, undercut bedrock or overhanging boulder. If a boater is swept under an undercut he will almost certainly be capsized. In some cases it may be possible to hold on to the rock above the undercut and work your way along the obstacle without being fed under it. The real danger is that there is some form of strainer hidden under the undercut, or that the undercut narrows and that the paddler is thus trapped underwater. Once again avoidance is the only real answer.

Spotting the Undercut

Undercuts are usually formed where the current sets onto a rock and erodes it. When the current sets onto a rock that isn't undercut it forms a cushion wave. (Fig. 3.4). If there is no cushion wave, or it is smaller than the power of the water would lead you to expect, suspect the presence of an undercut.

Fig.3.4 The cushion wave shows that the boulder probably isn't undercut. Photo: FF.

Sometimes undercuts are obvious because the rock has been eroded at high water and the river is being run in low or medium water. In this case, if the current sets under a overhanging section of rock, one should assume that the rock is further undercut beneath the water.

Siphon

A siphon is where water flows through a tunnel formed by a pothole in the bedrock or a gap between boulders. They can be a lot harder to spot than undercuts. In all other respects the dangers posed are of the same nature. (Fig. 3.5).

Spotting the Siphon

The only sure way to spot siphons is to inspect the riverbed in drought conditions! In normal river flows, if there seems to be less water coming out of a pool than is flowing into it, suspect the presence of a siphon. If the mouth of the siphon is near the surface it may cause the same sort of vortex effect on the water as you see when water goes down a plug-hole.

Sometimes the mouth may be inconspicuous but the exit point obvious, in which case one can make an educated guess as to where the water is coming from. Inspecting by working one's way upstream is a good way to spot siphons.

Dangerous Stoppers

As discussed in the previous chapter, deep recirculating stoppers will hold a swimmer whereas surface stoppers usually don't. None the less, a deep recirculating stopper may not be a killer. It may have a weakness, indicated by a tongue of water flowing through in the

Fig. 3.5 Unusually obvious siphon. Photo: Franco Ferrero.

opposite direction to the towback on either side. Through this weakness a bold and sufficiently skilled paddler could break through, or a swimmer could make his escape. Most but by no means all natural stoppers have one or more weaknesses. Whether an individual paddler has the skill or is cool headed enough to be able to use them is another matter.

Assessing Risk

By looking at whether a stopper is even or uneven, deep or surface, we can assess just how dangerous it is. (Fig. 3.6). There are other factors to take into account such as the size of the stopper, depth of the water and the power of the current, underwater and downstream hazards and the technical skill of the paddlers involved. If in any doubt, get out and walk!

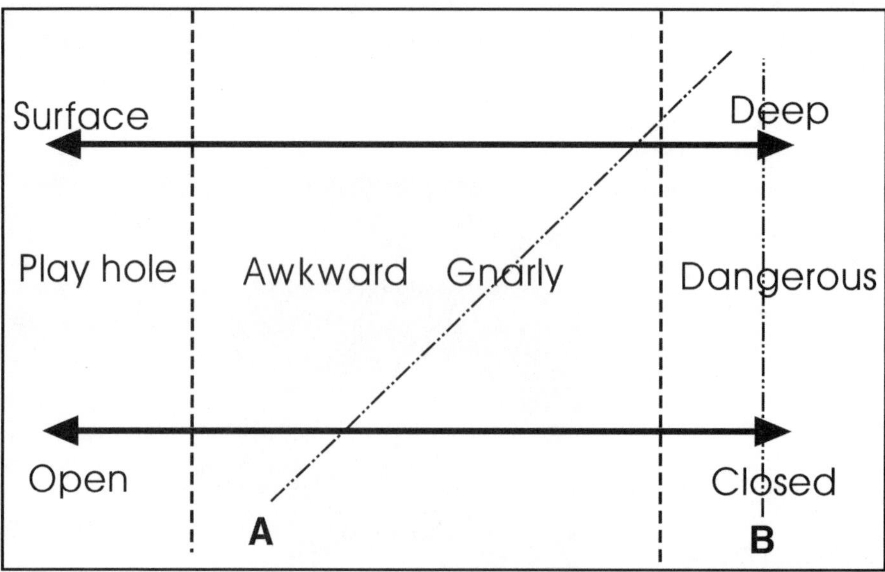

Fig. 3.6 On this scale Stopper A has a fairly uneven towback but is deep re-circulating and merits a rating of 'gnarly'. Stopper B is deep re-circulating and closed!

Double Recirculation

A particularly lethal kind of stopper is formed where water has undercut the base of a drop. This can cause a double recirculation, (fig. 3.7). Should a person end up recirculating in the undercut his chances of survival are slim.

Spotting a Double Recirculation

Any vertical or near vertical drop with a decent flow of water running over it should be considered suspect. Look for signs of erosion at the base of the rock face, behind or to the sides of the flow of water. Look for signs of water from the pool at the base of the fall recirculating behind the waterfall.

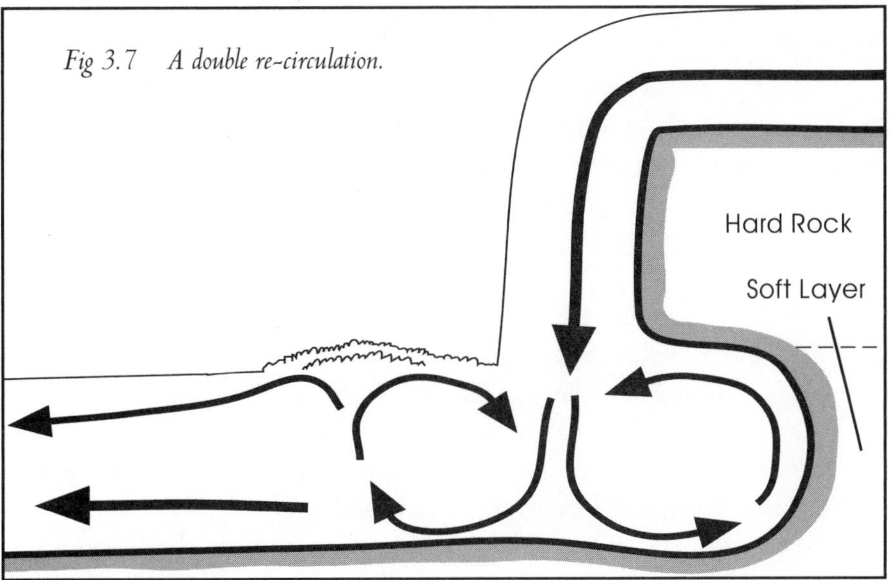

Fig 3.7 A double re-circulation.

River Goeddol, North Wales.
Kevin and I finished inspecting the two drops. On the first the water divided and fell as a near vertical fall on 'river right' and a shallower angled but more turbulent looking fall on river left. Both options looked straight forward, so we decided that whoever was not running it would stand by with a throwline by the second fall.
I had gone first on the last big drop so it was Kevin's turn. I signalled to confirm that I was ready and he paddled over the right hand fall of the first drop vanishing from sight into the plunge pool.
When after a few seconds neither he nor his boat had reappeared, I ran back up to the plunge pool and, my heart pounding, scanned the foaming water. After what seemed an eternity his boat reappeared but there was still no sign of Kevin. Time passed, and I began to wonder how I was going to break the news to his pregnant wife.
Suddenly he burst to the surface. He had kept his cool and, on feeling his foot touch bedrock, had kicked off it for all he was worth. Milliseconds later my throwline landed in his hands and I pulled him to safety.
We reinspected the fall, and ruefully I realised that we had missed the signs. They weren't obvious but they were there. The back of the fall was undercut producing a double recirculating stopper. I felt physically sick at the thought that because we had missed the vital clues my friend had come close to losing his life.
I'm not sure who was more shaken, but the decision to get off the river and retreat to 'Pete's Eats' for a monster 'pig out' was unanimous.

Weirs

Weirs or *'Low Head Dams'* often produce dangerous stoppers. This is because, being man made, they are symmetrical. Therefore they produce stoppers that are regular and have no weaknesses through which a jet of water can flow . To make matters worse the ends of the stoppers are often blocked off with high walls that offer no holds for a swimmer to grab hold of. Horseshoe weirs are particularly bad as they recirculate their victims to the middle of the river where it is hard to get to them. Anti-scour weirs have a 'lip' which is designed to prevent erosion, dissipating energy by creating a particularly powerful deep recirculating flow of water which **will** hold a swimmer, (fig. 3.8). In Britain the governing bodies of our sport are campaigning to stop any more of these lethal weirs being built.

Other ways that have been used to reduce the flow of the water include placing steel stakes, concrete 'dragon's teeth' and 'gabions', (wire-mesh baskets filled with rocks), on the bed of the river. As 'gabions' erode, the damaged wire mesh is particularly hazardous.

Some weirs are built with weaknesses designed into them, and broken weirs sometimes provide good play spots because, through damage or neglect they have become uneven. Beware, none the less, because broken weirs may have dangerous spikes in the form of exposed reinforcing steel rods.

Fish passes are best avoided. It is sometimes illegal to even paddle near them and they are often made in such a way that it is possible to become entrapped.

...'Weirs are either straightforward, or they kill you'...

Weirs are either straightforward, or they kill you. Therefore, if in any doubt, portage. The only way to be sure is to ask the locals. Always inspect weirs and the stoppers they create. Possible signs that you are approaching a weir are:

Calm Deep Water

Weirs are designed to hold water back, so upstream of the obstruction there is a 'weir pool'.

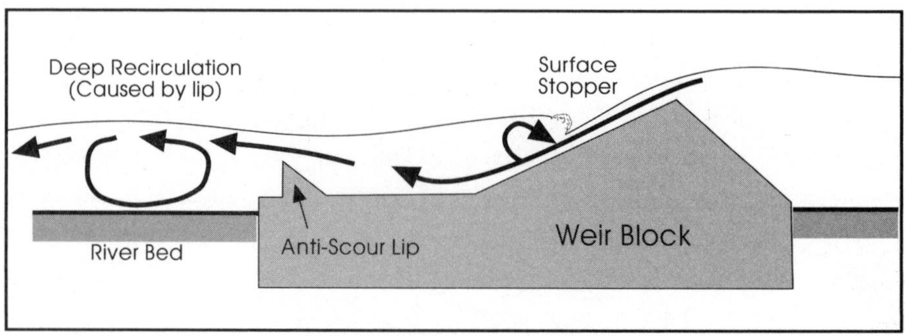

Fig. 3.8 An Anti-Scour Weir.

Noise

Created by the overflow of the weir. Be wary, some dangerous recirculating stoppers are very quiet.

An 'Event Horizon' (Fig. 3.9)

Due to the sudden drop created by the weir, you will see a foreground, a false horizon, and a background. The middle ground is missing, giving you an unusual perspective and a valuable early warning sign.

A Change in Height

A change in the height of the river banks.

Concrete Constructions

Concrete walls or small buildings.

Mill Buildings

Older weirs built during the Industrial Revolution were often built to power cotton mills. Old multistorey buildings are a useful warning sign.

A Warning Notice

These are unusual in Britain but common in parts of continental Europe where canoeists are seen as a valuable tourist resource. Even if you can't read French or German the skull and cross-bones is pretty clear in its meaning!

Don't get complacent! The absence of a warning sign doesn't necessarily mean that the weir is safe.

Other Paddlers

Other paddlers are potentially a very real hazard particularly at popular and crowded play-holes or play-waves. There is a form of etiquette that is best to follow:

1. On slalom sites it is usual to keep out of the gate-line and get out of the way of anyone who is doing a timed run or obviously training seriously.

Fig. 3.9 An 'event horizon'.

2. If the normal line of descent of a rapid goes through a play-wave or hole, boaters descending the river have right of way. Having said that, someone who is struggling at their limit to master a play-hole may not be looking upstream. It is therefore a good idea to stop where they can see you and wait for them to clear the hole. If you are playing the hole, be courteous and make a point of signalling them to come on down.
3. Don't drop in uninvited, even if the person concerned has been hogging the hole. The unwritten rule is that if there are other people waiting, you only stay on the wave or in the hole for two minutes. If somebody is hogging the hole, have strong words with them when they are in the eddy rather than risking physical injury by trying to barge them out of the hole.

Environmental Hazards

I have included a number of items in the final part of this chapter that the reader may have expected to find in the chapter on first aid. There are two reasons for this:

1. They are conditions brought about by environmental hazards.
2. They are all conditions that are easily preventable.

Sudden Immersion

In very cold water this can stop a paddler from thinking clearly and reacting. Prevention is simply a case of wearing a foam-lined helmet or a neoprene skull-cap under your helmet and suitable protective clothing. (See Chapter 12).

Another effect is a form of hyperventilation. The cold causes people to keep trying to breathe in and feeling unable to breathe out. With habituation cold water immersion is less likely to have this effect. Some raft guides brief their clients to counter this by shouting as loud as they can when they surface. This has the effect of expelling air from their lungs as well as attracting the raft guide's attention.

Hypothermia

Hypothermia is a condition brought about by a lowering of the body's core temperature, which can ultimately result in death. It is caused by a person being unable to generate enough heat to counteract the effects of cold due to exhaustion, or, more commonly with boaters, through the rapid lowering of the core temperature caused by immersion in cold water.

The difficulty of grading rivers. Both the photos are of sections of river that are given grade V.
Top: State Line Falls on the Wataga, North Carolina, United States.
Bottom: The Upper Oertz, Austria. Photos: Loel Collins

...'even in its mildest form, hypothermia can drastically affect a person's judgment.'...

Being mammals, humans need to maintain the vital organs of the body at a constant 37 degrees Celsius. The critical thing about hypothermia is that even in the early stages, in its mildest form, it can drastically affect a person's judgment. Therefore if you are feeling very cold, you should take remedial action or get off the river before you start making dangerous mistakes.

Prevention

Once again, the emphasis should be very much on prevention.

1. Avoid taking long swims by careful scouting, thorough assessment of the risks involved and skilful paddling.
2. Maintain a suitable level of personal fitness.
3. Eat well before and during a river trip. Complex carbohydrates such as rice, pasta, bread, cereals provide energy in a form that is made available to your body at a steady rate and over several hours.
4. Wear suitable clothing for the conditions and type of paddling.
5. 'Buddy' up and keep an eye on each other for the early signs of hypothermia.
6. Be prepared to shorten or abort a trip if members of the party show signs of getting too cold.
7. If one member of the party is suffering from hypothermia, there is a good chance that the conditions that affected them are affecting everyone else. Therefore action should be taken to protect the team as well as treat the victim.

Signs and Symptoms

The good news about immersion hypothermia is that if someone takes a long swim in glacial melt water it is obvious that we should suspect its onset. Unfortunately exhaustion hypothermia can easily go unnoticed in its early stages. Paddlers can fall prey to either form or a mixture of both. Therefore whenever we paddle in cold conditions or someone goes for a swim in cold water it is important to look out for the signs and symptoms.

In a hospital, doctors would take a core temperature. This involves the use of a rectal thermometer which is not very practical on the river bank and would probably result in the first aider being assaulted by the victim! The signs and

Top: John Moxham getting to know the deep re-circulating stopper (hydraulic) on the Wataga Gorge, North Carolina, USA. Photo: Paul O'Sullivan

Bottom: A 'mother of all stoppers'. The Zambezi River, Zimbabwe. Photo: Loel Collins.

symptoms are what matter. The figures in brackets indicate the core temperature at which they normally occur. Note that a victim may not exhibit all of the signs and the order they appear in may vary slightly. (Normal 37 degrees C)

Early warning :

- Feeling cold and tired (35°C)
- Numbness of hands or feet
- Blue lips
- Intermittent shivering

In an alert group of boaters who work as an effective team, hypothermia would rarely be able to progress beyond this stage unnoticed or untreated.

Serious :

- Continuous shivering
- Unusual, uncharacteristic behaviour (34°C)
- Physical and mental lethargy
- Slurring of speech
- Violent outbursts of unexpected energy
- Lack of muscular coordination
- Failure or abnormality of vision

Deep hypothermia :

- Shivering stops, lowered conscious level (33°C)
- Limbs stiffen up (32°C)
- Victim drifts into deep unconsciousness (31°C)
- Pulse irregular (29°C)
- Unconsciousness, coma, death (24°C)

Treatment

In the case of immersion hypothermia, the body hasn't depleted its energy reserves. This means that victims will respond more quickly to treatment and are more likely to make a complete recovery. The field treatment for both types of hypothermia is essentially the same, except that if exhaustion hypothermia is suspected, one should assume that victims are unfit to continue, even if they appear to have made a full recovery. If remoteness means that the easiest way to evacuate them is to continue paddling, they should be made to rest and eat for as long as is practicable before setting off.

Early Stages

Prevent Further Use of Energy. - Exercise will draw warm blood away from the core where it is needed and use up energy reserves which the body needs to generate heat for the core.

Prevent Further Heat Loss. - Provide shelter from wind and rain. Put extra clothing on victims. Put them in a bivvi-bag, (a two by one metre plastic bag). If available put them in a sleeping bag. Be aware that the insulation in a sleeping bag keeps heat out as effectively as it keeps heat in. Therefore it is best to put a warm bodied person in with the victim.

Slowly Reheat Victims - This is best achieved by providing an environment in which they are breathing warm moist air. In this way they are rewarmed from the inside. In a house this can be achieved by sitting them down in a steam filled bathroom heated to 40°C. In a hut or tent heat and humidity can be provided by boiling a pot of water on a stove, being careful not to knock it over and burn the victims. On the river bank the most effective way is to get the all the members of the party in a 'group shelter', (fig. 3.10). Once inside everybody's body heat and breath soon provides a warm moist environment. This has the added bonus of ensuring nobody else develops hypothermia as well as rewarming the victims.

Encourage the Victims to Eat - Give them food that will rapidly provide energy with which the body can generate heat; glucose and sugars, (Simple carbohydrates).

Serious Hypothermia

As for early stages plus:

Seek Hospital Treatment - Even if the victim appears to make a full recovery.

Stretcher Evacuation - Unless the victim appears to make a full recovery he should be evacuated on a stretcher and not permitted to use energy by walking or paddling.

Fig 3.10 A Group Shelter. Photo: Bob Timms.

Some Don'ts

- Do not rub victims
- Do not place warm objects on the victims' bodies
- Do not give the victims alcohol

The body's natural defence involves shutting off circulation to the limbs and surface blood vessels. This ensures that warm blood is retained in the core where it is needed and cold surface blood isn't allowed to cool the core further. All of the above 'treatments' have the opposite detrimental effect.

Sunshine

It is sometimes hard to believe this is a problem in Britain. Paddlers in sunnier climes are well aware of the potential damage.

Hyperthermia

Hyperthermia is caused by the body overheating and can be divided into two distinct stages.

Heat exhaustion is caused when the body overheats, and having lost too much water and salt through sweating, is struggling to maintain a normal body temperature.

Untreated it can lead to **heat stroke.** This occurs when the body is no longer able to sweat and the body's temperature rises unchecked. This condition can become life threatening.

Prevention

Prevention is simple, In warm climates drink plenty of water; don't put your wet suit on until just before getting on the water and have rest/lunch breaks in the shade. On white water stretches the constant splashing with cold water keeps paddlers cool. On long flat stretches it may be necessary to splash oneself or roll from time to time.

Heat Exhaustion - Signs and Symptoms

- Feeling unwell - headache - dizziness - nausea - cramps
- Weakness
- **Moist** skin

Treatment

- Remove to cool area
- Give fluids

Beware! Although not in itself a serious condition it will progress to heat stroke if the casualty is not removed from the source of heat.

Heat stroke - Signs and Symptoms

- Confusion/loss of consciousness
- Skin hot and **dry**
- High Temperature

Treatment

- Reduce temperature by removing to cool area
- Bathe with **tepid** water. (Drenching them with very cold water could cause heart failure)
- Fan the casualty
- Seek urgent medical attention
- If the casualty is unconscious, place in the recovery position

Dehydration

Peeling off layers of paddling clothing is very inconvenient. It is therefore tempting to drink as little as possible to avoid having to go to the toilet. This is a great mistake both in terms of the risk of hyper **and** hypothermia and in terms of reduced performance. Paddlers should drink frequently in hot and cold climates.

Sunburn

British paddlers abroad are particularly prone. They are so used to paddling in the rain at home they don't realise how quickly and badly they can burn.

Prevention

- Avoid the noon day sun and rest in the shade whenever possible
- Wear long sleeved garments and sun hats that protect the ears and neck
- Use water proof sun block creams on all exposed skin and apply frequently

Treatment

- Cool affected area by bathing in cool water for 10 minutes
- Prevent infection by **not** bursting any blisters and covering any that have burst with a sterile dressing
- Prevent any further exposure to direct sunlight
- Ensure that the victim drinks plenty of fluids
- If the sunburn is severe and covers an extensive surface area, medical attention should be sought

Eye Damage

Sun reflected off water can cause eye damage in the same way as sunlight reflected off snow. In the short term this can cause extreme discomfort and in extreme cases temporary blindness. In the long term the accumulated permanent damage can lead to cataracts and other forms of eye damage.

Prevention

Wear sunglasses and peaked hats.

Signs and Symptoms

- Headaches
- Tears
- Gritty painful eyes

Treatment

Rest in a dark room and seek medical treatment.

Aural Osteomata

This is also known as 'swimmer's ear' or 'surfer's ear'. Subjecting one's ears to frequent incursions of cold water causes bony growths to develop, which narrow the ear passage. Eventually this causes frequent ear infections and even deafness.

One method of prevention is to wear ear plugs. Even with the ear plugs in place, one can still hear well enough for normal river communication. It is also a good idea to tape up the ear-holes on your helmet during the colder months.

Some manufacturers now make very thin neoprene or lycra skull caps that fit easily under a helmet to cover one's ears and are designed to prevent surfer's ear.

Polluted Water

On our crowded planet it is a fact of life that many white water rivers or sites are polluted to some degree. Rivers that are heavily polluted with industrial effluent are out of the question, but many less polluted rivers.are paddled regularly. In 'developed' countries where sewage is treated the risk of getting a viral infection is **least** in the warm summer months when water levels are low. This is because the 'bugs' used in the treatment plants to break down the sewage are at their most efficient in the warm months.

...'Periods of higher flows are higher risk.'...

Periods of higher flows are higher risk, summer or winter, because accumulated rubbish is washed out of storm drains and high flows of water can cause the treatment tanks of sewage plants to overflow. This means that untreated or partially treated sewage gets into the river.

In poorer countries, the disposal of rubbish and faeces, and in some places, the bodies of those too poor to afford a funeral pyre, take place on the river bank. This is deliberately done above the normal high water mark. This means that the water is as clean as it can be for most of the year. In the monsoon all this detritus is swept downstream to fertilise the plains. During the early part of the monsoon almost everyone, canoeists and locals, are ill with some form of stomach bug.

Prevention

1. Avoid paddling polluted rivers in periods of high flow.
2. Remove wet clothing and wash hands and face in clean water, or better still, take a shower before eating or drinking.

When paddling in countries where the water is untreated:

1. Treat your drinking water. Either use one of the commercial systems where you pump through a filter that also adds iodine at the required dose, or, add two drops, (more if the water is heavily polluted), of tincture of iodine, (available from any chemist) and leave to stand for an hour before drinking. (Note that chlorine based water purifying tablets will not kill the cysts that transmit amoebic dysentery).
2. Only eat food that has been thoroughly cooked and is still hot.
3. Don't take milk in tea or coffee unless it has been boiled.
4. Don't eat locally made ice cream or items such as salads which have probably been washed in polluted water.

Leptospirosis or Weil's Disease

This is a potentially serious disease that is transmitted when rats' urine is washed into water courses. The main symptoms are very much like those of flu. Weil's Disease is not very common and is usually associated with sewage workers. This means that many doctors in general practice are unlikely to suspect it.

It is just as prevalent among paddlers as sewage workers. Therefore if you suspect you may have it, you may have to insist that they send off a sample of blood for testing urgently. If undiagnosed and untreated Weil's disease can be fatal.

Although safe in small quantities, iodine is a poison that builds up in the thyroid gland. Therefore if you are going abroad for an extended period it may not be a suitable solution.

Chapter 4
Skilful Paddling

The best way to become a safer paddler is to be a better paddler! When combined with the ability to read water, skill is a far better guarantor of safety than a full face helmet and body armour.

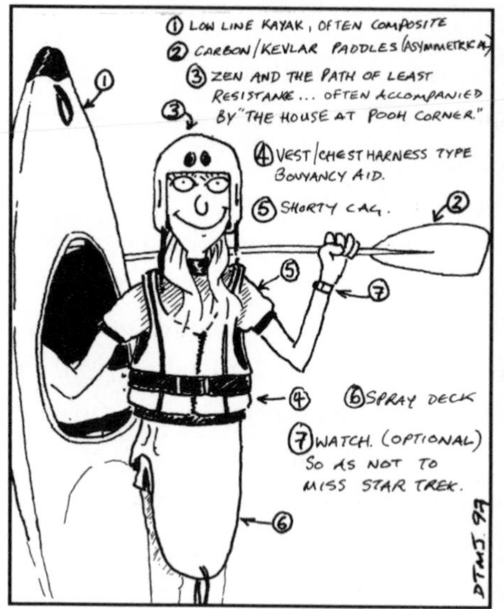

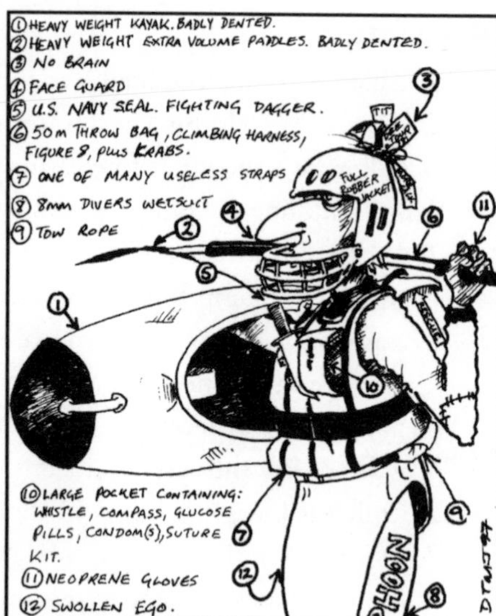

Fig.4.1 Skill versus Technoogy.

Skill

Skill in paddling white water is the ability to choose a line and paddle down it smoothly and efficiently. A truly skilful paddler makes it look effortless.

Fig. 4.2 shows a profile of all the parts that have to come together for a paddler to perform skilfully. When all these factors combine what we see is in essence good boat positioning. It doesn't matter in what proportion the parts are mixed, as long as the end result is that the paddler is in the right place at the right time. They also need to be pointing in the right direction, moving at the right speed and the right way up!

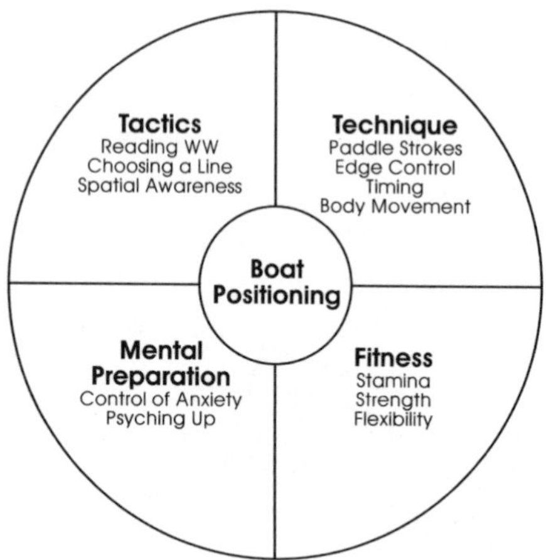

Fig 4.2 The components of paddling skill.

Tactics

Reading white water is covered in Chapter 2.

Choosing a line is the ability to 'see' a way down a rapid, that avoids all the hazards and uses rather than fights the water wherever possible. It is your brain's contribution to good boat positioning.

...'Choosing a line is the ability to 'see' a way down a rapid.'...

When choosing their line paddlers need to ask themselves the following questions:

1. Which way is the water flowing?
2. What hazards need to be avoided?
3. Will the water take the paddlers where they want to go?
4. Where it won't, what do they need to do to stay on a line that avoids any hazards.

Mental Preparation

This subject is covered in Chapter 5.

Technique

Good technique will serve a paddler far better than brute strength. It would take another book to cover technique, so for now I will refer the reader to other books. However, as it has a direct bearing on safety, we will look at some techniques that, when performed poorly, can lead to injuries.

In both the following cases poor technique can and frequently does lead to shoulder dislocations. If this injury ever occurs, help should be sought from a specialist sports physiotherapist. It is vital to build up the various groups of muscles that prevent instability of the shoulder joint. Repeated dislocations could lead to irreparable damage and the end of that person's paddling days. Prevention is better than cure. None the less, treatment is dealt with in the chapter on first aid.

High Brace

A kayak technique, the high brace is used to prevent a capsize. The kayaker reaches out at 90 degrees and gains support by laying the drive face of the blade on the water and pulling down, with his wrists underneath the paddle shaft. The stroke can be used statically, as a 'brace', where a water feature provides so much uplift that it feels like one is resting the paddle on a firm cushion. Alternately, it can be used dynamically, as a 'support stroke'. In this case the paddler gains enough support to bring the boat back upright by pulling down powerfully on the paddle.

Good technique consists of keeping the mid point of the shaft no more than forehead high and keeping both elbows bent, (fig. 4.3). Bent elbows act as shock absorbers relieving the pressure on the shoulder joint.

Fig 4.3 A safe form of high brace.

Bad technique is illustrated in fig. 4.4. The shoulder joint is already at the extreme end of its range and the elbow is already fully extended. Should there be a sudden increase on the force applied to the paddle there is no way to safely absorb the energy. The only way of relieving the pressure is for the shoulder to dislocate, or for the paddler to let go of the paddle. Unfortunately it often happens too quickly for the latter to be an option.

Fig. 4.4 A dangerous form of the high brace.

Fig 4.5 A dangerous form of bow rudder.

Bow Rudder

The bow rudder or *'Dufek stroke'* , is a very variable stroke. It has been suggested that a better name for it would be the Vertical Paddle Turn. The blade that is in the water may, depending on the situation, be held in a position that can range from almost touching the hull of your boat forward of your knee, to reaching out to the side level with your hip. In the latter case the placement should be achieved by rotating the trunk, (fig. 4.6), rather than by just using your arms, (fig. 4.5).

Try the following exercise:

Sit upright on a bench or hard backed chair. Now hold one arm so that your elbow is touching your side and your forearm sticks horizontally out in front of you at 90 degrees to your upper arm. Keeping your upper body still and your elbow at your side, rotate your forearm out to the side and see how far it will go. The position your arm is now in is the extreme range of movement permitted by your 'outer rotator cuff muscles'. In most male paddlers the range of movement will be about 80 degrees. In female paddlers it may be over 100 degrees. Memorise this position and then go back to the original position.

Fig. 4.6 A safe form of bow rudder. Photos: Bob Timms.

This time, by rotating your trunk, turn your shoulders through ninety degrees and place your forearm in the same place it reached in the first movement. Now try and rotate your forearm even further. You should find that because you have rotated your trunk you can now rotate your forearm through another 20 degrees or more. This represents the safety margin that is introduced through good technique.

Fitness

The best way to get fit for paddling is to paddle **regularly**. Even if paddlers live a long way from white water they can still paddle on flat water to build up stamina and strength, and maintain flexibility. If paddlers don't paddle for months and then jump straight onto a demanding white water run, their bodies may not be able to deliver the fitness component of the skill required. If you have had a long break from paddling, **build up slowly.**

Geographical location and work patterns may make it impossible to paddle as regularly as is necessary to maintain the required standard of fitness. A carefully thought out fitness training regime, designed to build up strength and stamina in the right proportions, and at the same time, maintain flexibility, can pay dividends.

Seek expert advice. Poorly thought out training can do more harm than good. If the right muscle groups are not built up in a balanced way it can set up an instability in the muscles that affect the shoulder joint. This can make paddlers more prone to dislocations. Strength training must be complemented by stretching to maintain flexibility. Stretching should be used to promote the **normal range** of movement required for paddling. Research carried out by Chris Lund, who is the physiotherapist for the GB youth slalom team, shows that over-flexibility in the shoulder joint can make paddlers more prone to dislocations. The shoulder is a very poorly designed joint and it is only the tension of the various muscle groups that hold it in place.

Boat Positioning

There are four ways paddlers can go about staying on their chosen line:

- By moving **faster** than the current
- By choosing to drift at the **same speed** as the current
- By moving **slower** than the current
- By **using water features**

Boaters involved in competition such as slalom try to always move faster than the current. They need to be fast and accurate.

Traditional open boaters and rafters generally try to go slower than, or at the same speed as, the current. They need to use their buoyancy to ride over the waves, because if they go fast and plough through them, they will get swamped.

Kayakers, closed deck C1 paddlers and people paddling specialist white water open boats, (with asymmetrical hulls, saddles and buoyancy bags), will benefit from using a mixture of all three approaches. (Fig. 4.7)

Faster

The times you **need** to be moving forwards are to accelerate into or out of an eddy, to 'punch through' a stopper, or when paddling across a fast flowing current to avoid an obstacle or hazard. In each of these cases there needs to be a distinct change of pace. If you are only paddling forward because you have **chosen** to in preference to other methods then you can afford a more leisurely pace. In both cases good forward paddling technique will pay dividends, either gaining more speed or saving energy.

Same Speed

If the flow of water is taking you where you want to go, then you can afford to drift. Your paddles should still be in the water, either moving the boat sideways using draw strokes to make small corrections to keep you on line, or in the low brace position to keep you stable.

When deliberately allowing yourself to drift you should be very aware of where the water is taking you and ready to change mode when the flow is no longer going your way.

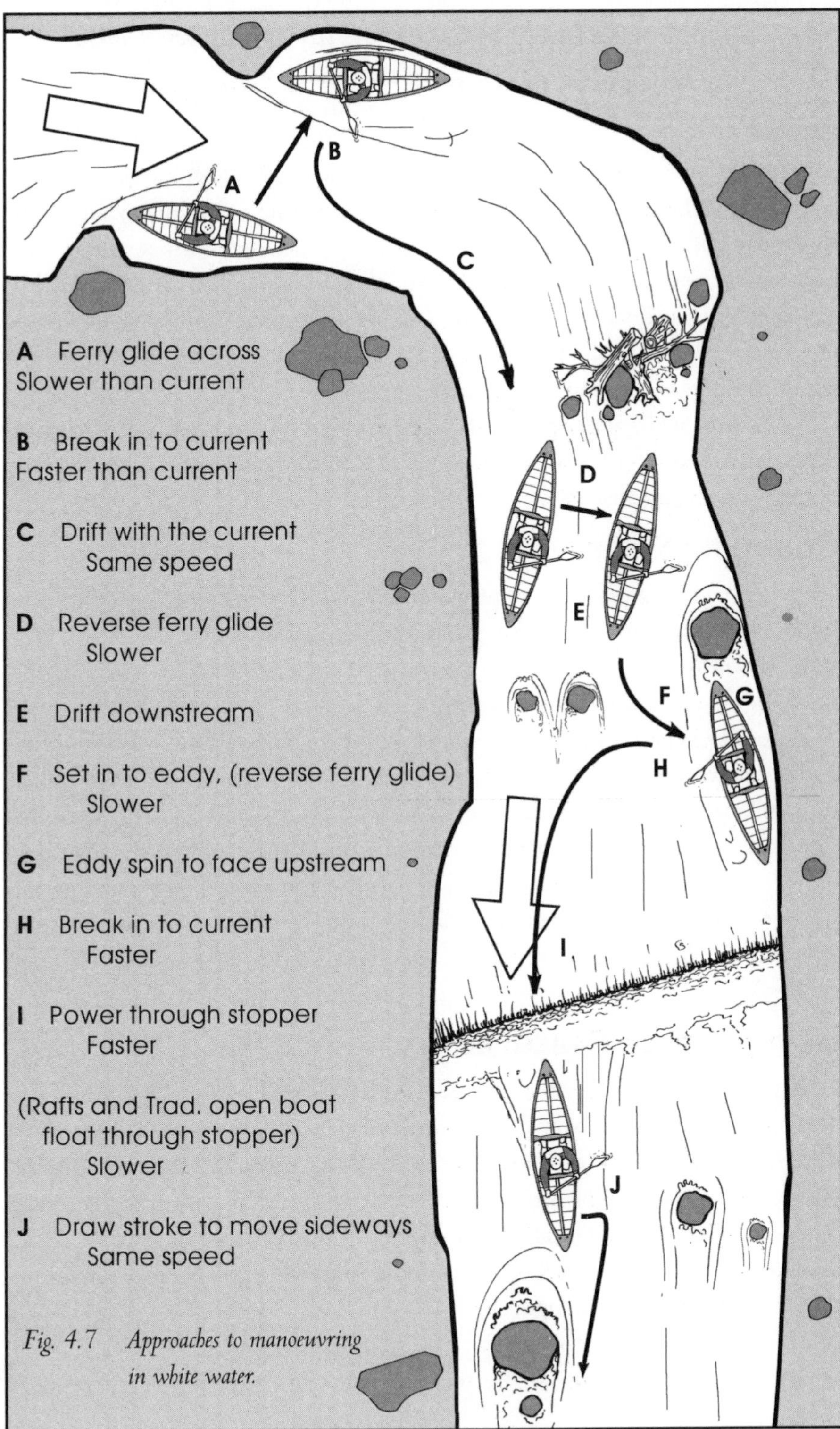

Fig. 4.7 Approaches to manoeuvring in white water.

...'When deliberately allowing yourself to drift you should be very aware of where the water is taking you.'...

Slower

Apart from not swamping open boats, the main advantage of slowing your boat down is that you get more time to see what is coming and plan your moves. By reverse paddling with your stern pointing directly upstream, you slow your boat down, or even hold your position in relation to the bank. By reverse paddling and angling your boat to the current, (reverse ferry glide), you slow down and move across the current. This allows you to adjust your position and stay on line whilst moving slower than the current.

In modern white water playboats that have very low and flat back decks it is necessary to lean right forward when reverse ferry gliding. Failure to do this may result in an involuntary 'tailie'.

Changing Gear

When paddling on white water you need to be either 'idling', paddling at a steady rate or, if only briefly, going flat out. It is important to:

1. Know when to paddle in which mode.
2. Be able to 'change gear' instantly.

A good exercise is to set up a circuit on a section of easy rapid. Plan your line, decide how you are going to stay on your line, where you can afford to idle, where to paddle at a steady rate and where you need to accelerate. Then paddle the circuit, consciously and deliberately changing speed at the points you identified earlier. At the points where acceleration is called for, shout **"now"**, and paddle flat out. The shout will let your companions know at which point you intended to speed up, allowing them to feed back to you how effective your acceleration was.

Using Water Features

Every paddler must be able to read white water well enough to choose a line down a rapid. The sign of an advanced paddler is the ability to read the water well enough to make use of water features, large and small, to accurately work his way down a rapid with the least effort. A tired paddler makes mistakes, so whenever possible use the water rather than fight it, (fig. 4.8).

The most commonly used ways of doing this are:

- Surfing standing waves
- Side -surfing stoppers
- Using the edge of a stopper to turn

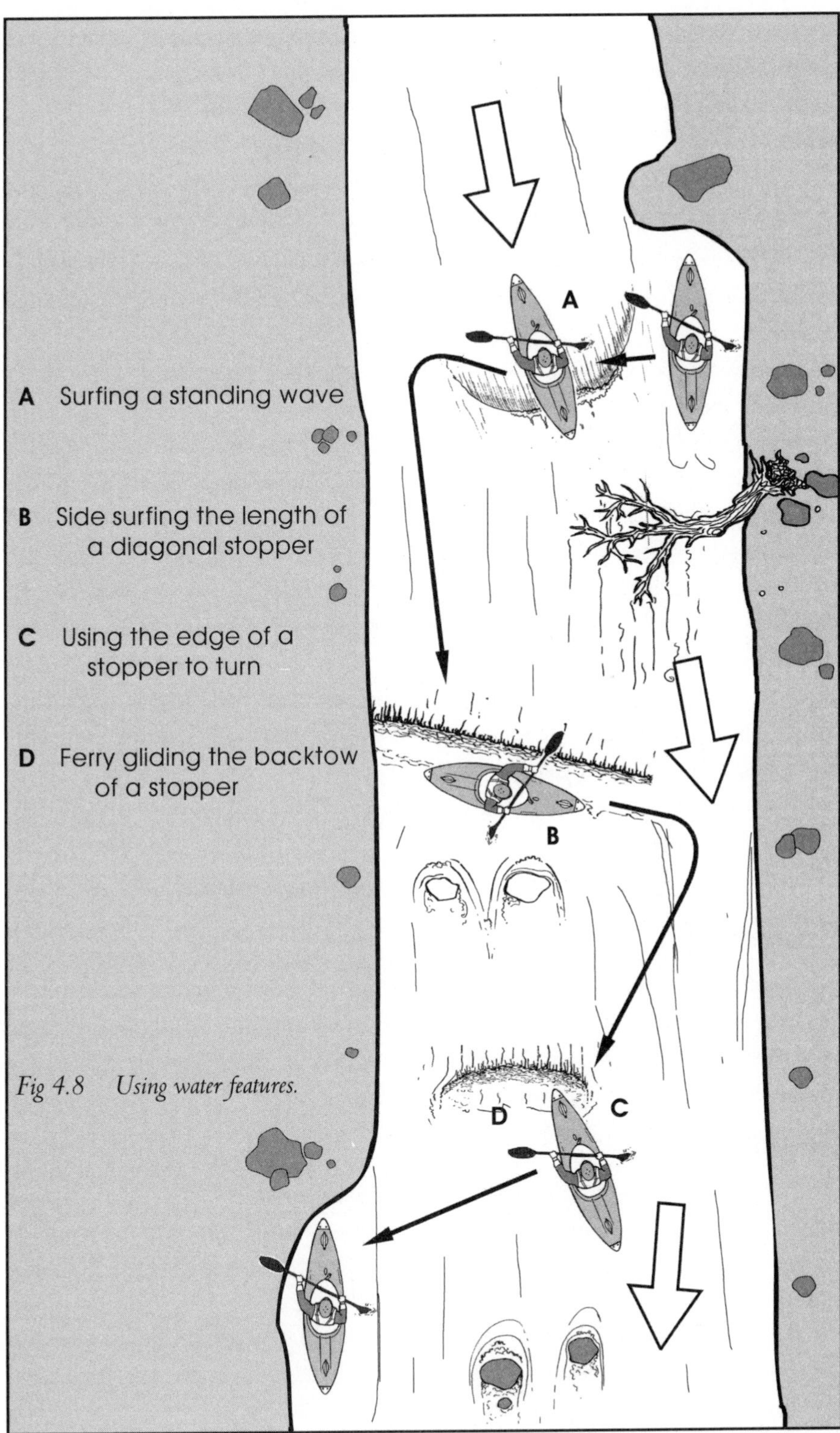

Fig 4.8 Using water features.

These skills are best practised by getting involved in playboating, or rodeo as the competitive version is known. All that is needed is a standing wave, a 'friendly' stopper and a group of friends.

...'Train Hard, Paddle Easy!'...

It is quite possible to have a grade III and a grade V rapid that require the same level of technical skill to follow the chosen line. If the paddlers end up off line on the grade III, they will probably be able to fight their way down anyway. If they lose the line on the grade V they are in serious, possibly life threatening, danger.

I believe that grade II is where we should learn our basic white water skills. Beginners shouldn't move on to harder rivers until they are in control at this level. That is to say that they can follow a predetermined line down a rapid and make a number of predetermined eddies on the way, rather than simply get to the bottom of the rapid still upright.

Grade III is where we hone our skills and ensure that we are sufficiently skilled to cope with the demands of hard white water paddling before we move up the grades. Before considering themselves ready to move on to harder things, paddlers should practice until they are competent, confident and fluent on grade III. They should also make the relatively safe IIIs that they are paddling as technically difficult as IVs and Vs, by deliberately choosing the most difficult line down the rapid, and making as many eddies as they can. In this way it is possible to simulate the difficulty of grade IV and V paddling without paying such a high price if mistakes are made.

...'good coaching is a valuable investment.'...

Coaching

Good coaching is a valuable investment. It can lay firm foundations for future skill by ensuring that the basics are learnt well and that bad habits are not 'grooved in'. Experienced paddlers can benefit from it to help them get over a 'learning plateau' or iron out bad habits.

Practice

Practice, and lots of it, is what is needed but beware, practice doesn't make perfect. Perfect practice makes perfect. So, when training, someone else needs to observe the paddler, and give him some constructive feedback that will help him improve.

The other important thing about practice is that it should be as varied as possible. Use different locations, practice on the left and the right, vary the angles, speeds, stroke work and approach.

Chapter 5
Mental Preparation and Warm Up

As mentioned in the previous chapter, mental preparation is a crucial aspect of skilful boating. A skilful paddler, who stays in control, is safe.

Stress

To paddle well, one has to be sufficiently stimulated or 'aroused'. The **right** amount of stress heightens awareness, speeds up reactions and ensures that brain and body are on full alert; (excitement or healthy fear).

Too little stress and we 'wind down'. This leads to a lack of concentration and a tendency to make stupid mistakes. Most boaters can think of times when they have run a difficult rapid perfectly, only to foul up on the easy section.

Too much stress and we become over anxious. Our performance decreases dramatically to the point where a paddler may even 'freeze'; (unhealthy fear or terror).

Catastrophe Curve

As we become more stimulated, the standard of our performance steadily increases. (See fig. 5.1). Eventually we reach the point where the stress becomes harmful and our performance starts to suffer. The bad news is that after a brief initial gentle decline, performance doesn't decline steadily, it plummets!

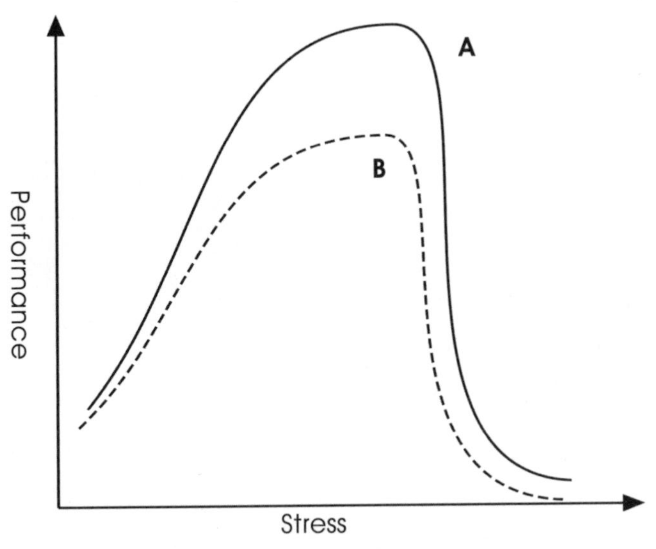

Fig. 5.1 The 'Catastrophe Curve'.

Individual Differences

Some individuals can cope with much higher levels of stress than others, (curve A). Others people's performance curves peak at a much lower level, (curve B). (See fig. 5.1)

Some people perform well at high levels of stress but are easily stimulated and have to be careful not to become over stressed. Others only perform well when highly stressed and find it difficult, on all but the most dangerous rapids, to be sufficiently stimulated to perform at their best.

Comfort Zones

If we look at fig. 5.2 we can think of how an individual reacts to different levels of stress in terms of three zones:

- The Comfort Zone
- The Adventure Zone
- The Disaster Zone

The Comfort Zone

If we never allow ourselves the stimulus created by straying into the adventure zone, our comfort zone, (i.e. the amount of stress we can deal with without becoming at all anxious), will shrink.

The Adventure Zone

If we constantly jump in and out of the adventure zone, our comfort and adventure zones expand. The closer we go to the outer edge of the adventure zone, the quicker we expand and the better we become at controlling anxiety.

The Disaster Zone

This is where anxiety changes to uncontrolled terror. If we misjudge our abilities or allow others to pressurise us into a situation where we step over this line, our self-confidence takes a massive blow and our comfort and adventure zones shrink dramatically.

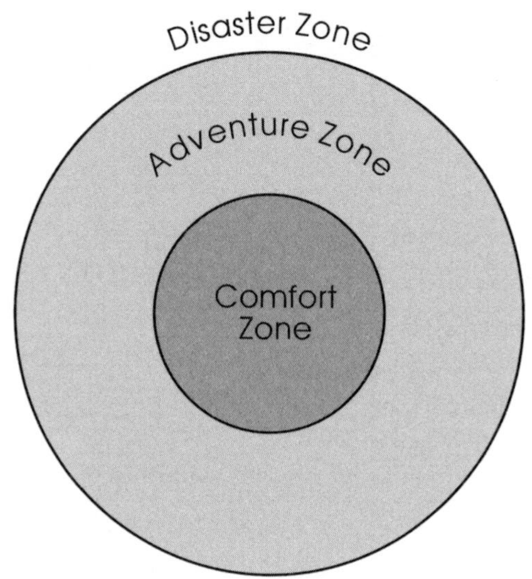

Fig. 5.2 Comfort Zones.

Coping With Stress

It is important that we recognise that we are all different and develop mental preparation strategies to suit our individual requirements.

The presence of physical danger obviously induces stress and anxiety. As paddlers become more technically proficient, if they wish to paddle on harder, more dangerous rapids, they will have to learn to control their anxiety levels.

Habituation

By gradually exposing themselves to more challenging situations, people find that they get used to the feelings produced by these situations. This has two effects on the persons concerned:

1. They are able to cope with higher levels of stress.
2. The situation becomes less stressful.

...'It is vital that we manage this process of habituation carefully.'...

Ritual

Before getting on the water, there are a number of things each individual must do, such as getting changed and checking one's equipment. There are also a number of things that perhaps we ought to do, such as a physical warm up and mental preparation exercises. If we learn a routine and do these things in the same order and the same way, they become a kind of ritual. Their familiarity is in itself reassuring, and has a calming effect.

People who need to increase their stress levels may benefit from deliberately varying the way they prepare and the order in which they do things.

Music

People who need to lower their stress levels should listen to peaceful, soothing music on the way to the river. People who need to 'psyche-up' should travel in another car and wind themselves up with some 'heavy metal'.

Warm Up

If you need to 'psyche-down' you should plan your physical warm up sessions so that they are slow and gentle. That way they will have a calming, rather than stimulating, effect.

If you need to psyche-up you should start your warm ups gently so as not to cause any injuries. As the warm up progresses the pace should become fast and frantic.

Breath Control

This is an exercise, borrowed from Yoga, that can be performed just prior to running a difficult rapid or drop. It is a technique that I have taught a number of paddlers I have coached, most of whom found it beneficial.

1. Sit in an upright but relaxed posture.
2. Think only of the act of breathing.
3. Take a long, slow, deep breath. Visualise the air flowing into every corner of your lungs.
4. When your lungs are full, hold your breath for about 3 seconds.
5. Breathe out, visualising the air flowing out of your lungs.
6. When your lungs are completely empty, pause and repeat the exercise three or four more times.

This exercise helps one relax and reduces physical and mental tension.

People who need to 'psyche-up' can perform the breathing exercises described later in this chapter. These can be performed in a much more energetic manner so that one gets the physical benefits without the calming effects.

Visualisation

Perform this exercise immediately after the breath control exercise and immediately before running the rapid or drop.

1. In your 'mind's eye', picture the rapid, complete with the flowing water, obstacles and hazards.
2. See yourself paddling in complete control down the line that you have chosen.
3. Picture yourself arriving in the safe eddy at the bottom of the rapid smiling with pleasure at the successful outcome.

This act of visualisation has a number of positive effects:

1. It habituates you to that particular rapid, even though you haven't physically been there yet.
2. It prepares you mentally and physically for the demands that are about to be made of you.
3. It instils a positive view of the outcome which reduces anxiety.

...'If you cannot visualise a successful outcome, don't run the rapid!'...

Mental Rehearsal

Experienced paddlers, who have had considerable practice of visualisation, will be able to take this a stage further, visualising the sequence of manoeuvres, and even the stroke sequences that will be needed to stay on a complex and technical line.

It has been shown that athletes who are practised in these techniques actually send the same signals through their nervous system that they will use when they perform the actual task they are visualising. The difference is that the brain sends much weaker versions of the signals so that they don't actually result in physical movement.

Fig. 5.3 Psyching down.

Positive Focus

When deciding whether or not to run a rapid, the risks posed by the level of difficulty and the seriousness of the hazards are assessed. Once the decision to run the rapid is made we must focus our minds on where we want to be, **not** where we don't want to be. If you are thinking of the stopper that you wish to avoid, that is precisely where you will end up! Focus your attention on the route that you have chosen, on the path that you wish the boat to follow.

1. Visualisation can be used by relative novices, mental rehearsal cannot because they do not have the memories on which to base their rehearsal.
2. If you cannot visualise a successful outcome, don't run the rapid!

'Psyching Up'

There are a few things that people who feel the need to 'psyche up' ought to consider seriously:

1. Although it works for them it may be the last thing that other members need.
2. Is it really for them, or do they do it because their mates have always done it?
3. At what point should they stop? No matter how high their optimum arousal level, once they go beyond that point their performance will crash as quickly as anyone else's.

Fig. 5.4 Psyching up!

Warming Up

If there is a long easy section at the start of your river run, then the very act of paddling gently is sufficient to warm you up before the more difficult sections make sudden and strenuous demands on your body. **However,** if you are going to be committed to difficult and demanding paddling within minutes, or even seconds, then a more 'formal' warm up session is essential. These can be done on the river bank or on the water, providing there is at least a short easy section above the first rapid or drop.

Physically warming up **before** taking on a demanding section of white water has a number of benefits:

Injury Prevention

If the body isn't properly warmed up before strenuous exercise we run the risk of torn muscles and ligaments. Having warmed up, we are able to use the whole of our normal range of movement without risking injury and have therefore, in effect, increased our range of available movement.

Reactions and Coordination

If the body is thoroughly warmed up, the efficiency of the transfer of messages from the nerve ends to the muscles is increased. This results in improved coordination and faster reactions.

Mental Preparation

It is worthwhile going through a 'formal', bank based, warm up even on easy rivers. This is because it enables paddlers to develop a routine, so that when they warm up before a difficult run it becomes part of a calming, reassuring ritual.

Techniques

Those with a background in physical training will probably already have a warm up routine that they can easily adapt to the needs of white water paddling. The following approach to warming up is one that most people can use, even if they aren't 'into' fitness training.

In my view, a warm up session should contain the following elements in the order shown:

- Gentle exercise
- Moderate exercise
- Mobility exercises
- Breathing exercises

A good start to the process, when paddling in cold climates, is to change in a warm place and travel to the river in a warm car.

Gentle exercise

This should last for a **minimum** of five minutes, preferably nearer ten. On dry land a gentle jog along the river bank is fine. On the water a leisurely paddle, against the current if necessary, is all that is required. The pace of this session should be such that the paddler is breathing deeply but never 'out of breath', and should carry on until he develops a light sweat.

Moderate Exercise

This should only last for 1 or 2 minutes, as we don't want to build up lactic acid. On the bank, this could consist of a short run at a pace which would no longer allow you to talk, followed by standing still and going through the movements involved in normal forward paddling. The arms, shoulders and trunk should start at a gentle pace and then move on to a brisk pace, (**not** flat out). On the water, a short brisk paddle will suffice.

Mobility Exercises

These are intended to warn your body of what is to come and ensure that your body will not be caught by surprise if it is asked to suddenly operate at the ends of it's range of **normal** movement. The joints and groups of muscles that paddlers need to prepare are in the following areas:

- Neck
- Shoulders
- Those involved in trunk rotation
- Hamstrings, (simply because of the sitting position in kayak)
- Wrists
- Ankles, (in canoe)

Neck

Stand in a relaxed but upright posture, feet slightly apart, looking straight ahead. Keeping your eyes at the same level, gently turn your head so that you are looking over your shoulder. Stop when you feel your muscles beginning to resist, hold the position for a couple of seconds, then face forward again. This initial movement is to warn your muscles of the movement to come. Repeat the movement and this time hold the position for a minimum of a slow count to ten. As you feel your muscles relaxing turn your head a bit further till you feel resistance again. (At no time should you feel any pain or even discomfort).

Repeat the whole of the procedure, this time looking over the other shoulder.

This exercise can be done sitting in your boat.

...'At no time should you feel any pain or discomfort.'...

Shoulders

Exercise One - Standing in the same position as for the neck exercise, starting with your hands by your sides, gently swing your arms forwards till they are above your head and then behind you in a circular motion. Repeat the action without stopping so that it is a continuous action. Keep the action going for a slow count to ten.

In your boat, start by sitting upright and relaxed, holding your paddle so that it is resting on the front deck of your boat or on your knees. Hold your paddle with your hands wider apart than usual. Keep your arms fully extended and slowly lift the paddle with the shaft vertical and raise it above and then behind your head, stopping **before** you experience discomfort. Hold this position only for a couple of seconds and return to the start position. Repeat the procedure, this time holding the position for a slow count to ten.

Exercise Two - Stand in an upright position again and, keeping your hands by your sides, 'shrug' your shoulders and then keep the movement going so that they move in a circular fashion. Keep it up for a slow count to ten and then repeat the action with your shoulders rotating in the other direction.

This exercise can be performed sitting in your boat.

Trunk Rotation

Stand with your feet shoulder width apart and your hands on your hips. Keeping your feet still, slowly rotate your upper body, once again stopping before you experience discomfort. Hold the position for a couple of seconds and then return to the start position. Repeat the movement, this time holding the position for a slow count of ten.

Repeat the whole sequence, this time rotating in the other direction.

In the boat you can use the same sequence except that you are sitting down. Instead of putting your hands on your hips, reach round with your paddle blade and place it on the back deck. (Fig. 5.5)

Fig. 5.5 Trunk rotation exercise.

Hamstrings

Stand with your feet together, bend at the waist and reach down to touch your toes. Once again only bend as far as it takes to feel some resistance, stop before you feel any real discomfort. Hold the position for a couple of seconds and stand up. Repeat the exercise, this time holding for a slow count to twenty.

In your boat reach forward to touch your toes and try and kiss the deck of your boat at the same time. (Fig. 5.6)

Fig. 5.6 Hamstring exercise.

Wrists

1. Stand with your elbows at your side and your hands held out in front of you. Extend your fingers so that they are fully spread out and then curl them up to make a fist. Repeat this action twenty times.
2. With your hands forming the same shape they would make if they were holding a paddle shaft, gently roll your hands around in a circular motion. Ten rotations in one direction and then ten in the other.

These actions can be performed equally well on the bank or in the boat.

Ankles

Sit down, keep one leg extended and cross the other so that your ankle is resting on your thigh. Hold the crossed leg in position with one hand and using the other hand to guide it, gently rotate your foot in a circular motion, ten times in one direction, and then ten in the other. Repeat with the other ankle.

This exercise can be performed on the bank or in an open boat.

Breathing Exercises

These can be done purely for the physical benefits of increased oxygenation of the blood and the flushing out of fatigue by-products and also as a deliberate mental relaxation technique.

On the bank immediately after your mobility exercises, start by standing upright with your hands held above your head. Crouch down so that your knees are touching your chest and your hands are on the ground. At the same time breathe out so that your lungs are empty. Hold this position for a second or two and then stand up and reach for the sky. Take a deep breath as you do so and hold your breath and the outstretched position for a couple of seconds. Repeat the cycle several times.

Warm Downs

After strenuous exercise it is a good idea to 'warm down' with 5-10 minutes of gentle exercise. This ensures that well oxygenated blood flows throughout your body, flushing out harmful fatigue poisons, ensuring a more rapid recovery and preventing sore muscles.

The pace should be even gentler than the warm up. Whereas on the warm up exercise you should be able to talk in short sentences interspersed with a breath or two, on the warm down you should be able to hold a continuous conversation.

Posture Correction

Sitting in a kayak forces paddlers to adopt a very poor posture. The spinal column is designed to remain curved. By sitting in a kayak we straighten out this natural curve in such a way that the discs that separate our vertebrae are squeezed outwards. This results in stiffness and even considerable discomfort if the disc bulges sufficiently to put pressure on nearby nerve bundles. Picking up a heavy plastic boat with your discs already weakened could easily result in a 'slipped disc'.

The following exercise is a good way to help your spine recover. Lie face down on the ground and leaving your hips where they are, raise your shoulders off the ground in a 'press-up' like motion. Hold this position for about a minute. Repeat if necessary. (Fig. 5.7).

Fig. 5.7 Posture correction exercise.

Upper Conwy, North Wales

Ian sat in the eddy staring at the entry to Bryn Bras Falls. We had inspected from the bank, chosen our line of descent and positioned other members of the group with throw lines. He didn't look too confident, so I decided to give him a final pep talk.

"Forget the obstacles and focus on being on the line." He didn't look convinced, so stupidly I went on to leave him with a negative mental image, "Come on, you've decided to do it because the worst that can happen is a cold swim. You'll do fine, but if you do go for a swim, remember: positive mental attitude. You're not a victim, you're a canoeist in temporary difficulties."

Ian nodded, so I paddled to an eddy half way down the rapid, got out of my boat and positioned myself where I could help anyone who didn't manage to avoid a rock that the main flow of the current ran straight in to.

I gave the signal and after a brief hesitation Ian set off. I couldn't help but notice that the other paddlers waiting at the top of the rapid were rolling about, shaking with laughter. Needless to say, Ian blew the line and was swept up against the 'magnetic rock'. When later I asked the others what had struck them as so funny, they told me that as Ian set off they heard him muttering: "Positive mental attitude, you're not a victim, you're a temporary canoeist in difficulties."

Chapter 6
Scouting Techniques

Throughout this chapter, when reference is made to a group, it can mean a group of boaters or a number of rafts travelling in convoy. The lead paddler or raft guide has to:

1. Spot potential hazards.
2. Work out which way the water is flowing.
3. Choose a line that all the members of the group will be able to paddle.
4. Decide at what point to get off the water and inspect from the safety of the bank.

Factors Affecting Choice of Technique

One of the basic principles of safe river running is that you never run anything blind, (the line of sight principle). If the river is straight forward and the lead paddler can see a reasonable distance ahead, decisions can be made without even needing to slow down. On a technically difficult stretch of river where visibility is limited by tight bends and drops, it may be necessary to inspect every rapid from the bank.

The above examples represent the two extremes of a continuum. In between there are a whole range of techniques we can employ, (fig. 6.1). As the river becomes more difficult, (in relation to the group's ability), and visibility deteriorates we have to 'change down a gear' and adopt a slower but more appropriate approach. As the river gets easier and we can see further, we can speed things up again.

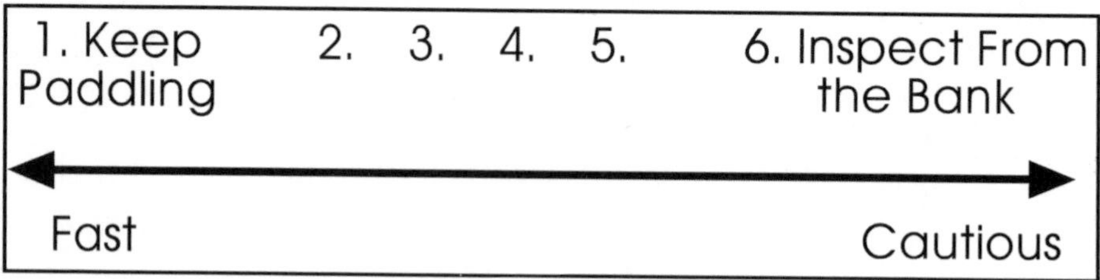

Fig. 6.1 A range of paddling techniques.

Technical Difficulty / Level of Ability

The smaller and more skilled a group, the more difficult the stretch of river they can paddle without changing to a more cautious approach. Whereas one group may decide to bank inspect a grade III rapid, another may choose to leap-frog from eddy to eddy down a grade IV. If both parties have correctly assessed their ability, then both parties have made the correct decision and shown good judgement.

Visibility

This is an entirely different matter. If a flat but fast moving stretch of water disappears around a blind bend and there is no other way of seeing what lies around the corner, someone has to get out and have a look. This is as true of the most technically competent 'hair boater' as it is of the complete novice. If there is a river-wide strainer caused by a recently fallen tree, and they decide not to inspect, the only difference is that there will be a few more famous paddlers at one of the funerals.

...'never run anything blind.'...

Techniques

By constantly switching techniques as the nature of the river changes we can descend a river quickly but safely. The following techniques are available to us:

- Keep paddling
- Slow down and manoeuvre
- Move from eddy to eddy
- Scout, using micro-eddies
- Lead paddler inspects from the bank
- Whole group inspects from the bank

1. Keep Paddling

On straight sections of river where it is possible to see far enough ahead to assess the difficulties and choose a line, the whole group can move together and move as fast or as slow as they wish.

2. Slow Down and Manoeuvre

As the river gets more difficult or bends reduce visibility, it may be necessary to slow down, or even reverse paddle to give the lead paddler more time to assess the situation and make decisions. In order to get a better view of the way ahead, the lead paddler may decide to go around a bend as far on the outside as possible even though this may mean going close to overhanging trees and other obstructions. The lead paddler will probably therefore signal the rest of the team to take a safer route.

Open boaters in non-specialist boats can do all the above, and stand up in the boat to get a better view.

3. Move From Eddy to Eddy

Where visibility is further reduced, it may only be possible to see the line as far as the next eddy or pool. If the line is straight forward and the eddies large the group may move down to the next eddy one behind the other. If the lead paddler isn't sure if the whole group can fit in the next eddy, or exactly how difficult it is going to be to make the eddy, he may choose to run the rapid first and then signal the rest of the group to come down or not. If the eddies are obvious but small, the group will have to leapfrog or eddy-hop. (See Chapter 9 Organisation).

4. Scout Using Micro-Eddy

Often it will be possible for the lead paddler to get to a position where it is possible to see round a bend by getting his boat into a micro-eddy. It doesn't matter if he is the only member of the group who has the skill to make the eddy. This is because from his observation post he is able to signal the rest of the group, (see Chapter 10), to either follow on down, run it one at a time, or get out and inspect.

Fig. 6.2 The joys of being lead paddler.

5. Lead Paddler Inspects From the Bank

If there is no way the lead paddler can inspect from the water, he will have to get out and inspect from the bank. If the way forward turns out to be straightforward, the lead paddler simply gets back on the water and leads the team down.

This technique is especially useful in open canoes and rafts where it is so much easier to hop in and out of the boat than in a kayak.

6. Whole Group Inspects From the Bank

This technique is the only option when the way forward involves a complex line that has to be memorised, or a risky line where each individual will need to decide whether to run it or not. (See Chapter 7: Assessing Risk).

Markers

When scouting a rapid and discussing or memorising a line, paddlers will refer to markers. These will be used to indicate a change of direction or the position of a feature that can be used. These may be bank features or, particularly on big volume rivers, water features. There is plenty of room for misunderstandings here; to less experienced members of the party one standing wave may look much the same as another. One way around this is to throw a stone at the feature to ensure that everyone is talking about the same one.

Early Warning Signs

The two main reasons for a loss of visibility are a tight bend or a sudden drop. Other signs may tell us that there is a dangerous hazard immediately around the bend or that the drop is large enough to be considered a hazard in itself. If these signs are present, a prudent lead paddler will get off the water well ahead of the hazard and not risk trying to get as close as possible using micro-eddies.

Noise

When paddling on a river we soon get used to the general background noise of the rushing water. If the roaring of a particular rapid or fall can be heard above this background noise, it is probably worth getting out and inspecting from the bank.

Spray

Big drops on volume rivers are often indicated by the spray created by the mass of falling water.

The Tree Line

Sometimes it is possible to see across the land in a bend in the river, even when it isn't possible to see around it. If you are level with the tops of the trees that grow on the river bank on the far side of the bend, there must be a considerable increase in the gradient of the river ahead.

The tree line is often a useful indicator of gradient on straight sections of river, where it is possible to see some distance ahead.

Event Horizon

Upstream of a drop, a paddler will be able to see the foreground, the background, but not the middle ground. Trees and other tall objects in the middle ground will appear to have their lower parts missing. This odd perspective gives the impression of a false horizon, and is a warning sign that should not be ignored.

Landmarks

There are some hazards where the river is fast flowing and lacking in eddies for some considerable distance upstream. Wherever a guidebook, or information from other paddlers, indicates this to be the case, it is **imperative** that paddlers inspect the section on foot before running the river and choose landmarks that will warn them when to get off the river.

There is a serious rapid just below the bridge to Cwm Penmachno on the Afon Conwy in North Wales where this is the case. It is notorious, and it is clearly indicated in the guide book that it should be pre-inspected and that it is normally portaged. None the less, every year, groups of paddlers find themselves huddled on a large boulder in midstream, waiting to be rescued by local paddlers on their way home from work, or by the local Mountain Rescue Team. They are the lucky ones, others have been drowned there.

Lead paddlers can make mistakes or overestimate other paddlers' ability. If you feel the need to bank inspect a rapid that the lead paddler thinks the group can run on sight, head for the side.

Quite often lead paddlers may choose a more difficult line than necessary because it will enable them to see further; therefore be prepared to make your own decisions and choose a different line.

Top: Oar rig on the Grand Canyon, USA. Note the broken oar!
Photo: Ray Goodwin
Bottom: Pinned raft, the wilder side of commercial rafting, Gore Canyon, Colorado River, Colorado, USA.
Photo: Paul O'Sullivan

Chapter 7
Assessing Risk

All adventure sports involve taking risks. Whether making lightening fast decisions as they descend a river, or calmly weighing up the various factors from the safety of the bank, paddlers should always assess the level of risk involved. They also need to decide what level of risk they are prepared to take on. Although a leader can advise, and where they have a legal or moral responsibility, reserve the right to veto a rash decision, all paddlers should make their own individual risk assessment.

When deciding whether or not to run a rapid, it is best to break the rapid down into sections, i.e. from one place of safety to the next. When trying to work out the level of risk one has to ask the following questions:

1. What hazards are there?
2. What are the consequences should you fail to avoid any of the hazards on a given section?
3. Does the flow of the water avoid or feed into the hazards?
4. What line will you need to stay on to paddle the rapid safely?
5. What manoeuvres will you have to effect to stay on your chosen line?
6. What is the probability of you being unable to stay on your chosen line and avoid the above hazards?

Consequences

When working out the consequences of failing to avoid a particular hazard we are looking at the **objective** dangers. That is to say that if a riverwide strainer is terminal, it will just as surely kill an expert as a novice should they get swept into it.

Rating the Consequences

One way of trying to quantify the consequences of falling foul of a hazard or series of hazards, (which can have a cumulative effect in terms of exhaustion and hypothermia), is to rate them on a scale of 1-5. One being the least serious and five the most. On this scale the **consequences** of failing to stay on one's chosen line would be rated as follows:

1. An easy swim.
2. Knocks and bruises and/or a long cold swim.
3. The potential for serious injury and the certainty of a considerable fright.
4. A risk of death and a high risk of serious injury.

Top and bottom: It's not only on the river that we take risks. Shimshal Gorge, Pakistan. Photos: Loel Collins.

5. Almost certain death.

Although the above is similar to the a-f system used in Terry Storry's guidebooks, it is important **not** to rely on a guidebooks assessment of the possible consequences. Each paddler should make his own observations and assessments. Besides; rapids change. Trees fall, boulders move, sections of bedrock collapse and water levels fluctuate wildly.

Probability

When working out the probability of avoiding hazards we are trying to quantify something that is very **subjective.** That is to say that it will be different for each individual. It is quite possible to have a hazard that is positioned in such a way that an expert will almost certainly be able to avoid it and a novice will almost certainly be swept into it. The key safety factor here is the ability to make an honest self-assessment of one's own capabilities.

Variables affecting the probability:

- The technical difficulty of staying on line
- The skill of the individual paddler
- How the individual feels on the day

The importance of the last of these variables cannot be emphasised enough. It doesn't matter if you've run the rapid a hundred times before. If it doesn't 'feel' right, don't do it! If we look at the scale below, a skilled paddler, looking at a relatively straight forward section of grade lll, could rate his chances of a successful outcome at anything between l and 3, depending on how well he was paddling on the day.

Rating the Probability

On this scale, the **probability** of blowing the line and failing to avoid the hazards would be rated as follows:

1. Almost certain success.
2. It would require a major 'pilot error' to end up sufficiently off line and it may be possible to avoid the hazards by paddling a different line than the one you had in mind.
3. A simple mistake could result in failing to avoid the hazards, but prompt remedial action would probably retrieve the situation.
4. It would only require a small error to end up off line and in trouble.
5. Almost certain failure.

Combining Probability and Consequence

In order to decide how high the risk factor is, we need to combine the probability of failure with the consequences. It is relatively low risk to run a rapid where failure to make the line would result in certain death (5), **if** the chances of blowing the line are virtually nil (1). Equally, the risk factor is relatively low where the paddler is deemed to be almost certain to end up in the hazard (5), **if** the consequences of such an action are only an easy swim and a dented ego (1).

In practice, it will be a case of: "I don't like the look of that. There is quite a difficult approach. I'm not paddling particularly well and if I do end up under that undercut it could get very serious. I'll portage." However, **purely to illustrate** various combinations of factors and the risk they pose, we can give a number to the risk factor by multiplying the probability rating by the consequence rating. This gives us a scale of risk that runs from 1 (negligible) to 25 (almost certain death).

Profiles

Consider the four people in illustration 7.1. Each of them will come up with a different risk rating for the rapid they are looking at, and each of them will have a different level of risk that they are willing to take.

Fig 7.1 Decision time!

The rapid is serious enough to rate a consequence rating of 3, this being an objective factor which is the same for all the paddlers. The rapid is also technically tricky which means that some skilful manoeuvring will be required to ensure success.

Jane enjoys paddling white water and taking reasonable risks. She would rate her risk factor limit at 12.

She is a highly skilled paddler and feels 'on form'. Therefore she rates her probability factor as a 3. When combined with the consequence rating of 3 this gives Jane a **risk factor of 9**. She therefore has no qualms about running the rapid.

Eric has a similar outlook to Jane and also rates his risk factor limit as a 12. However he is only an averagely skilled paddler and is feeling 'off form', having missed a few simple break-outs higher upstream. He therefore rates his probability factor as a 5. When combined with the consequence factor of 3, this gives Eric a **risk factor of 15**. He has no qualms about portaging.

Sue enjoys white water paddling and playboating. However, she doesn't particularly enjoy risk taking and is very aware of her responsibilities to her young family. She would rate her acceptable risk factor as 8.

Sue is also an averagely skilful paddler but unlike Eric is feeling on form. She therefore rates her probability factor as a 4. Combined with the consequence factor of 3, this gives Sue a **risk factor of 12.** Sue will also hit the portage trail.

Paul enjoys risk taking and regards the prospect of 'a good trashing' as part of the learning process. His awareness of his lack of experience and skill means that he will 'only' accept a risk factor of 16! As he improves he will probably go on to accept a risk factor as high as 20.

Despite the fact that he is feeling 'on form' he is almost certain to blow the difficult line. He therefore has a probability factor of 5. Combined with the consequence factor of 3 this gives Paul a **risk factor of 15.** Despite being the least able paddler in the group Paul will run the rapid. He does so knowing that his actions pose no threat to the other members of the group and in full knowledge of the risks involved.

Assuming the above people to be a group of friends, every member of the group has made a careful risk assessment and behaved accordingly. However it is worth pointing out that in a situation where a leader has a legal or moral responsibility for the other members of the group it would be foolish of the leader to allow Paul to run the rapid. No responsible leader could allow a person in his charge to tackle something he was almost certain to fail on where there was a potential for serious injury.

Chapter 8
Planning a Descent

Whether it be an 8 day unsupported trip in Nepal or a day's paddling on one of the local rivers, the factors that affect our planning from a safety viewpoint are the same:

- The skill level and experience of your team
- The difficulty of the rivers you would like to paddle
- Water levels
- How committing the river is
- How the individual feels on the day

The Team

A sizeable portion of the time I have spent teaching on white water has been spent rebuilding individual paddlers' shattered confidence. The story is nearly always the same. Their 'friends' tell them not to worry that it's a grade harder than they've ever paddled. "It's easy for the grade. You'll be fine." What the so called friends really mean is that they are determined to paddle a given river for their own selfish reasons, and if our paddler isn't up to it, tough! Inevitably our paddler gets 'trashed' and his self confidence plummets.

...'paddle with people who will support each other.'...

It is important to create a team environment. On wild rivers, one should paddle with people who will support each other. Competition is a luxury we can only afford on safe sites and play waves!

Rivers should be chosen on the basis of what the **least** able paddler can manage. Many rivers have sections of differing levels of difficulty. This allows the 'hair boaters' to warm up on the easier section whilst the less able paddlers have a stretching but enjoyable time. The more able paddlers then go on to test themselves on the harder section and everyone goes home happy.

If you are choosing a trip for a team that includes people you haven't paddled with before, be careful. When some people say they paddle grade V they mean that they have paddled the odd V where a positive mental attitude and good reactions will get you down in one piece. Their boating skills and ability to 'work the water' may not be up to more technically demanding grade Vs.

Difficulty

When taking on a river that has rarely or never been run before, paddlers have to make some 'guestimates' about the difficulty of the river based on it's volume and it's gradient. The steeper a river is, the less volume of water it needs to be a difficult paddle. Equally, the more volume it has, the less gradient it needs to reach the same level of difficulty, all be it in a very different way. Most of us are quite happy to gather information on a river from a guidebook or paddlers who have first hand knowledge of it.

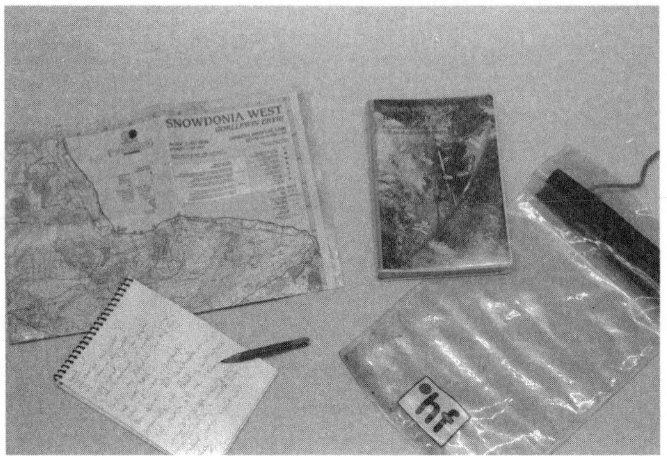

Fig. 8.1 Planning.

Guidebooks

It is important to remember that a guidebook's function is to give a **rough** idea of what we are in for. It is not supposed to be a substitute for our eyes, ears, brain and 'river sense'. In my view a guide book should provide the following information:

- Local customs and attitudes. (This can be a very important safety factor)
- The general layout and character of the river system
- The volume and gradient
- The overall difficulty of the river
- The difficulty of any rapids or drops that are markedly harder than the rest of the river
- The position of any mandatory or advisable portages
- Information on any hidden or easily overlooked hazards
- Where to start
- Where to finish
- Other points at which it is possible to get off, (escape routes)

Everything else should be down to personal observation and judgement. Trees fall across rivers, boulders move, eroded bedrock collapses, water levels change. If you get into difficulties it is your problem, not the guidebook writer's.

...'it is your problem, not the guidebook writer's.'...

River Grades or 'Class'

The way we try and define difficulty is by use of a grading system. Although adequate, this system has lots of flaws. How can a 5 cumecs (cubic metres per second) creek, so steep you get vertigo, be given the same grade as a river like the Sun Khosi in Nepal, which has a very low gradient but can run at 400 cumecs? As outlined in chapter 3, I feel that the system breaks down completely when it comes to big drops.

The truth is that the system does work quite well; providing the guidebook also tells you if the river is:

Low, high or medium volume.
Continuous or Pool/Drop.

Only with experience will we get to know what a high volume grade III or grade V is like, and what makes a low volume steep creek just as difficult, all be it in a completely different way.

The International River Grading System

In 'normal' water levels you could translate the table, (fig. 8.2), as follows:

Grade I

Even complete novices could paddle on this provided they can be kept away from overhanging trees.

Grade I	Grade II	Grade III	Grade IV	Grade V	Grade VI
	Passage free	Route recognisable	Route not always recognisable. Inspection mostly necessary.	Inspection essential	Generally speaking impossible
Regular stream Regular waves small rapids	Irregular stream Irregular waves Medium rapids, small stoppers, eddies, whirlpools and pressure areas.*	High irregular waves Larger rapids Stoppers, eddies, whirlpools and pressure areas	Heavy continuous rapids Heavy stoppers, whirlpools and pressure areas	Extreme rapids Stoppers, whirlpools, and pressure areas.	Possibly navigable at particular water levels. High risk
Simple obstructions	Simple obstructions in stream. Small drops	Isolated boulders, *(small)* drops, and numerous obstructions in stream.	Boulders obstructing stream, big with undertow.	Narrow passages, steep gradients and drops with difficult access and landing	

* 'Pressure areas' refers to water piling up against a rock or other obstacle, (sometimes called cushions in this country).

N.B. Weirs are not classified as white water and as such are not evaluated. They are either easily navigable or very dangerous.

Fig. 8.2 The International River Grading System

Grade II

The ideal grade on which to learn and hone basic white water boating skills. There are some dangers but they can be easily manoeuvred around, provided you recognise them.

Grade III

At this grade you can come across nearly all the water features and hazards there are. However, a 'line' down the rapid is clear enough that a competent paddler could tackle it without the need for a bank inspection. Dangerous hazards are few and easily avoided by those with the skill to manoeuvre. Bank based protection may, in places, be a good idea with relative novices.

Grade IV

The line can be scouted from your boat but it is advisable to bank inspect. The line is difficult to manoeuvre down, even for skilful paddlers. Mistakes can be costly. Bank based rescuers, positioned in advance may be helpful, especially with less experienced paddlers.

Grade V

The line is complex due to the increased number of dangerous hazards that have to be avoided. Bank inspection is essential. Staying on your chosen line will require a high skill level and a cool head. Mistakes will involve risk to life and limb. Where feasible, bank based rescuers, positioned in advance, are the norm.

Grade VI

Only runnable at specific water levels. The slightest mistake will involve risk to life. Even the most skilful and cool headed paddlers will need to feel 'on form' to take one of these on.

If you paddle regularly on, say, Grade IV water at home on low and medium volume rivers, when you go on holiday and paddle high volume rivers, stay on grade III until you get used to the differences. The same also applies to the volume paddler who has a go at creek boating. Drop at least a whole grade until you learn the different style, skills and approach demanded.

Other Systems

In many guide books there are variations on the I - VI system. Many guidebook writers use the symbols + or - to let you know whether a rapid is at the harder or easier end of the grade. It is also common practice to use brackets to indicate isolated rapids that are harder than the rest of the river and easily portaged. If a river was mostly grade III but had a couple of short sections of V it would appear as III (V).

One of the ideas put forward at the International Safety Symposium meeting held in North Wales in 1994 was that we should add the following letters to the grade to provide more information:

S = Steep rivers, those with an average gradient above 1:50.

T = Technical rivers, generally lower volume where rocks are a major hazard to the paddler.

C = Continuous sections of white water (more than 400 metres in length) are present.

R = Remote rivers which are more than ten miles away from the nearest road or habitation.

P = Portages are a likely prospect.

Another idea put forward was to add a seventh grade.

Terry Storry, whose guidebooks are very popular in Britain, uses a dual grade system. In his system the numbers I - VI tell you the degree of technical difficulty. The letters a-f tell you how potentially dangerous the rapid is should you end up swimming it. His seriousness grades are defined as follows:

a = Safe

b = Little Danger

c = Some Danger

d = Dangerous

e = Very Dangerous

f = Extremely Dangerous

In this system one would normally expect a grade of Ia or VIf. However, it does allow for the odd exceptions. It would be possible to give a rapid a grade of IId or even IIe if failure to perform a simple manoeuvre would result in the paddler ending up in a potentially lethal strainer.

Whilst I agree that it can give a more complete picture, I am not that keen on the system. This is because I believe that too many paddlers are already over-reliant on the guidebook writer and not reliant enough on their own eyes and judgement.

...'paddlers should make their own individual risk assessment.'...

Maps

I find that conventional maps are of little, if any, use once you are afloat. They are however very useful in the planning stages for identifying access and egress points and finding landmarks to warn you of the approach of major rapids or portages. In Switzerland and other parts of Europe there are maps made specifically for boaters that contain the above information. They also use a colour code to let you know at a glance what grade any given section of river is. These maps **must** be used in conjunction with the guidebook as they give no indication of what 'normal' water levels are. On remote rivers it is essential to carry maps in case you are forced to walk out, through boat loss or injury.

Water Levels

As discussed in Chapter 2, changes in water levels can make your intended paddle considerably harder or easier. Most guidebooks will tell you how to work out what the average or guidebook level is. This will usually involve water gauges, which are often positioned near bridges, or failing that, local landmarks such as prominent boulders. Study them carefully and try and find out how much these changes affect the river you have in mind. If no information is available, assume that the higher the water level, the more serious / dangerous the river becomes.

Seasonal Changes

All the river systems of the world are either fed by melting snow/glaciers or rain. Snow and ice act as a reservoir, making the release of water predictable on a seasonal basis. So, if for example you are planning a trip with the 'Wild Bunch', you would go to the French Alps in May and the rivers would almost certainly be huge. On the other hand, if you wanted to paddle some of the more technical gorges you might choose to go in early August when the rivers are low but still runnable.

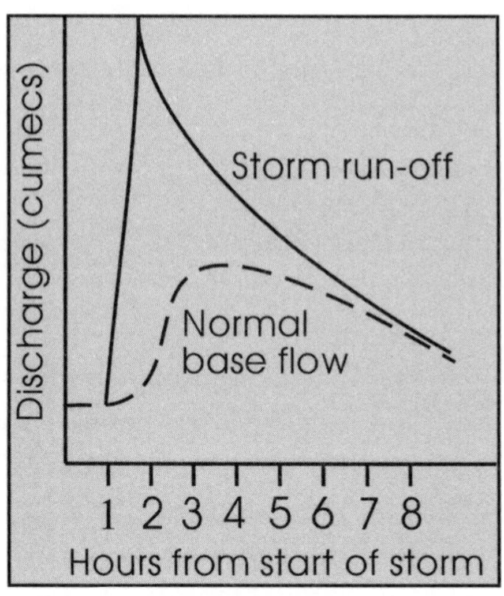

Fig. 8.3 Water flow on spate rivers.

Unfortunately, in Britain the only seasonal change is that it is more likely to rain in the colder months.

Daily Variations

In snow melt rivers the water is usually lower in the morning and at its highest in the late afternoon, due to the influence of the midday sun.

In rain fed systems water levels go up and down like yo-yos. Keep an eye on the weather charts for some days before your planned trip. Cultivate local paddlers who won't mind you phoning them for a rain check. Spate rivers come up far faster than they go down. Therefore it is safer to get on them when they have reached the optimum level and are on the way back down. (Fig. 8.3). Mature rivers, fed by heads of water such as large lakes come up more slowly and hold their water for longer.

Commitment

If a river trip involves being several hours from help should someone get injured, it raises the seriousness stakes considerably. A multi-day trip will involve you paddling a boat that is much heavier and therefore less responsive. I believe that such considerations take a good half or even a whole grade off what I am prepared to paddle. A laden boat increases the probability of error and remoteness increases the consequences.

How You Feel on the Day

This factor really can't be emphasised enough. When planning a day's river running, paddlers should always have a number of rivers on their tick list. This allows considerable flexibility to take into account unseasonable water levels or members of the party feeling off form.

Only once you have taken the above factors into consideration can you decide on which river to paddle, what gear to take, transport arrangements and so on.

Tamba Khosi, Nepal
After a twelve hour bus journey on the most frightening roads imaginable, a meal of 'Dhal Bhat at a local tea house, and a bivvi at the water's edge, I was raring to go. I had already packed and was watching Ray check, for the third time, that he had packed everything.
I couldn't help chuckling. Untypically, he had been very disorganized at the start of the trip. We had even had to take a detour into Central London on the way to the airport to pick up his visa. I had given him no end of 'stick' about this; as you do.
At long last he looked up, a satisfied grin on his face. "No, I haven't forgotten anything," he announced. I looked down at my boat and suddenly felt as 'sick as a chocolate parrot'. "Ah," I groaned, "I have. I've left my helmet at the hotel!!"

Chapter 9
Organisation

Once afloat, small groups of experienced paddlers often find that they have no need for a leader as such. Each paddler assumes a position or role they are happy with and, should a decision be necessary, or a rescue need dealing with, whoever is in the best position to do so temporarily assumes the role of leader/ coordinator.

Unfortunately this state of perfect cooperation is rare. Teams are seldom so well matched. The greater the disparity in experience and the larger the group, the greater the need for organisation and leadership.

No matter how little need there is for a formal leader, any group that wishes to paddle in safety will need to be organised. Each member of the group needs to know:

- The role of each team member
- The way in which the group is going to tackle the river
- The order of descent

Roles

In order to make a safe descent of a river each member of the group will have to accept responsibility and take on one or more roles.

Team Member

All members of a team must have the safety and well being of the whole group as their top priority. We all paddle for our own selfish reasons; however, if these come before our concern for the safety of the other members of the team we are a liability.

All team members need to be honest about what they have to offer, and their own limitations. It is better to say that you are not prepared to take on a certain role than to accept it and foul up through lack of skill or confidence.

The 'Buddy' System

This system involves every member of the party pairing up with another. From that point on, as well as their normal responsibility for the other members of the team, each person is particularly responsible for the welfare of their buddy. This is particularly useful in large groups where it might otherwise be possible for someone to go missing without anyone realising.

Lead Paddler or Raft Guide

This person is not necessarily the leader. This role is often taken on by the more experienced and skilled paddlers or by the person in the group who has paddled the river before. Because of the linear nature of rivers, whoever is out in front has the following responsibilities:

- Choosing a line
- Spotting and avoiding hazards
- Deciding when to bank inspect
- Getting the group off the water well above any portages

Being lead paddler is an exciting, challenging and satisfying role, (see Chapter 6, Scouting Techniques). Taking a turn at being lead paddler on a suitable stretch of river is an important part of a paddler's personal development. If you don't normally take the lead, insist on having a turn out in front on the easier sections. Don't let anyone 'hog the lead' and have all the fun.

Back marker

Sometimes known as 'Tail-End Charlie'. This is another role that is usually taken by one of the more experienced paddlers. This is because they have to pick up the pieces and therefore must be able to take on the role of 'chase boater'.

Fig. 9.1 Tail End Charlie.

They are also at extra risk because everybody else tends to look down river. If they get into trouble there is the possibility that it won't be noticed for some time. When boating, I prefer to have two people take on this role, frequently changing places as back marker. That way they act as a team within a team and feel a special responsibility for each other. (The 'Buddy' system).

Chase Boater

Chase boating is the art of rescuing swimmers or their equipment from your boat rather than from the bank. (See Chapter 15). It is a high risk activity requiring a high level of skill and confidence, fast reflexes, even better judgment and the ability to think on the move. In some groups every paddler will be able to take on this role. In others there may be only one or two people willing and able to take it on.

Specialist Rescue Roles

There are some situations that may require specialist knowledge, skills or aptitude. Examples are rescues that might involve rope-work skills or where there is a risk of ending up in, or a need to enter the water. In the case of the latter it is important that such roles be taken on by people who are strong swimmers and water confident.

If you are not keen on such a role, don't buy a chest-harness buoyancy aid.

Should such a rescue situation arise, time will be precious, so it is better to identify who can take on these roles in advance.

Motivator / Agony Aunt

Not all team roles involve paddling skills. Everybody needs a shoulder to lean on or a sympathetic ear at some stage.

Team Leader

The leader takes on a multitude of roles. At the very least he is an organiser, motivator, risk assessor and communicator. He may well find himself having to be counsellor, psychologist, coach, pillar of strength and wisdom, to name but a few!

A team leader will also have a role as a safety advisor. Where there is a legal or moral obligation, or the consequences of someone else's poor judgment puts the welfare of the team at risk, he may have to veto an individual's decision.

Tackling The River

How a group is best organised will depend on:

- The size of the group
- The nature of the river
- The nature of the group

Size of Group

It is seldom a good idea to solo paddle on white water. To paddle as a pair is acceptable although, if one paddler gets into trouble, that only leaves one potential rescuer, which would limit the number of options available. With two rafts working in tandem this is less of a problem as there will be plenty of person power even if only the two raft guides are experienced. If you decide to paddle as a pair, bear this in mind when assessing risks and err on the cautious side.

Three is a good number from a safety point of view. Four is probably the ideal. This is because it allows people to 'buddy up' and operate as two pairs who, although still members of the team of four, are **particularly responsible** for the welfare of their 'buddy'. It is also a small enough team to operate with a minimum of organisation.

The River

Different types of river require different approaches.

Low and Medium Volume Rivers

On low and medium volume rivers that are fairly straightforward it is usually best to travel as one small group, one behind the other, keeping fairly close together. If the leader is not the lead paddler he may well position himself in the centre of the group so that he can see both the lead paddler and the back marker.

High Volume Rivers

On high volume rivers the distance between safe eddies, and the size of the water features mean that there has to be a reasonable gap between each paddler. It is probably best to travel as semi-independent buddy groups, (pairs). One of the good things about the buddy system is that you can pair a young 'hot shot' paddler, with an experienced paddler. The experienced paddler will have the 'eyes' to choose a safe line and the 'hot shot' the skills to stay on it. With this arrangement, instead of being able to see the whole group, paddlers will only be able to see the pair immediately in front and behind them, and only then intermittently, from the top of waves. It is therefore vital that the lead pair stop whenever they find a large enough eddy to re-group and count heads.

'Technical' Rivers

On technically difficult low and medium rivers it may also be better to travel as semi-independent groups of two or three paddlers. The twists, turns and drops restrict visibility and the technical difficulty means that paddlers need more space.

A group of six would split into two semi- independent groups of three. Each group of three would act independently, obeying the 'line of sight' principle within the subgroup. Whenever the back marker of the first group lost sight of the lead paddler of the second group, the first group would stop and wait until the second group came back into view.

Group Control

In the above section we looked at how different factors might make us choose different ways of moving together as one group. On some sections of river, it may be preferable that not all paddlers are on the move at once. With all the following techniques it is essential that every member of the group understands what is required and that a simple and efficient system of signals is agreed on. (See Chapter 10, Communication).

One at a Time

In its simplest form, the lead paddler runs the rapid first and then makes a signal. On seeing this, a second member of the group runs the rapid. Everyone else stays put until the lead paddler/raft guide signals again for the third person and so on.

On harder rapids where a bank inspection has taken place, most or even all of the other members of the team may provide bank protection while one member of the team runs the rapid. In a large group it is essential that the group are well briefed and that the leader uses a clear set of signals to keep things moving.

As soon as the paddler reaches the bottom of the rapid he must get out and change places

Fig. 9.2 One at a time with bank support.

with one of the people on the bank who is then free to get ready to run the rapid. If possible it is best to keep two people free of bank protection jobs. That way, while one person is running the rapid, another is getting ready to run it. This speeds up the process considerably.

Leapfrogging

This works particularly well with **small** groups of boaters on rivers where there are lots of small eddies that will only take one boat at a time. A large group of paddlers would have to break into subgroups (ideally pairs) to make this work. Often this technique and eddy hopping are only used for short technical sections, the group reverting to moving together, or one at a time, as the river becomes easier or harder.

With this method every paddler in the group takes it in turn to be lead paddler and back marker. The lead paddler signals the back marker, who leapfrogs the whole group, becoming the new lead paddler and so on.

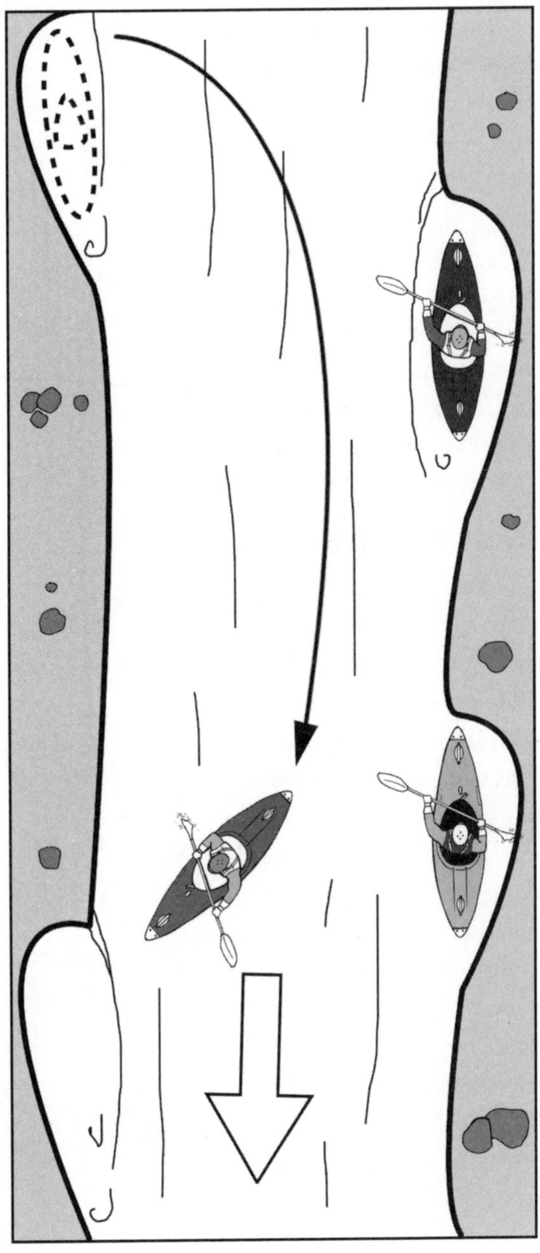

Fig. 9.3 Leapfrogging

Eddy Hopping

This works in similar situations to leapfrogging. A possible advantage over leapfrogging is that the order of descent doesn't change. Strangely enough the disadvantage is that it is harder to keep control of the group.

The lead paddler moves down to the next eddy that he thinks all the other members of the group will have the ability to paddle in to. On the lead paddler's signal, the rest of the team move down one eddy. It is vital that paddlers do not set off until the paddler downstream of them is well clear of the eddy they want to move down to. (See fig. 9.4).

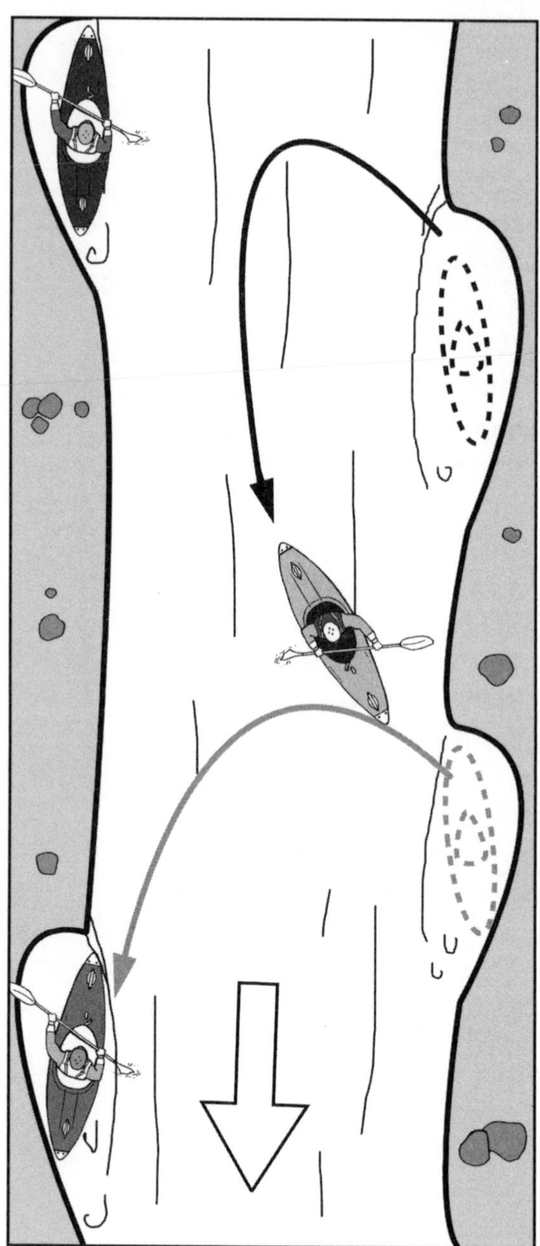

Fig. 9.4 Eddy hopping.

Order of Descent

With a group of evenly matched paddlers it is only really necessary to decide on who is the lead paddler and who are the back markers. Everyone else can paddle in any order they like, as long as they keep an eye on the person in front and the person behind them. With a mixed ability group it is best to pair people up so that the more skilled/experienced paddlers are teamed up with the less able. The exception being the back markers who both need to be good paddlers.

Chapter 10
Communication

Good communication avoids misunderstandings, and their subsequent mistakes. Over the years, I have been asked to look into a number of kayaking accidents. In almost every case such misunderstandings were key contributory factors.

Briefings

In some ways, avoiding misunderstandings is much more difficult when paddling with a group of friends than as a group of people who have paid or formally asked someone to guide or instruct them. In the latter case, people will expect the leader to allocate roles and give a formal briefing so that everyone knows what's happening.

...'clear and concise.'...

Formal briefings

At the beginning of a trip a number of things need to be made clear to all members of the team:

- The nature of the river and likely hazards
- Who is taking on which role and the responsibilities it entails
- The order of descent
- Who is who's buddy, if you decide to use the buddy system
- Who is carrying what items of rescue equipment
- What signals the group is going to use
- Any pre-arranged actions in the event of someone getting into trouble

Leaders should ensure that their briefings and any instructions given are clear and concise. They should know exactly what they are going to say **before** they say it, rather than 'thinking out loud'.

...'use questions to confirm understanding.'...

Members of the party may be apprehensive or distracted, so it may be a good idea to use **questions** to **confirm** that they have understood. The end of a briefing might go something like this:

"If anyone goes for a swim on this section, leave the chase-boating to Angela and me. If you see someone swimming, shout "SWIMMER" to let everyone else know; make your way to the side and then run down the bank and offer what assistance you can.

Eric, if you see a swimmer, who does the chase-boating?"

Informal Situations

In a less formal situation, it may not be at all clear who is responsible for what. Even worse, different members of the group may have completely different views of what their roles are. Often people are loathe to offer leadership which they believe may be unwelcome.

Here, a more subtle approach may be needed. If you feel that all is not as clear or as organised as it might be, it may be better to ask questions, rather than try to give orders.

For example:

"Hey, just so there is no confusion, what signals do you use?"

Or:

"I'm feeling a little off form today; I'd feel a whole lot better if we buddied up."

Or:

"I've brought a first aid kit, whose carrying the split paddles?"

If paddlers feel that they or other members of the group are not clear on what is going on, **they owe it to themselves and the rest of the group to clear things up.**

...'If you aren't sure of what is going on you can be sure that you're not the only one!'...

Signals

A clear set of hand and/or paddle signals can help avoid confusion, save time and increase flexibility. Often, when on or near white water, it is difficult to hear and visual signals are the only practicable option.

Basic Criteria

It really doesn't matter what signals are used, providing they meet the following criteria:

1. Each member of the party is using the same signals.
2. Each signal used has one specific meaning, i.e., is not a mime.
3. Signals are kept to a workable number, (unless you paddle regularly with the group, I would suggest no more than three).
4. Signals are visually sufficiently different that they can't be confused with one another.

Acknowledge Signals

When a signal has been given, the people to whom it is being sent should, if they are not too busy staying upright, repeat it. This achieves two things:

1. The signal is passed on to any member of the group who is out of sight of the original signaller.
2. It confirms that the correct signal has been received and understood.
3. It acts as an acknowledgement so that, if for some reason you can't act on the signal immediately, the person sending it knows that you have seen and understood.

Fail Safes

The following two rules ensure that people don't get into trouble because of a simple misunderstanding:

Fail Safe No. 1

If someone is in a safe position waiting for a signal, the rule is: No signal, no move!

...'No signal, no move!'...

Fail Safe No. 2

Always point away from the danger, and in the direction of safety.

...'Always point away from the danger'...

Three Basic Signals

It is possible to develop a complete river runners' sign language, if you paddle with someone often enough. At one stage, I teamed up with a friend to run trips in the French Alps for four seasons running. We eventually had about forty hand signs we could use with each other, but we only taught our customers a few, to avoid confusing the issue.

These are some basic signals that are in fairly common use:

Stop

Fig. 10.1 and 10.2 Stop! Photos: Bob Timms

Description: Paddle held horizontally above the paddler's head or, both arms held upright with palms facing outwards.

Meaning: Essentially: "stop". However, depending on the situation, it can mean:

- Get to the nearest safe eddy
- Hold your position

Important: This signal should only be used to stop someone who is moving down river. If someone is in a safe position waiting for a signal, the rule is: No signal, no move! (**Fail Safe No.1**).

One Person To Paddle

Fig. 10.3 and 10.4 One person to come down. Photos: Bob Timms

Description: Paddle held vertically in the air or, **one** arm held upright, palm of hand facing outwards.

Meaning: One person **only** to leave the eddy and paddle the rapid. The next person should not set off until he is signalled to do so.

Go More to the Left or Right

Description: Shuffle your hands along the shaft of the paddle and extend it horizontally in the direction you wish the paddler to move or, extend your arm out horizontally palm outward in the direction you wish the paddler to move.

Meaning: Move in the direction the paddle or arm is extended.

This is used to help other paddlers to stay 'on line', if necessary a sense of urgency can be imparted by using short jabs of the paddle or finger.

Six Other Useful Signals

If people paddle regularly together it is worth learning a few more signals that will enable the team to communicate more effectively.

Everyone Come on Down

Description: Clenched fist held above head and pumped up and down as if repeatedly flushing a toilet.

Meaning: Everybody follow the lead paddler, leaving a suitable distance between each paddler or, if the lead paddler has gone ahead to inspect the rapid, everyone paddle the rapid and join him, again leaving a suitable distance between each paddler.

Fig. 10.5 Everybody come down.

Send 'X' to join me

Description: One hand held palm down on the top of the signaller's head.

Meaning: Send whoever has been designated down to join the lead paddler. (This is usually one of the better paddlers who is able to chase boat, often the paddler who brings up the rear).

Fig. 10.6 Send 'X' down.

Often, when the lead paddler has gone ahead to inspect a rapid, he may decide that it can be adequately protected by having one good paddler stationed near a hazard that is half way down the rapid and another stationed at the bottom of the rapid. By having the above signal, this can be arranged quickly, allowing us to have the best paddlers where they are going to be of use, rather than sat in a safe eddy at the top of the rapid where people don't need any assistance.

Put Your Boat Over There

Description: Thump your fist on the front deck of your kayak or the gunnel of your open boat and then point very deliberately with your forefinger at the place where you want the boater to stop.

Meaning: This is usually used when the signaller doesn't want the other boater to break out in the same eddy that they are in. It can also be used to position the stronger paddlers in such a way that they are in the best place to effect a rescue prior to the less able boaters shooting the rapid.

Make Ready With Throw line

Description: Mimic the action of an over arm throw **twice**, then point very deliberately with your forefinger at the place where you want the person to position themselves.

Meaning: This can be used to instruct a paddler to get out onto the bank and be ready with a throw line, or to move a rescuer who is already on the bank to a better place.

Fig. 10.7 Making a throw bag action.

Fig. 10.8 Pointing at the location.
Photos: Bob Timms

Close Up

Description: Hold your arms out horizontally and, keeping them outstretched, bring them together directly over your head. Repeat this action several times.

Meaning: Keep closer together.

Space Out

Description: Hold your hands, palms together in front of your chest. Keeping them at the same level, move them out to the side until your arms are fully outstretched. Repeat this action several times.

Meaning: Keep further apart.

I used to use signals to indicate hazards to be avoided. I no longer do this on the water because, if the paddlers following you missed the first part of the signal, they may think that you want them to move in that direction. Always point away from the danger in the direction of safety. **(Fail Safe No. 2).**

Sound Signals

In the noisy environment of a white water river it is best to keep these to an absolute minimum. I only use two:

1. A single whistle or shout means: "look this way".
2. Continuous whistling or shouting means that someone is in serious trouble.

Other paddlers may use different signals so check it out **before** getting on the water.

Briefing a Novice Raft Crew

Bob Timms - See Appendix C

Fig. 10.9 A novice raft crew.

Chapter 11
Leadership

Good leadership is an essential aspect of paddling a white water river in safety. Whereas previous sections have dealt with many of the tasks that usually fall to a leader, such as planning and organizing, this section concentrates on **how** a leader behaves. A planner works with ideas, a leader is the person who can get a group of individual people to work as a team and make the plan work.

'Natural born leaders', if such a thing exists, may not need to think about what leadership entails, they just do it. The rest of us may well benefit from consciously trying to improve our performance, through a better understanding of the processes involved.

Once the planning and organising are done and we actually get on the river, the leader's main concerns are: the safety and well being of the team members, morale, and making decisions.

Fig. 11.1 Attilla the Hun?!?

How they perform in the eyes of the other paddlers will depend on:

1. Their personal qualities.
2. The way they go about leading, (their leadership style).
3. The way they go about making decisions.
4. The effectiveness of their leadership.

Leadership Qualities

If you asked a number of people to list the qualities they would expect to find in an effective leader they would come up with similar answers. What would differ is the amount of emphasis they would place on different qualities. One person would say that decisiveness was far more important than, say, honesty. Another would put the emphasis the other way around.

Every 'quality' has a dark side. Decisiveness can become inflexibility. Honesty can become insensitivity. An effective leader will have these qualities in the right balance. Some qualities, such as decisiveness, determination and assertiveness are essential in terms of getting the job done. However, they need to be counterbalanced by other qualities such as honesty, empathy and openness, which help a leader to understand and manage people.

Leadership Styles

Both Mahatma Ghandi and Attilla The Hun were great leaders. Their approaches or styles of leadership couldn't be more different; but they were both effective!

A leadership style is not the same as a leader's personality, although a leader's personality will affect which styles he is happiest using. If we think of the range of leadership styles available to us, then at one extreme we have an authoritarian style, a dictatorship, and at the other a laissez-faire style, in other words, let everyone get on with it. Between the two extremes there are a whole range of styles available. (See Fig. 11.2) Most leaders will tend to operate left or right of centre but nowhere near either of the extremes.

Factors affecting which style will be most effective or appropriate are:

- The leader's own personality
- The expectations / personality of the individuals he is leading
- Time
- Lack of time

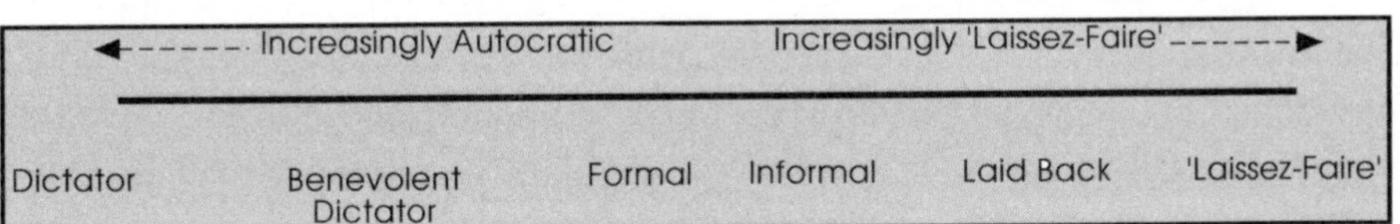

Fig. 11.2 A spectrum of leadership styles.

Fig 11.3 Time for 'laissez-faire'?

- Immediate danger
- The nature of the task being undertaken

Personality

Because of their own personality, leaders will tend to have a preferred style of leadership that, all other factors being equal, they will work within. The most effective leaders will, subconsciously, use different styles in different situations. It is possible for leaders to increase their effectiveness by consciously trying to expand the range of styles they are comfortable using.

Group Expectations

People's background will affect their view of what effective leadership is. So if, for example, a person who is comfortable with a very 'laid back' approach, finds himself asked to lead a group from a military background, he may well find that the group's expectations force him to adopt a **more** authoritarian approach than usual. Otherwise the group may refuse to accept what they **perceive** to be weak leadership.

Equally, an authoritarian leader, faced with the average anarchic group of paddlers, will have to adopt a more relaxed style, or there will be a mutiny. Given enough time, a group will accept that a leader is effective and the leader may be able to revert to his preferred range of leadership styles.

Individual Expectations

Certain individuals within any group may, due to their own personality, feel that certain approaches give them more confidence than others. An effective leader will soon realise that John is happiest if he is **told** what to do, whereas Anna will be a more willing and effective team member if she is **consulted**; her views having being taken into account, she will probably offer to take on a particular task.

Time

If there is no need for an instant solution, it may be that a far more relaxed approach is advisable. A calm, unhurried approach will reduce tension. Consulting other members of the group may produce a less risky solution to the problem that the leader hadn't considered.

Fig. 11.4 Not the time to be laid back!

Lack of Time

If time is precious, this will greatly restrict the choice of leadership styles available. If there are only minutes or even seconds in which to act, then I'm afraid that Attilla the Hun is your man. There simply isn't the time to consult and cajole. This is particularly true when lack of time is combined with the element of danger. The good news is that in these emergency situations even the most anarchistic people will accept an authoritarian style because the need for it is obvious. All other needs are irrelevant compared to the need to get a friend out of a dangerous situation quickly.

The Task

Sometimes the nature of the task being undertaken will virtually dictate what style the leader must adopt. Imagine a complex rescue where each member of the team has to do a different job at the same time and the noise of the rapids makes communication difficult. In addition, the leader has to do one of these jobs himself due to the fact that the team is a small one. The leader will have little choice but to delegate, and having done so, to let them get on with it.

Flexibility

The most effective white water leaders will probably have a preferred style but will switch styles as appropriate. It is quite possible to use the whole range of styles we have identified on a single trip. Imagine the following:

Our leader, Lisa, has been asked by a group of club paddlers to lead them down a river they haven't paddled before. Lisa starts the day in a 'formal' style. She hasn't paddled with them before and wants to ensure that everyone is clear about how they are going to run the river. The river is at the easy end of grade III at this point. She stays in this mode for a while, keeping tight control of the group and telling everyone exactly what she wants them to do. Eventually she realizes that everyone is working well together and that the group are more competent than she was led to believe. She therefore allows herself to change to a more 'informal' style, allowing group members more freedom of action.

Eventually they get to a short but technically demanding grade IV rapid which they inspect from the bank. Everyone decides to portage except Wayne, who is only 15 years old, and for whom our leader has therefore, a greater legal and moral responsibility. What is more, it is obvious to Lisa that Wayne's wish to run the rapid isn't matched by his ability as a paddler. Wayne also seems determined to ignore good advice. Having sent the others off to start the portage, Lisa goes into 'benevolent dictator' mode and lets Wayne know that he isn't going to run the rapid on this trip and that is that.

A little further down, one of the paddlers loses concentration and ends up stuck on a rock in a way that could deteriorate into a life threatening situation if it isn't dealt with immediately. For the one minute that it takes to deal with the problem Lisa becomes a total 'dictator', issuing orders, expecting and getting instant obedience.

The emergency dealt with, everyone feels euphoric with relief. Lisa reverts to a 'formal' style till the group settles down.

The last couple of kilometres of river are of pleasant straight forward grade II paddling. The group are quite capable of running this section without much guidance so she adopts a much more 'laid back' style.

Decision Making

Most decisions have to do with picking one of a number of ways of solving a problem. Problems range from: "Shall I wear my sports sandals or my wet suit booties today?" to: "How do we get Wally's boat out of that strainer without killing anyone in the process?"

There are a number of ways in which we can come to a decision. Which way a leader decides to operate will be influenced by the same factors that affect their choice of leadership style. The nature of the decision being taken plays a very important part in this. There are some decisions that must have the backing of the whole group.

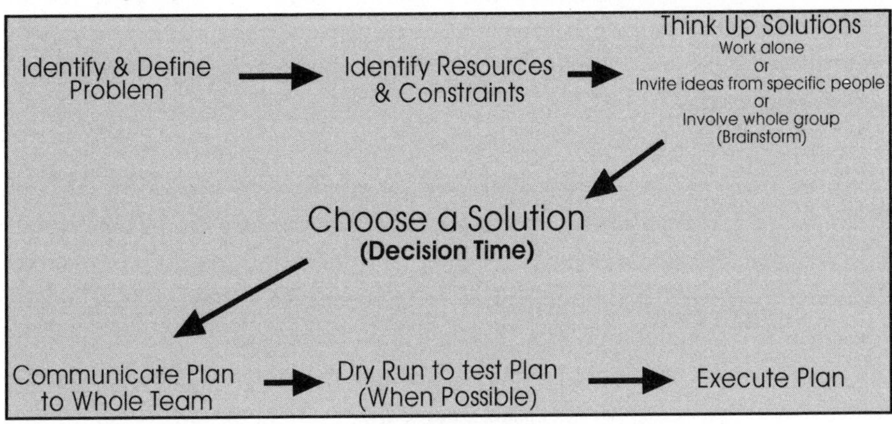

Fig. 11.5 One approach to problem solving.

Authoritarian

This is the method where the leader makes the decisions without any reference to the rest of the team. Even if the leader has involved the rest of the team in thinking up or 'brainstorming' possible solutions, he doesn't take into account the team members' preferences when it comes to deciding which plan they are going to use.

Pros: Fast, appears very decisive, which can be good for morale.

Cons: The leader may choose a plan that the team have little faith in, causing morale to plummet.

Democratic

This is where the various options are compared and the group agrees to accept the plan that the majority approve of.

Pros: The group feel more involved in the decision making process and may well try that bit harder to make the solution work. Reasonably quick.

Cons: Can result in a split in the group where a significant minority feel their views have been ignored. Doesn't necessarily come up with the best solution, only the most popular one.

Consensus

This is where the matter is discussed until every member of the group accepts that the plan decided on is the best one.

Pros: Every member of the group is committed to, and feels a part of the solution.

Cons: Can be a very slow process. Usually only works with small groups.

False Consensus

This is where one or more members of the team accepts a decision even though they don't actually believe it to be the best solution. This is normally done to preserve unity or because they have had enough of discussions and would rather get on with it.

Whichever system is used a decision must eventually be made. An effective leader will seek consensus if it is necessary and if he thinks it can be obtained. If a degree of acceptance is essential for the plan to work but it is obvious that one or more members of the group will never agree with the majority, then seeking consensus is a waste of time. The leader will go for majority rule. If time is of the essence or the group expect the leader to make all the decisions, then the leader will have to make the decision unaided.

There is no 'right answer'; no one way to lead a group. All leaders have to find a way that works for them and for the people they are leading.

Top: Slowing the canoe down to avoid swamping. River Garry, Scotland.
Bottom: Paddling a swamped but well kitted out with air bags open boat. River Tryweryn, North Wales. Photos: Ray Goodwin

Chapter 12
Safety in Equipment Design

In recent years there has been a great deal of effort on the part of innovative paddlers and equipment manufacturers to design and make equipment with safety as a major consideration. Whilst this has made safe paddlers even safer, there has been a down side. This is that many paddlers seem to believe that if they have the right technology they are safe. This in turn led to equipment being designed with rescue in mind rather than paddling. Buoyancy aids were produced that were great for swimming in, but so restrictive that paddling skill suffered. In the very worst excesses, buoyancy aids have been produced with so many unnecessary loops and attachment points for rescue equipment, that they can easily be snagged. Many white water paddlers buy specialist rescue equipment as a 'fashion accessory', without the faintest idea how to use the equipment safely.

...'no matter how well equipped paddlers are, without awareness, judgement and skill, they are still unsafe.'...

Well designed and manufactured equipment is a wonderful bonus. However, no matter how well equipped paddlers are, without awareness, judgement and skill, they are still unsafe.

The more forward looking and responsible manufacturers have started to address these concerns by improving and simplifying their equipment, and providing much more comprehensive written instructions.

Helmets

A good helmet should :

- Protect the wearer's head from direct contact with hard or sharp objects which would otherwise lead to cuts, lacerations and fractures of the skull
- Absorb the energy of blows to the head that would otherwise cause concussion
- Protect as much of the head as possible without impairing vision, hearing or balance
- Stay firmly in position, even if the wearer is being thrown around in turbulent water

---

Top: Preventive action, bank protection on Big Sandy Creek, W Virginia, USA.
Photo: Paul O'Sullivan
Bottom: Andy Knight takes preventive action of a different kind in Nepal.
Photo: J Smith

In order to check that a helmet will be able to achieve the above, paddlers should look for the following features:

Outer Shell

The outer shell should be made of a tough but lightweight material. Most helmets are now made of plastic although there are some good helmets made with carbon/kevlar or other Glass Reinforced Plastics. Colour is also important because, when you are a swimmer, your helmet may be the only part of you that is visible. There is some debate at the moment as to which colours show up best if someone is under the water. It would seem best to steer away from colours that are too light or too dark. White or pale yellow won't show up in aerated frothy water and black won't show up in peaty or muddy water.

Shock Absorbing Layer

The inner layers of a helmet are usually made of closed cell foam, some form of cradle, or a mixture of both. The main advantage of cradles is that they can be adjusted to fit more than one size head. They are also cooler in hot climates.

Closed cell foam absorbs energy efficiently and leaves few spaces for water to fill if you capsize. Providing it is the right size, it is more comfortable to wear, and in cold water environments, it keeps your head warmer.

A few people wear full face motorcycle helmets on white water. The lining used in these helmets absorbs water. This makes them very heavy once they get wet and increases the risk of neck injuries. They are not recommended.

Fit

The front of a helmet should come well down over the wearer's forehead and protrude sufficiently to provide protection to the area around the wearer's eyes. There are many helmets available that either don't cover this area, or ride up and expose it.

The rear should come down far enough to cover the whole of the back of the cranium and the sides of the helmet should protect the temple and ear. Blows to any of these areas can lead to brain damage. There are many helmets on the market that are designed to 'look good' or comply with **minimum** standards to satisfy competition rules. They do not provide adequate protection for serious white water use. If a helmet meets the above requirements and fits well it will stay on with only a minimum of help from the chin strap.

Helmets that are marketed for other sports often contain fittings and fastenings that corrode in water. They may be a little cheaper but they are not a bargain.

Face Guards

If you train yourself so that on capsizing you tuck into a screw roll position, with your face touching the front deck of your boat, your face will be well protected. This is because only the back of your helmet is exposed to the river bed. For this reason, and the fact that face guards inhibit vision and look very aggressive, few paddlers wear them.

If boaters feel the need for facial protection, then it is important that they wear a helmet with a good face guard that has been designed for the job. One quite often sees paddlers wearing canoe-polo face guards. Whilst these are perfectly adequate for keeping paddle blades out of your face in a swimming pool environment, the manufacturers stress that they are not designed for white water situations. Their cage like construction means that they could easily be snagged and the lack of quick release means that this could lead to a broken neck.

There are helmets on the market that have a removable face guard. The guard is made in one piece, limiting the snag potential. As an added precaution the guard is locked in place with special clips which release if the guard is pulled rather than pushed.

Buoyancy Aids

When trying to evaluate a buoyancy aid I ask myself the following questions:

1. Is it comfortable to wear?
2. Does it contain sufficient buoyancy to do its job if I go for a swim?
3. Does it allow sufficient freedom of movement so as not to inhibit good paddling technique?
4. Does it provide good body protection?
5. Is there somewhere to stow a knife and a spare karabiner?
6. Is it as 'clean' as possible? In other words are there any unnecessary attachments or pockets that inhibit movement or increase the risk of getting snagged?

Buoyancy

The minimum buoyancy that a buoyancy aid may contain is now regulated by law. In Europe, the regulations come under The European Community Directive on Personal Protective Equipment and in the United States, P.F.D.s (Personal Flotation Devices), are regulated by the Coastguard.

In Europe buoyancy aids come under one of two categories:

CEN 50N

The British Canoe Union recommends this as the **minimum** standard for all canoeing and kayaking activities. 50N stands for 50 Newtons, which is a measurement of force. Put simply, this means that a 50N buoyancy aid should be able to support a 5.5 kg lead weight. This is for a person weighing 70 kg or more. The table in fig. 12.1, shows the sliding scale used to determine the minimum buoyancy needed for a given weight.

CEN 100N

Buoyancy aids that meet this standard must contain a minimum of 100 Newtons of buoyancy for a person weighing 70 kg or more. They must also have a flotation collar which makes them impractical for canoeing and kayaking. However on high volume runs some raft companies prefer these for inexperienced customers.

Size	Weight	Chest	Buoyancy
CEN 50			
	30-40 kg		35N
	40-50 kg		40N
	50-60 kg		40N
	60-70 kg		45N
	>70 kg		50N
Competition Plus (Palm)			
XS/S	30-50 kg	76-96 cm	55N
S/M	50-60 kg	96-102 cm	65N
L/XL	60-70+ kg	102-120 cm	65N
Extrem River Vest (Palm)			
XS/S	30-50 kg	76-96 cm	60N*
S/M	50-60 kg	96-102 cm	70N*
L/XL	60-70+ kg	102-120 cm	70N*
*When worn with the optional buoyancy pad in the front pocket, a further 10N is added.			
Grade 6 (Palm)			
S	40-50 kg	86-96 cm	80N
M	50-60 kg	96-102 cm	85N
L	60-70 kg	102-110 cm	90N
Xl	>70 kg	110-120 cm	110N
XXL	>70 kg	120-130 cm	110N

Fig. 12.1 Table showing CEN minimum and actual buoyancy in a range of products.

Rib and Slab

Most white water buoyancy aids are now made of large slabs of foam rather than lots of thin ribs of foam. Slab buoyancy has several advantages:

Less wetted surface area means that the foam degrades more slowly. There is more actual foam for a given surface area which allows manufacturers to make shorter garments that are more suited to boaters.

Slab buoyancy makes for a more effective 'body armour'.

Vests and Jackets

There are two basic designs available. The way they are cut, the accessories they have and their colour may vary immensely, but they are all variations on a theme.

Jackets

Jackets consist of a rear piece and two front sections of foam encased in a nylon based material. When worn the jacket is kept in place by a full length front zip and some sort of draw-cord or tape at the waist.

The main advantage of this design is that it is easier to put on and remove than a vest.

Vests

Vests have only two slabs of foam, (one front and one rear). The material is sewn to form a one piece vest and when worn it is held in place by two or more 'cinch' straps on each side.

There are a number of advantages to this design:

1. The lack of a zip dividing the front buoyancy means that room doesn't have to be found elsewhere for the missing buoyancy. This means that there is more scope to cut the vest in such a way that your freedom of movement is less restricted.
2. The use of a number of 'cinch' straps to secure the garment means that it is easier to adjust the fit to your body shape.
3. Although awkward to put on and take off, they are usually more comfortable to paddle in.

Ageing

Paddlers should be aware that the foam used in buoyancy aids does degrade. Manufacturers deliberately put more foam than is needed in a new garment to allow for this. At the rate they expect it to degrade in normal use it should remain within the design specification buoyancy for three years. However, in certain circumstances, such as when used in polluted water, the foam can deteriorate a good deal quicker.

If there are any doubts, the buoyancy should be 'tank tested', by seeing if it will float with the appropriate amount of weight tied to it. (See fig. 12.1).

Spray Decks (Kayaks and C1)

As cockpits have become larger, so the amount of tension required to keep the spray deck in place has increased. This is achieved by using very 'stretchy' neoprene material and holding the deck on the cockpit rim by using either:

1. A 'bungee' cord sewn around the edge of the spray deck 'skirt'. Or:
2. A flat band, which can be made of solid or hollow tube rubber sewn in the same place.

The bungee type is harder to put on when you are sat in your boat but is relatively easy to remove. This makes it better for use by less experienced white water paddlers.

The flat band type is preferred by experienced paddlers as it is easier to put on and sticks so firmly that it is almost impossible to remove it accidentally. This has had the unfortunate side effect of ruining the classic post-swim excuse: "Honest ....my spray deck imploded!!"

Quick Releases

The other effect this has had is to make it imperative that the quick release fitting cannot become detached. In the past a length of nylon tape was sewn directly onto the rim at the front of the spray deck. Most manufacturers now sew the tape as a loop that goes right around the rubber band. (See fig. 12.2). This ensures that even if the stitching that secures the tape to the band should fail, the loop of tape would still enable you to release the spray deck.

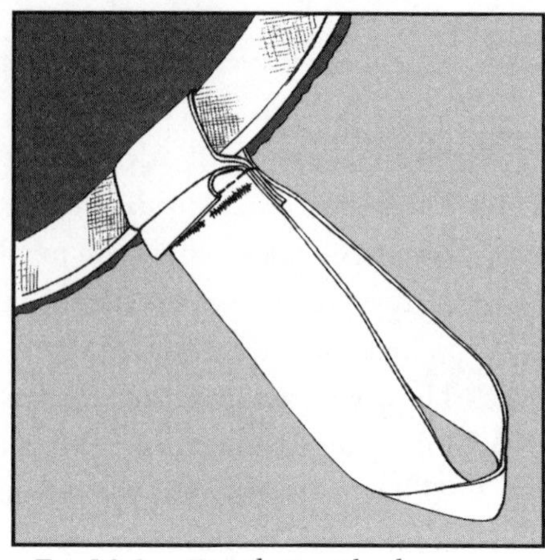

Fig. 12.2 Detail of quick release strap.

On some decks there is a back up system in the form of a tape sewn to both edges of the spray deck. This is adjustable so that it is just in tension when the spray deck is fitted. The idea is that if a paddler is unable to use his hands to release the spray deck, he can release it by pushing his knee against the tensioned tape.

Thermal Layers

The layers of clothing worn under a waterproof outer shell has one purpose, to keep you warm. In cold climates that means in the boat and, if necessary, if you go for a swim. In many countries the air temperature is high but the water, being provided by melting snow or glaciers, is freezing. This means that paddlers need a combination that will not cause them to be too hot in their boat, yet will prevent them from succumbing to hypothermia should they go for a prolonged swim.

Wetsuit and Thermals

When paddling on a river with a warm air/ice cold water combination a 'Long John' wetsuit with a thin thermal top is a good combination. Wetsuits are designed to work in the water. They work by warming a thin layer of water and retaining it close to your skin. This means that if a paddler has a long swim the wetsuit works very efficiently. If a paddler only has a short swim, as soon as he gets out of the water the thin layer of warm water drains away and he cools down.

The other advantage of a wetsuit is that it offers a paddler's legs and bottom some protection against the battering they can receive in a swim down a rocky river. For this reason this is probably still the best combination for use by novices and people who swim a lot, supplemented in cold climates by a 'fleece' top and thermal under-trousers.

No Wetsuit

If you don't go swimming very often or you wear a drysuit, a combination of layers of thermal underwear and fleece garments may be more efficient. By adding or removing layers it is possible to cope with any conditions. In addition, this type of clothing is a lot more comfortable if worn for several hours or even days.

Paddlers from a competitive background or those who are used to playboating on a site, close to changing rooms and cafes, often wear a minimum of clothing and items like wetsuit shorts, even in cold climates. This approach is fine in such situations. When undertaking a longer trip on a wild river it should be remembered that such clothing may not be adequate.

Shell Clothing

A wind and waterproof outer layer is essential to keep the paddler warm and dry. In Britain, most paddlers wear a 'drycag' cagoule and either waterproof trousers or salopettes. Good spray decks and 'drycags', with their latex wrist and neck seals, keep virtually all the water out whilst the paddler remains in the boat. The overtrousers are needed to keep one's legs warm and dry when out of the boat.

In warmer climes or in a rare hot British summer a 'cag' with neoprene cuffs and a neoprene adjustable neck fastening, or even a short sleeved cagoule, may be more appropriate.

Fig.12.3 Venting a drysuit.
Photo: Bob Timms

In very cold conditions it may be worth considering a drysuit. It is essential, when wearing a drysuit, to vent all the air out of the suit before getting on the water. This is achieved by pulling the neck seal away from your neck with your finger whilst at the same time forcing the air in the suit upwards by crouching in a 'foetal' position. If this precaution is not taken and you capsize, the water pressure forces all the air into the legs of the suit. If you were then to come out of your boat you would float with your head down and your legs in the air! Should this happen a paddler would have to rip the latex ankle seals to allow the air to escape from the suit.

Foot Wear

When choosing footwear for white water boating one would expect it to:

1. Provide a good grip when moving over greasy rocks or muddy banks.
2. Have a thick enough sole to protect feet from broken glass or sharp rocks.
3. Protect the bony protrusions on one's ankles from knocks.
4. Keep one's feet warm when it is cold and wet.
5. Keep one's feet cool when it is hot.

The choices of footwear that are available to paddlers are:

- Wetsuit bootees
- Sports sandals
- Specialist 'extreme' white water boots

The truth is that no item of footwear can meet all of these criteria. Sports sandals are comfortable in warm weather, wetsuit bootees in very cold weather. 'Extreme' boots are appropriate on rivers where there are committing gorge sections, difficult portages or where there is likely to be a great deal of bank protection needed.

A good compromise is to buy a pair of sports sandals and a pair of wetsuit socks to wear with them in cold weather.

Paddles

In the eighties and early nineties the trend towards paddling rocky technical rivers led to a demand for extremely strong paddles that wouldn't break at a critical moment and literally leave you ...'up the creek without a paddle'. We got our strong paddles but paid for them in terms of their weight. If you were built like Arnold Swartzenegger they were fine. For most of us there was a considerable loss in our ability to 'feel' the water through the blade, and for smaller paddlers they were a disaster.

The advent of playboating and rodeo has meant that there has been a lot of crossover between competition and recreational paddlers. There are now a whole host of paddles made in carbon-fibre and thermoplastics to choose from. This means that we can have paddles that are strong and light!

Stiff shafts and large blade areas can lead to tendonitis in the elbows. I would advise recreational paddlers to buy the most flexible shafts they can get and a medium or even small blade area. (Flexible 'carbon' shafts are normally made from a combination of ordinary glass-fibre and carbon-fibre).

Kayaks

There are three questions we should ask when looking at a kayak from a white water safety point of view:

1. Does it have the white water safety features that one would expect to find in any design of white water kayak?
2. Is it the right size for its occupant?
3. Is its design suitable for the kind of white water paddling it is going to be used for?

Safety Features

These are:

- Keyhole cockpit
- Full-plate footrest
- Buoyancy
- Grab/Attachment points

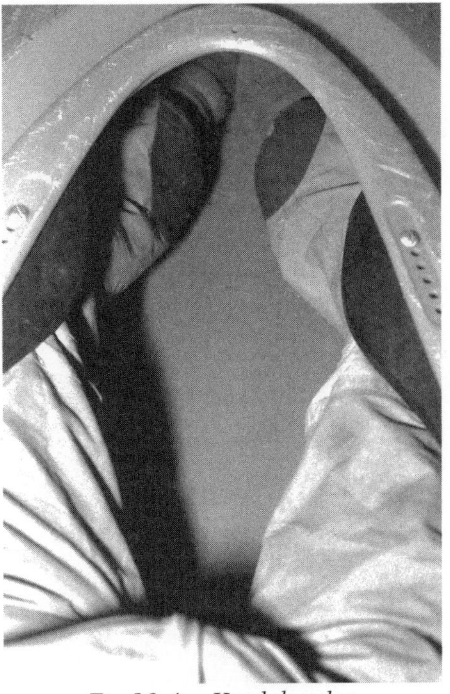

Fig. 12.4 Key-hole cockpit. Photo: Bob Timms

Keyhole Cockpit

When the very first plastic boats came on the market, the materials used in the manufacture of spraydecks were not very 'stretchy'. As a result cockpits were made as small as possible to minimise the chances of a wave collapsing the spraydeck. Boats made in ordinary glass-fibre tended to break up if they were badly broached giving the paddler a chance to fight his way out. With plastic and diolen/carbon fibre combinations this no longer happens; therefore cockpits must be designed in such a way as to make it possible to exit the boat even if the deck is collapsing.

This is achieved by making the cockpit much larger and by making it a 'keyhole' shape. (See fig. 12.4). When the paddler's knees are splayed out, they grip the thigh braces and when the knees are brought together, they are no longer held in.

An easy way to test the effectiveness of your boat's cockpit is to get some friends to stand your boat up against a wall with you in it to simulate a vertical pin. If you can get out unaided its fine; if you can't, get another boat.

Full-plate Footrest

Full-plate footrests are essential in a white water boat because, if a paddler hits a hard surface, they spread forces involved over the whole of the soles of both feet. This and the shock absorbing properties of the foam pad reduce the risk of ankle and lower limb injuries. (See fig. 12.5).

European manufacturers have opted for designs which don't require a foam block between the boater's legs, which does make it easier to get out of the boat in an entrapment situation.

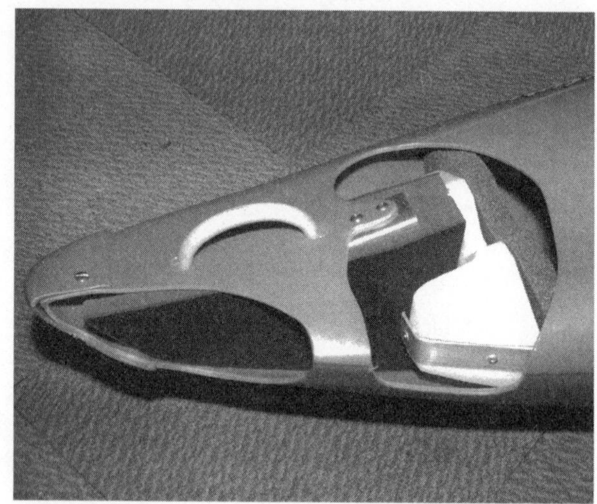

Fig. 12.5 A full plate footrest.
Photo: Pyranha

North American manufacturers still use a foam block to stiffen the front deck. This does make getting out of the boat more difficult, although the designs have improved by making the cockpits larger and shaping the central block so that it tapers towards the boater.

Buoyancy

The foam buoyancy that is used to strengthen most boats and provide a minimum of buoyancy is not sufficient for white water use. Paddlers should supplement this with air-bags so that any space not filled by the paddler or equipment is buoyancy.

This has two effects:

1. The boat is far easier to recover as it contains less water and therefore weighs less.
2. Experience and tests carried out at Plas-y-Brenin in the late seventies show that, because a boat filled with buoyancy floats so much higher in the water, it is much less likely to fold if broached.

Grab/Attachment Points

When these are fitted they may be present for the following reasons:

1. To give the swimmer something to keep hold of the boat with.
2. To provide a strong attachment point for boat recovery purposes.

End Grabs

These need to be strong enough to be used as attachment points, so most manufacturers now make them strong enough to withstand a static load of at least 500 Kg. Swimmers also use them as grab points, so they need to be made in such a way that it is impossible for a swimmer's hands or fingers to become trapped or injured. (Fig. 12.5 and 12.6).

Fig. 12.6 Grab handle
Photo: Bob Timms

Broach Loops

These are not very common. When present they are situated near the middle of the boat, just in front of the cockpit, or just behind it, or both.

They are intended purely as attachment points for equipment recovery purposes and are usually made in such a way that it would be dangerous for a swimmer to hold onto them. There is a strong argument that the dangers they pose to swimmers' fingers more than outweigh their advantages.

Streamers

A streamer is a piece of nylon tape about a metre long that is attached to the rear grab handle so that it 'streams' behind the boat. It has two main uses:

1. In a very short boat, by the time a paddler has got out of his capsized boat the boat may have floated far enough away that the grab handle is out of reach. The swimmer can grab the streamer instead.
2. Even with a keyhole cockpit, a long legged paddler in a vertically pinned kayak will find it easier if they can pull on the streamer. In this situation the streamer hangs down the length of the rear deck.

Some boaters attach streamers to bow and stern.

It is essential that the streamer is fitted in such a way that it does not form a loop or have any knots that could get snagged.

Deck Lines

As kayaks have got shorter and cockpits longer the use of deck lines has almost ceased. This is because it is now easy to get a firm grip of the cockpit rim with one hand whilst still holding the end grab with the other. If you paddle a 4 metre boat or for any other reason decide to use deck lines, bear in mind the following points:

1. The deck lines should be made of rope of at least 8 mm diameter so as to be thick enough not to cut into a person's hand.
2. The rope used should be of a colour that contrasts vividly with the colour of the boat.
3. They need to be fitted in such a way that they remain taught and flush with the deck so as not to get snagged.
4. Unless your boat comes fitted with broach loops you will have to engineer strong attachment points, just in front and just behind the cockpit for one end of each deck line. The other ends are usually attached to the end grabs.

Size

Every boat will perform best if the person paddling it comes within a certain body weight range. Therefore a boat that performs well for a paddler who weighs 50 kg, (8 stone or 112 lbs), will wallow hopelessly if paddled by a 100 kg, (16 stone or 224 lbs) paddler. Equally, if a 50 kg paddler tries to paddle a boat that suits a 100 kg paddler he will be unable to edge, accelerate or manoeuvre effectively. That is assuming he hasn't already injured himself trying to pick the boat up!

We all come in different shapes and sizes, therefore manufacturers have to design their kayaks so as to fit the largest person that is likely to paddle it. Good kayak control demands that your kayak fits like a glove. To this end, boaters should invest some time and effort in 'customizing' their boat.

Hip Pads

Pieces of 'minicell' foam can be cut to size, shaped with a 'former' and then glued to the side of the seat. This ensures that any movement of the hips is transmitted to the boat, improving edge control and the ability to roll in rough water. Some manufacturers now sell these in kit form.

Thigh Grips

Some modern kayak designs have adjustable thigh grips, which are a real bonus for people with non standard leg length. It is well worth spending some time finding the ideal position for comfort and effectiveness. Any thigh grip can be further improved by gluing on pieces of the closed cell foam used in 'camper mats'. This improves the comfort and one's ability to grip. On non-adjustable thigh grips it is possible, by experimenting with different layers of foam, to improve the fit.

Design

It is true that, if a boater is good enough, he can paddle any kind of boat on any kind of river. It is, however, also true that certain types of boats perform better on certain types of water.

Squirt boats are extremely specialist, being designed to spend as much time under water as they do on it, and I will leave them to the specialist books. In order to make the distinction, all other kayaks that are used on white water are sometimes referred to as 'float boats'.

These can be split into four broad categories:

- Long boats
- Short boats
- Mega-short boats
- Specialist play boats

Long boats

These are boats that are 3 metres or longer, have pointed ends and distinct, angular edges. Their length and shape give them a greater forward speed. Their edges make it easier to 'carve' turns so that they can turn without losing forward momentum. The pointed ends help achieve the hull shape needed for the above characteristics and makes it easier to 'ender' out of holes. These features make them better suited to high and medium volume rivers where water features are the challenge.

Short boats

These are boats of less than 3 metres with rounded ends and much less distinct, if any, edges. Their relative shortness and more rounded hull mean that, although relatively slow, they can change direction quickly. The lack of hard edges means that if the paddler makes a mistake, he is less likely to capsize. The rounded bow and stern mean that they are less likely to get pinned. These features make them better suited to low and medium volume rock-strewn rivers and rivers with lots of vertical drops.

Mega-Short Boats

At the time of writing we are talking about Prijon Spuds and Pyranha Microbats. These can spin on a sixpence and are excellent for paddling steep gradient, low volume mountain streams, vertical drops and playing on short steep waves.

Although people can, and do, paddle high volume rivers in them, their tendency to get back-looped in big stoppers and their lack of forward speed mean that a different style of paddling is required. This is best learnt **before** committing oneself to this kind of water. Another consideration is that their lack of speed and their inability to carry a swimmer on the back deck make them a questionable choice from a rescue/chase-boating point of view.

Specialist Play Boats

The range of vertical moves now being performed in rodeo has caused these boats to evolve to the point where the front end is a pointy 'float' boat and the rear end is a squirt boat! Although people can and do use them for river running, it should be remembered that reverse paddling can result in an unwanted tail dip and that mistakes are always paid for because of the very hard edges. On the other hand, **once these different techniques are mastered**, they can be put to good use on a river run.

There are of course kayaks that don't fit neatly into these categories. If we use our eyes and our brains it won't be too difficult to work out what kind of white water they best suit.

Traditional Open Boat

by Ray Goodwin

An open boat that is used on white water needs to be thoughtfully outfitted. Pole, spare paddle, bailer, rucksacks, all have the potential to entangle the boater in the event of an upset. Simple and tidy is the answer.

End Loops

A small loop of 9 or 10 mm rope at each end of the canoe, threaded through holes drilled through the hull about 4 cm below the gunwale, provides a secure attachment point in any recovery. The carrying handles on the deck that are usually provided are not secured to a strong enough attachment point.

Attachment Points Along the Side

There are two systems in common usage:

Eyelets

This involves pop riveting (metal gunwale), or screwing (wooden gunwale) a series of eyelets into the gunwale.

Drill and Lace

A series of holes are drilled about 4 cm below the gunwale and about 10 cm apart. These are then threaded with 5 mm rope creating a series of attachment points inside the canoe; with a tight fit there is no perceptible leakage. As an extra, one can run shock cord down the inside of the boat by twisting it through the interior loops of the threaded rope; this enables one to quickly secure items such as a sponge or the end of a spare paddle, and yet have them readily to hand. Putting more shock cord under the seats allows spare paddles to be secured at the blade end.

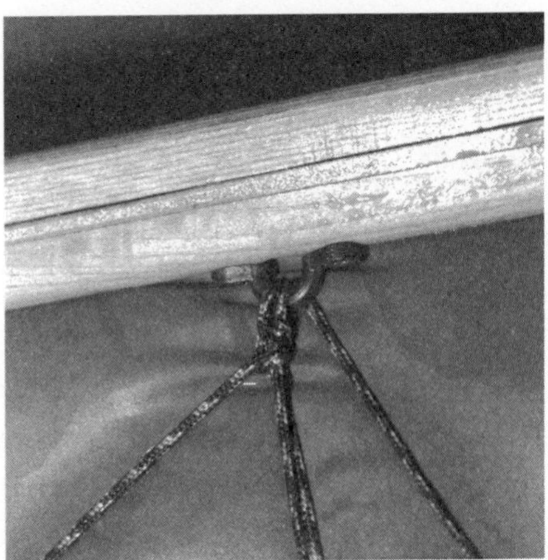

Fig. 12.7 Eyelet screwed in to wooden gunwale. Photo: Bob Timms

Buoyancy

All canoes used on white water should be fitted with extra buoyancy. I favour small buoyancy bags at each end of the canoe. By attaching a short rope to the end of the buoyancy bag, then threading it through the end loop where it loops through the boat, the air bag can be secured to the end of the canoe. A thin rope crisscrossed through the interior side ties or eyelets of the canoe and over the air bag hold it down. To complete the system, a 'D' ring is glued to the floor and a strap run up over the bag to hold it into the canoe. Do not rely solely on the bag's own tie-in points as these can rip off.

Fastening Kit into the Boat

There are two distinct systems for fastening barrel, kit bags, etc. into the canoe; both have their advantages.

Leashed

One is to attach the kit via a long leash. The leash should be no longer than half the length of the canoe, and tied to the central thwart. The great advantage, particularly when paddling solo, is the ease with which the load can be moved around to adjust the trim. For most situations the canoe is paddled with the bow just a little lighter than the stern. However, in some windy conditions or whilst doing reverse moves on the river, it can be better to be bow heavy. The trim is altered by moving the load or the paddlers.

Tied In

The other system is to lash everything into the canoe using a series of lashings from side to side. As extra security, 'D' rings in the floor can be used to run a strap over the load lengthways, so as to stop any kit movement in the event of a swamping. The kit bags now act as extra buoyancy bags enabling you to paddle the boat fully swamped and effect your own rescue. With a heavy load the canoe remains remarkably stable.

The disadvantage is the difficulty of changing the trim of the boat; none the less, in serious conditions I tend to lash everything.

Bailer

This can either be attached via a very short cord to a karabiner and clipped to the boat, or a ring of old car inner tube can be whipped to a seat and the bailer simply pushed into the rubber.

Recovery Ropes

The basic idea is simple. A throw line or swim rope is attached to the boat in advance. Upon capsizing, you grab the rope, swim for the bank, and then quickly run the rope around the nearest rock or tree.

Some people attach the throw line to the side of one of the seats. This system works well on some boats by flipping them on their side and emptying them of water as the tension comes on. However it can be difficult to find the rope.

Fig 12.8 Swim line attached to end loop. Photo: Bob Timms

Alternately a throw line can be secured to the end loop and kept in place on the deck with a couple of pieces of shock cord. It only takes a moment to locate and free the rope. Some people attach a throw line to both ends of the canoe to make finding a rope even easier. Twenty metres of rope is usual but on wide rivers some people use 30 to 40 metres of swim rope.

White Water Open Boat

by Dave Luke

Outfitting

Good control of a white water canoe requires an effective system of saddle, thigh straps and foot brace. It is possible to buy a canoe fitted out by the supplier but this is often a compromise as it may well be done with a range of different sizes and body shapes in mind. The type of water that you intend to paddle may demand a different approach to outfitting; big volume rivers, creeks, and rodeo/ play will change your method of outfitting your boat.

The Saddle

The saddle, or pedestal, is generally placed so that the canoe has a neutral trim. When the canoe is swamped the saddle needs to be small enough to allow water to flow freely across the bottom of the boat, so that stability is not upset by water being trapped on one side of the boat.

Thigh Straps

A strap system needs to do two things, in order of priority:

1. Have a 100% effective and simple release mechanism.
2. Hold your knees in contact with the hull and your butt on the saddle even when upside down.

When starting from scratch, I have found it better to position the rest of the straps and 'D' rings by using the release system as a reference point. If for one reason or other the straps can't be released, you still need to be able to get out. It may be possible to remove your feet from the foot brace and slide out backwards or build in a second point of release. Flap type 'fastex' buckles on the 'D' rings work well.

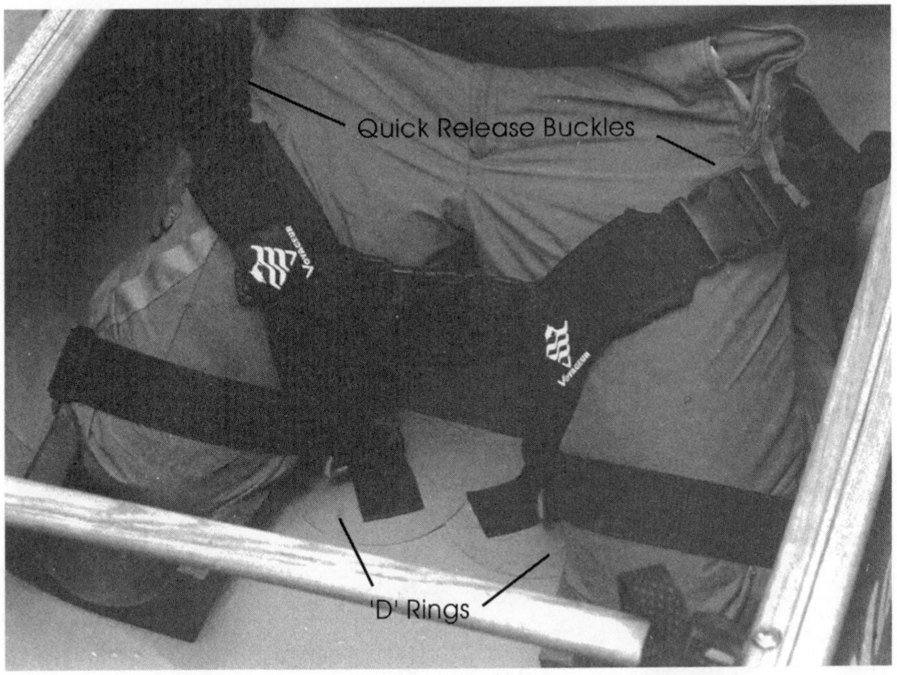

Fig. 12.9 Dave's thigh strap system Photo: Bob Timms

Foot Braces

Foot braces or toe blocks are an integral part of the system as they enable you to push forward and lock into the straps. My personal preference is for a 'keeper' style foot brace fixed to the saddle. This suits me because I prefer to paddle with my feet flat; it also enables me to slide my feet out easily. Alternatively, a range of toe-blocks that can be glued to the bottom of the hull are available.

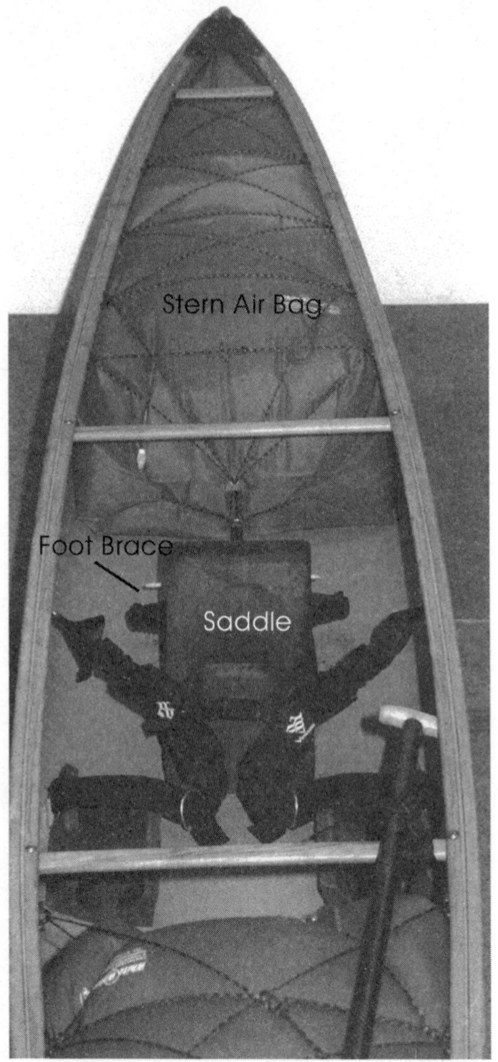

Fig. 12.10 Specialist ww open canoe or OC1. Photo: Bob Timms

Air Bags

Air bags come in a range of sizes and which ones you choose depends on the style of paddling you use. Generally the stern bag will fill as much space as possible although you might want to leave room for some kit behind the saddle.

The bow bag for a predominant play paddler would be as big as possible so as to exclude the maximum amount of water from the boat. When paddling on a river, a shorter bag has the advantage of allowing room to bail whilst on the water. In sticky situations, upside down on a shallow rapid, you will have space to duck forward and escape a trashing, your back being protected by your buoyancy aid and your head safely inside the canoe.

Rescue Considerations

A white water open canoe doesn't make the best of rescue tools so be prepared to rely on a good repertoire of self rescue techniques. How you set your boat up can save a lot of time and effort.

Painters.

Painters are short lengths of line attached to each end of the canoe which are normally used for tethering the boat while you inspect a rapid. Painters can also act as short recovery lines to pull the boat off a pin. The length of the lines should be just over half the length of the boat. They should be tied to each end loop and brought back to the thwarts behind and in front of the seat, and tied with a quick release hitch for quick access. Too long a line will result in loose rope flopping around in the bottom of the canoe.

Recovery/Swim Lines.

The most common method of creating a recovery line is to attach the bag end of a throw bag to somewhere secure at one or both ends of the canoe. Remember that any potential load on this attachment may well be huge, so do not use the handle on the deck-plate as they tend to pull off. The bag can be secured with elastic, with the end of the rope free, ready to be pulled out in an emergency.

In the event of a swim this line can be pulled out and taken to the bank, thus swinging the boat in. Do not, under any circumstances, attach yourself to this line. The same technique can be used in a pin or a broach situation. In a risky situation the line can be thrown to the shore or released into the water and picked up downstream of the pin. When recovering an open canoe from a pin it is usually better to try to roll the boat as it is pulled off, to spill the water and reduce the load that is being pulled. (See Chapter 28, Recoveries).

Chase Boating.

A white water open canoe is not a great deal of use as a chase boat, apart from giving emotional support to the swimmer. Generally open boats are too slow to give an effective tow and too unstable to carry a swimmer. Therefore the importance of being self-sufficient and confident with self-rescue is, if anything, more important to canoeists that to our kayaking buddies.

Rafts

by Bob Timms

Raft Designs

All rafts are constructed of a very strong oven rubber coated fabric which is highly abrasion resistant. They come in many sizes and widths, depending on the nature and size of the river. Big volume equals big raft, equals a larger crew. Technical manouvering equals a smaller raft, equals a smaller crew.

They generally have thwarts. The smallest 4 person rafts may only have one, a large big volume raft may have four. They have upturned ends to reduce taking on water and lead the bow up and over waves. Rafts can be paddled by a crew or rigged with oars, (see below). They are usually self baling with inflatable floors, though you may come across old 'Bucket Rafts' with a single sheet of material on the floor and no baling holes. These are a liability and inappropriate for serious water, as they become heavy and un-manoeuvrable when full of water.

Rafts, other than paddle rafts, fall into three main groups:

Catarafts.

These are two independent, inflatable tubes bridged and held together by a frame which is strapped to them. Suspended under the frame is a tensioned net to catch fallen guides and carry equipment. They are usually oar rigged and are great fun on big technical rivers. Imagine a sailing catamaran with inflatable hulls being rowed, and without its mast or rigging and you have a cataraft!

Transom Stern Rafts.

These are shaped like a motor launch with parallel side tubes tapering to a point at the front and the back section square cut and decked to spill off water. The stern is open to allow any water to drain out, and they are stiffened laterally with thwarts. They are usually more for low grade float trips than technical or bigger water, and are generally less stable than the standard rafts. They usually assemble from several sections that are laced together.

Oar Rigs.

Oar rigs are usually to power rafts either on big volume rivers where the raft's safety cannot rely on a rookie crew, so the guide does the work, or on a gear raft supporting paddle rafts by carrying their gear. They are very manoeuvrable and can pick up good speed, but require a deal of expertise to helm them. Both the oars and the rowlocks need to be tied to the rig on leashes, as to lose either part way down a rapid or trip can be disastrous!

Safety Features.

These are:-

- Self bailing
- Multi Compartment
- Removable thwarts/floors
- Hand, bow and stern lines
- Foot straps

Self Bailing.

Modern rafts are designed so that any water spilling into the raft runs over the floor and into a gutter which runs down adjacent to the side tubes. This gutter is full of holes and allows the water to drain out. It also means when loaded, that a small amount of water will sit in this gutter. The heavier the load the lower in the water, the more water comes into the raft. This is still preferable to 'Bucket Rafts' which have a non draining floor and need to be constantly 'Bailed out' after each rapid!

Multi Compartments.

Most rafts are made up of a number of inflatable compartments, usually between 6-8 including the thwarts and the floor. This means that in the event of a puncture the remaining compartments stay inflated, allowing the raft to be paddled to safety.

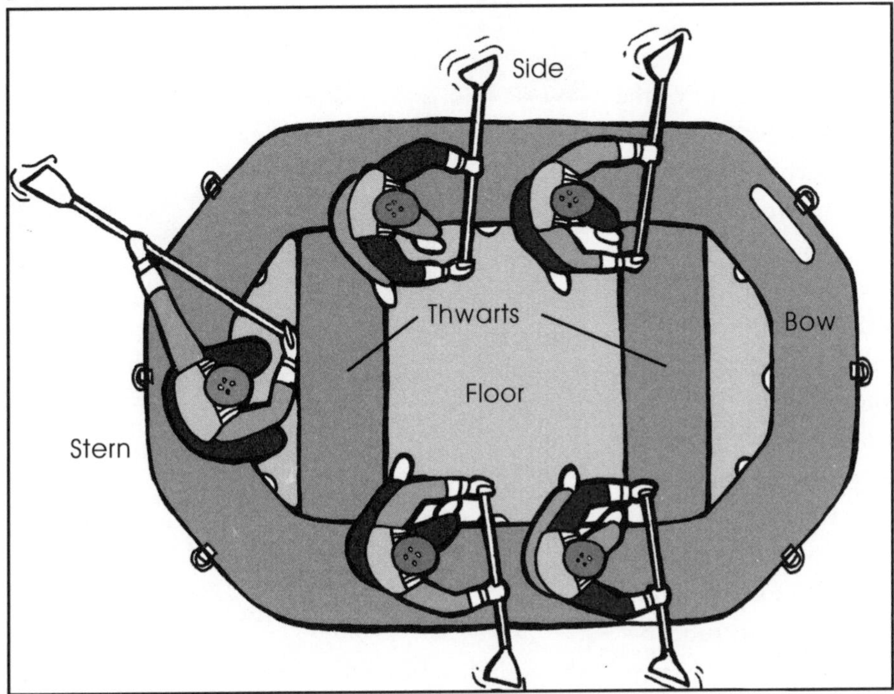

Fig.. 12.11 Main structural features.

Valves.

Valve designs vary a lot, but the biggest enemy of the valve is grit and sand, so designs with secure caps or covers are preferable!

Removable Thwarts/Floors.

Some rafts have thwarts which are removable to allow more equipment to be carried on long trips. These are also sometimes useful on very long portages and 'trek-ins' to rivers, where the weight of a raft can be split down. Removable floors also help this greatly. Floors are usually held in place using strong line. This lacing is vulnerable on rocky rivers; it can snag and wear out!

Hand Bow And Stern Lines.

Hand lines are tensioned lines all the way around the outside of the raft, positioned so as to be reached by the crew. They allow the crew to lean in and brace against the tensioned line in the event of a collision or rough water. They are attached to the raft via the 'D' rings which double as attachment points in the event of a pin or wrap!

Fig. 12.12 'D' ring and attached hand line. Photos: Bob Timms

Bow and stern lines are lengths of line attached each end of the raft for securing to banks and to aid awkward landings etc. The correct length for any raft is such that a line can be run to the central 'D' ring on a side tube, and then across to the opposite tube so it just hangs over the far side, thus can then be used as an emergency flip line!

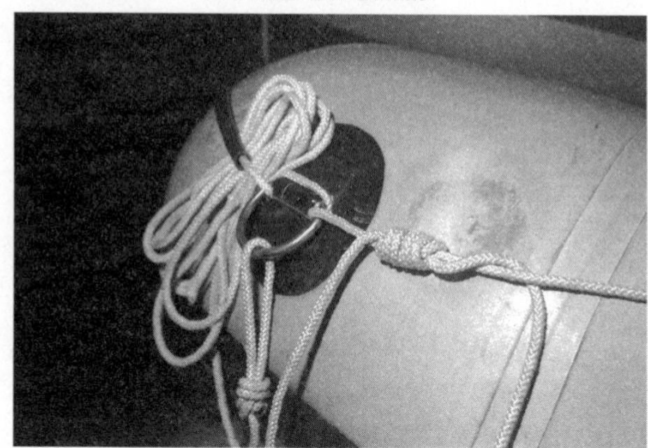

Fig. 12.13 Bow line.

Foot straps.

Most rafts have foot straps fitted in the rear compartment for the guide to help stay in position. If fitted in the right place and of the right size they are invaluable. If poorly positioned and oversized they can be dangerous, leading to lower leg sprains and twists and the possibility of a foot entrapment! Occasionally some rafts will have them fitted for the crew. In inexperienced 'hands' a foot strap is a liability, not an aid!

PART

WHITE WATER RESCUE

II

"Rescue is when safety has gone wrong."
Dave Mamby

Chapter 13
Principles of Rescue

Principle of Personal Safety

"Rescuers should not take unnecessary or unjustified risks."

Potential rescuers are of no use to the victim or anyone else if they become victims themselves.

Principle of The Victim's Best Interest

"No action by rescuers should place victims in more danger than they were already in."

Principle of Simplicity

"Keep it simple, keep it fast."

In most rescue situations, time is of the essence. The simpler a solution, the quicker it can be put into practice, and the less there is to go wrong.

Principle of Maximum Usefulness

"Rescuers should position themselves so as to cover the highest risk."

Risk being defined as the combination of consequence and probability. As most people have the sense to keep well away from life threatening hazards, this usually means the most likely occurrence, rather than the most dangerous hazard.

Principle of the Clean Line

"Ropes and water are a bad mix."

The chances of a rope snagging is substantially reduced if handles are removed and hitches are used instead of free-standing knots, whenever possible.

Principle of Presumed Insanity

"Contact rescues are dangerous by definition."

When deciding whether or not to make physical contact with a victim, the rescuer must assume that the victim is in a dangerous state of panic, until his actions and responses prove otherwise.

Chapter 14
Basic Rescue Equipment

Rescue is what happens when preventative measures have failed and we need to retrieve the situation. It is about safeguarding or saving people. In rescue situations involving water the time available is often limited to a few minutes. In such situations use of equipment should be kept to a minimum, as solutions need to be simple and quick. On the other hand, it is imperative that we become thoroughly practised and competent in the use of the equipment that we **do** need to use.

If the following items are carried by every member of the team, they will have the tools needed to deal with almost any situation:

- Throw bag
- Knife
- Nylon tape sling
- Two karabiners

Any person prepared to contemplate entering the water during a rescue should also possess:

- A white water chest harness

In committing technical gorges or waterfalls, specialist equipment and techniques may be required in order that rescuers can get into a position to protect difficult sections. These techniques are dealt with in Part Four.

Raft guides, river guides and instructors who may be working with people who will not have their own rescue equipment will obviously have to carry enough to make up the shortfall.

The Throw Bag

The main use of the throw bag is to get a line to a swimmer in order to help him reach safety. It can also be used to ensure the safety of rescuers, recover equipment, or rig a tarpaulin.

Where difficult recoveries are envisaged, and ropes are likely to be needed for access purposes, it may be necessary to carry different types of ropes, (see Chapter 26 Specialist Equipment).

With the above uses in mind, the following features should be considered when choosing a throw bag.

The Line or Rope

The line should be made of a floating material. A line that floats is less likely to become snagged on the river bed. The material should be woven in such a way as to provide a 'soft' comfortable grip and not damage a user's hands even when considerable forces are involved.

...'less than 8 mm in diameter....... can slice through muscle and sinew like a cheese-wire.'...

To meet these criteria throw lines are usually made of braided polypropelene rope of **no less than** 8 mm in diameter. Any smaller is extremely dangerous in that it can slice through muscle and sinew like a cheese-wire.

It is now possible to get throw lines made with an outer sheath of polypropelene and a core of aramid fibres such as Kevlar, Spectra or Dyneema. These have the advantages of being twice as strong as conventional polypropelene and the disadvantages of being twice as expensive. With boaters, storage space is at a premium, so it may make sense to have a throw bag made with kevlar core line that can also be used for more specialist access and recovery situations.

Length

Most commercially available ropes come in lengths between 10 and 25 metres, (33 and 80 feet).

Short ropes of 10 metres or less are useful on narrow technical rivers or for use by raft guides to throw to customers who have fallen out of the raft. This is because in both cases the distances involved are small and it is more important to be able to re-pack the rope quickly than throw long distances.

Medium length ropes of between 15 and 20 metres are the most useful as throw lines. It all depends on how much rope the individual concerned can throw accurately.

Long ropes of over 20 metres are difficult to throw and are usually used for recovery or protecting and positioning rescuers. For this reason they are often made out of stronger, thicker diameter rope, (10 mm or more).

Colour

Both the bag and the rope should be constructed of highly visible materials. Bright primary colours such as yellow or orange are best. 'Day-glow' colours are great when new; unfortunately they tend to fade very quickly. If carrying more than one rope it is a good idea to have different coloured ropes.

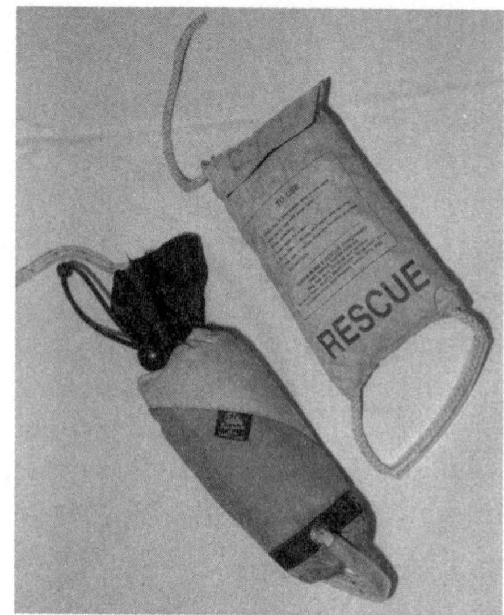

Fig. 14.1 The two main throw bag shapes. Photo: Bob Timms

Shape

From the point of view of being easy to throw and easy to re-pack, a roughly cylindrical, or 'bucket' shape is best. Ideally, it should taper so that it is narrower at the leading end and wider at the end that the rope comes out of. (See: fig. 14.1.)

Flat envelope shaped bags are easier to stow, particularly if kept in a buoyancy aid pocket. However, they are difficult to throw accurately, particularly in windy conditions and are awkward to re-pack.

Principle of the Clean Line

Although the throw line is one of the most basic and most useful rescue tools, it can, through misuse or misfortune become a hazard in itself. Moving water and ropes are a bad mix.

...'Moving water and ropes are a bad mix.'...

If the situation arises where the rope is worsening the situation, and the victim is unwilling or unable to let go of the rope, the rescuer's only option is to let go of his end of the rope. In order to minimise the risk of the rope snagging in such a situation, it is best to remove any handles or knots from the thrower's end, **permanently!** If your brand new throw bag comes complete with a handle at the thrower's end, cut it off! In the unusual event of the rescuer needing a handle, it takes less than a second to tie an overhand knot on a bight.

The other advantage is that if the force of the water is such that rescuers are unable to hold the rope without the aid of a knot or handle, it will almost certainly pull them into the water, and they are better off letting go of the rope.

Care and Maintenance

During use, rescuers should take care not to tread on the rope as this pushes grit in between the fibres. The grit can then abrade and damage the rope from the inside.

After use, ropes should be rinsed in clean water to remove mud, sand and grit, dried and inspected, both visually and by running them through one's hands for any sign of damage. If a rope is obviously damaged, retire it. If you are in doubt, retire it. A rope that doesn't inspire confidence may or may not be physically safe but it is by definition bad for morale.

Ropes should be stored out of direct sunlight as they are weakened by prolonged exposure to UV rays. They must also be stored well away from any petroleum products, as any contamination will weaken them and may go unnoticed.

It also a good idea to store throw lines coiled and out of their bags. This ensures that they are inspected and correctly packed before use, by the person who is going to use them.

Stowage

Some people like to carry their throw bag on their buoyancy aid and others prefer to clip it to a strong point in the raft/open boat or behind the backrest of their kayak. A bag stowed on the rescuer's body has the advantages of being instantly accessible and impossible to leave behind during bank inspections. The disadvantage is that it impedes a paddler's freedom of movement.

Knife

Paddlers who carry or use a throw line should carry a safety knife. If the rescuer or victim become entangled it may be necessary to cut the rope immediately.

A safety knife designed for use on white water should be securely retained when not in use, yet easy to get hold of with one hand and easy to release or open. Most boaters and raft guides use small sheath knives or lock knives that have been specifically designed for the purpose, (fig. 14.2)

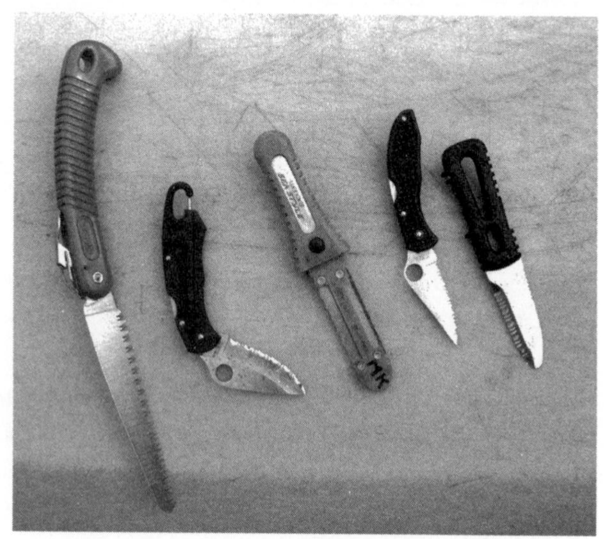

Fig. 14.2 Saw and a selection of safety knives.
Photos: Bob Timms

Large, 'Rambo' style knives are awkward to carry, likely to snag and present an aggressive image that many people find offensive or threatening. They are also illegal in some countries. I would therefore suggest that they have no place on the river.

Sheath Knives

In the case of a sheath knife there must be some mechanism that holds the knife securely in the sheath when not in use. The rescuer must be able to remove it from the sheath one handed, so it must be possible to operate the release mechanism one handed and **with either hand.** It will also be necessary to attach the sheath to one's buoyancy aid in such a way that it is accessible to either hand.

Lock Knives

Lock knives have the advantage of being more discreet and virtually impossible to snag. However, they must be designed so that they can be opened one handed and with either hand. Care should also be taken to select a buoyancy aid that has a suitably positioned knife pocket.

Other Design Features

Many knives have serrated edges which are specifically designed for cutting ropes.

There is some debate as to whether a sharp point or a blunt end is best on a knife. The blunt ended knives are designed so that they can be used to cut but not to stab, which means that the risk of accidental injury to a person or damage to a raft is considerably reduced. The down side is that there are some extreme situations where it might be desirable to deliberately puncture a raft, or cut away part of a kayak, where having a pointed end on the knife is essential.

Lanyards

Some people attach their knife to their buoyancy aid by means of a thin piece of line, so as not to lose it if they let go of it. I would suggest that this is not good practice, as a razor sharp knife flailing around in a strong current could do the rescuer considerable damage.

Saws

Small folding saws were very popular in the days of small cockpit kayaks. Modern 'keyhole' cockpits make the prospect of needing to cut somebody out of a boat less likely. However **it is certainly worth having one between the party** as it may have other uses, such as the preventative removal of strainers.

Tape or Sling

An **eight foot sewn** sling of tubular nylon tape or 'spectra', can be used for a whole variety of purposes: to quickly create an anchor point, to make a rescued boat fast to the bank, to make your own boat fast while you clamber on to a rock in midstream, to name but a few. It should be kept in a pocket so that it can be got at quickly. Shortening it with an overhand

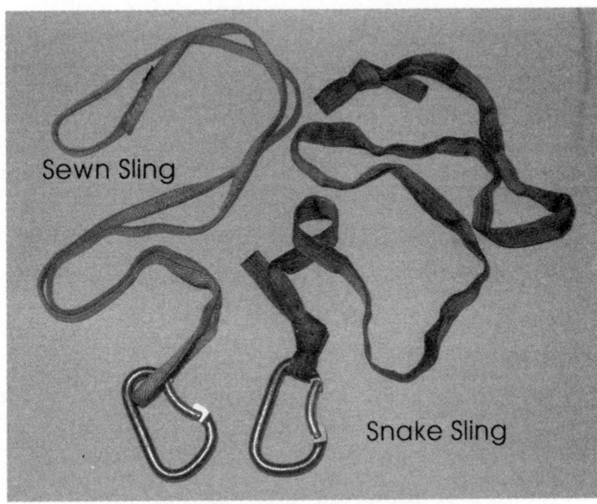

Fig. 14.3 Tape slings.

knot and wearing it clipped around the waist using a karabiner is **not a good idea.** This is because it forms a potential snag loop that will take a 2,500 kg load before breaking.

Alternatively, a **'snake sling'**, (fig. 14.3) can be used and carried in a similar way. For raft guides this is the better choice, as it doubles up as a 'flip line' which is used to right upturned rafts. The length of the sling will depend on the size of the guide and raft.

Karabiners

There are two shapes of karabiners: 'D' shaped and Pear shaped, and two types: snaplink and screwgate.

Shape

'D' shaped karabiners are lighter but are designed to be strong only at key points where the shape of the karabiner feeds the ropes. (Fig. 14.4).

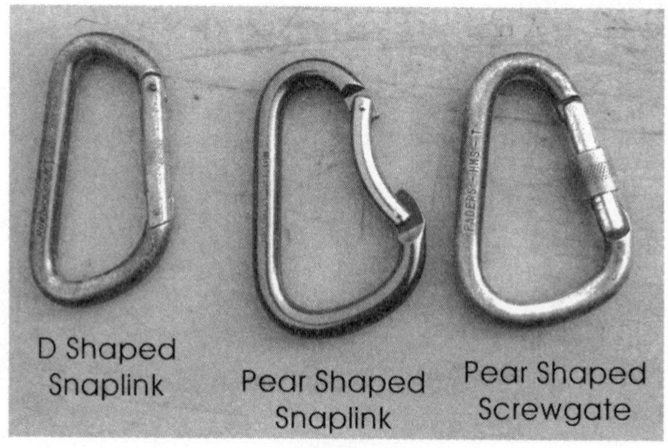

Fig. 14.4 A selection of karabiners.
Photos: Bob Timms

Pear shaped or H.M.S. karabiners are engineered to take the strain over a much greater area of the karabiner. This makes them much more versatile as they can safely take more than one rope and can be used with a greater variety of knots and hitches.

I would therefore recommend that if paddlers are only going to carry a couple of karabiners, they should be pear shaped ones.

Snaplink vs. Screwgate

Snaplinks are lighter and quicker to use. Screwgates are stronger and, providing you remember to screw the gate shut, more difficult to accidentally become detached from. (Fig. 14.4). Professional rescue teams only use screwgates. However they usually only get involved in situations which are relatively stable, such as people stranded on a rock in midstream, or to recover bodies.

....'a 'window of opportunity'...

Boaters or rafters involved in an incident have a 'window of opportunity', a period of about four to seventy seconds after an incident starts, during which prompt action can sort out a situation before it develops into a major problem. This is why many of them prefer to use snaplinks for water based incidents.

A compromise is to use a snaplink to secure your throw bag and a screwgate on your tape sling.

Improvised Paddle Hook

A paddle hook is used to attach a line to a victim or piece of equipment that is out of reach. By using some surgical strapping tape from a first aid kit, or some 'gaffer tape' from a repair kit a paddle hook can be made using a snaplink karabiner. The karabiner is securely taped to the end of a paddle or better still a long pole; an open boater's pole is ideal. A line is attached to the karabiner and then the absolute minimum amount of tape necessary is used to hold the gate open. (Fig. 14.5).

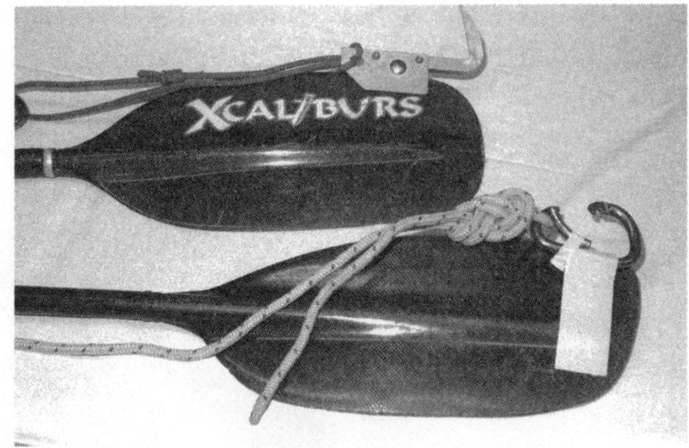

Fig. 14.5 Commercial and improvised paddle hooks.

Once the karabiner is hooked, a sharp tug is usually enough to dislodge the small piece of tape and close the gate. If the minimum amount of tape necessary is also used to attach the paddle to the karabiner it is usually easy to detach the paddle, which might otherwise get in the way.

White Water Chest Harness

Chest harnesses designed for use in white water rescue have only one function. They are designed as a 'safer' way of attaching a swimmer to a line in fast flowing water. To achieve that simple objective they have to meet the following criteria:

1. They must reliably release under a relatively light load right through to extreme loading.
2. They must self-release before pressures can reach levels which would result in chest injuries.
3. It should be difficult, if not impossible to release them accidentally.
4. The attachment point of the line should be high enough up the centre line of the rescuer's back so as to ensure that rescuers are held in such a way that fast flowing water will surf them to the surface and maintain them in a stable position that ensures that they can breathe, (Fig. 14.6).

Design

Although the actual detail may vary, all the designs currently available tend to be similar. The design criteria are met by:

1. Integrating the design into a buoyancy aid. This means that the whole system is more stable and less likely to let the attachment point move from it's optimum place than a separate harness.
2. Using purpose built release buckles that are designed to break **or** allow the belt of the harness to slide, if the loading reaches an injury threatening level.

It is important to realise that considerable time, money and experimental models are involved before manufacturers come up with their final product. These are not the sort of items that lend themselves to being improvised or 'home made'. It is also important to read the manufacturer's instructions or seek professional guidance on a safety and rescue course, to ensure that they are used correctly.

Fig. 14.6 Rescuer being surfed to the surface.
Photo: Bob Timms

Release Buckles

The problem of having a release mechanism that will release or not release in different situations has led some manufacturers to add a friction plate that the paddler threads the belt through prior to fastening the quick release buckle itself. The plate is threaded in situations where it is essential that the harness does not allow the belt to slide, even under quite high loads, such as when being used to anchor a belayer to the river bank. **It is not threaded when the rescuer may wish to release the harness under much smaller loads, as is the case in most swimming situations.**

Top: Using a swim line on the River Tryweryn, North Wales.
Photo: Ray Goodwin
Bottom: Throw line rescue on the Bhote Kosi, Nepal.
Photo: Mark Nichols/Palm

However, some systems are designed in such a way that it is the manufacturer's intention that the plate should always be threaded. If this is the case I would advise that people check, through cautious experimentation, whether the buckle will release under the lower pressures sometimes encountered in swimming situations.

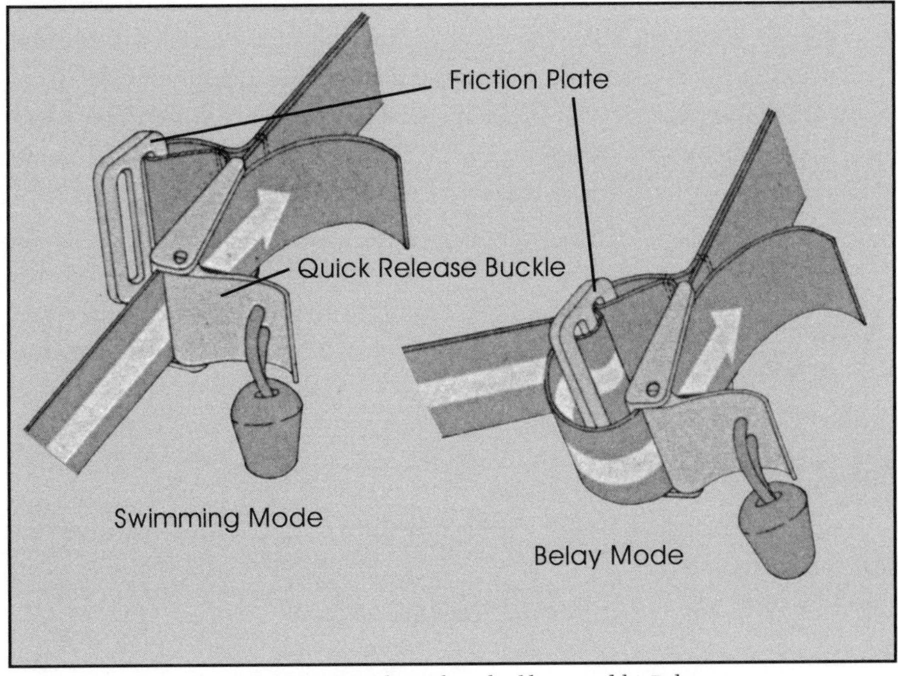

Fig. 14.7 Detail of release buckle as used by Palm.

Cows' Tails

Cows' tails act as an extension, so that the rescuer doesn't have to get someone else to clip the line into the attachment point, or perform contortions to do it himself. When not in use the end that would clip into a line is clipped to a quick release point on the front of the buoyancy aid, so that the cow's tail fits snugly against the rescuer's chest. They are very convenient but some paddlers prefer to do without them. This is because, if they are worn loose they can snag an obstruction, whereas if they are worn tight they reduce mobility. Elasticated cows' tails go some way towards reducing these concerns.

Top Left: Swimmer just below Lava Falls on the Colorado River, Grand Canyon, USA.
Bottom: One chase boater goes for the swimmer, onefor the kayak and another keeps an eye on everyone else!
Top Right: Carrying the swimmer.
Photos: Ray Goodwin

Chapter 15
Swimmers, Boats and Paddles

A boater failing to roll, a rafter catapulted into the water; these are common everyday occurrences on a white water trip. The first priority is obviously to get the swimmer out of the water, but the abandoned boats and paddles also need to be dealt with. Strictly speaking, I should deal with these items in the part of the book that deals with 'recovery'. However, the techniques used for dealing with swimmers or items of equipment that are floating in the current are so similar that I have chosen to deal with them in the same chapter.

We can never justify a high level of risk taking when attempting to recover drifting equipment. If in doubt, leave it and wait until a more favourable situation develops.

Self Rescue

Self rescue is by far the most reliable form of rescue. The main requirement is a positive mental attitude.

...'a positive mental attitude'...

Two people swimming on the same stretch of water who have a different mental approach are in two completely different situations! One is a helpless victim, the other is a paddler in temporary difficulties.

As soon as a swimmer's head breaks the surface he should shake the water from his eyes and ears, and look around. Information needs to be gathered and conscious decisions need to be made:

1. Where is the nearest point of safety, and how to get to it? (In a rafter's case, this is normally the raft. However, there will be times when it will be easier and safer to make for the shore).
2. Is anyone in a position to effect a rescue and if so, how can the swimmer best cooperate?
3. Whether to hang on to one's equipment or whether to ditch it so as to be able to swim more effectively?

Having gathered the information and decided on a course of action, the swimmer will need to be aware of, and preferably have practised, good white water swimming techniques.

Swimming in White Water

When swimming in fast flowing water the greatest danger is getting a foot or hand caught between two boulders, or trapped in some other obstruction on the river bed. This would result in the swimmer being forced to the bottom by the current and drowned.

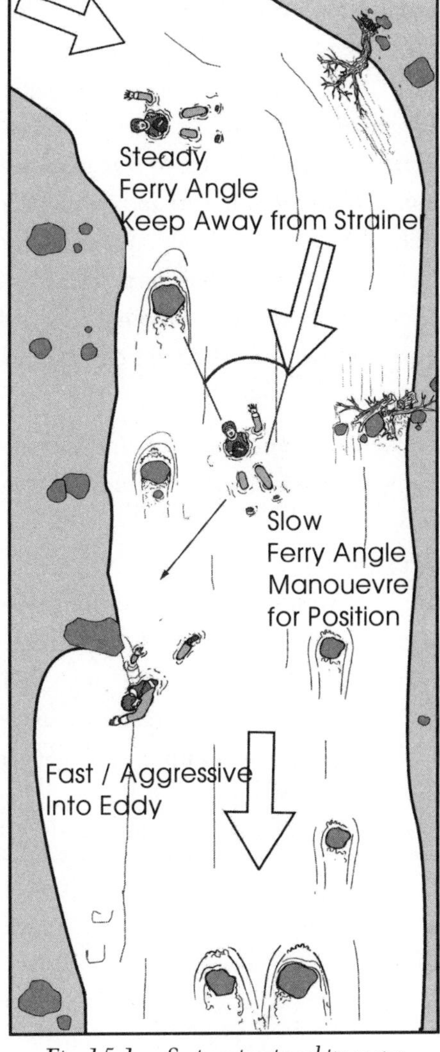

Fig. 15.1 Swimming in white water.

Basic Position

By swimming on our backs and keeping our feet and hands on the surface we can avoid the risk of foot entrapment. By keeping our heads upstream and our feet downstream we gain the following advantages:

- We can see where we are going
- Our head is protected from impacts
- We can fend off boulders with our feet
- If we do make contact with the bottom, the knocks are taken on the back of the buoyancy aid or our buttocks, which means bruises rather than fractures

Progress is made around hazards or obstacles and towards safety by swimming at a ferry angle, (i.e. about 45 degrees to the main flow).

Deep or Slow Moving Water

If the water is deep or slow moving, we can use front crawl or breast stroke.

Passive or Aggressive?

Swimming in cold turbulent water is an exhausting business. Unlike in normal swimming, the swimmer has to have a reserve of oxygen in his blood, and air in his lungs, to survive sections where he is forced below the surface. These factors mean that it is not a good idea to swim 'flat out' for more than about ten metres.

On narrow creeks the distances involved are so short that the only sensible option is to swim aggressively to the shore. Anyone falling out of a raft will usually be within a few metres of the raft. If they act quickly and swim aggressively they will regain contact with the raft within seconds.

If the distance to safety is too great, the swimmer should husband his strength. He should swim steadily towards safety but not so fast that he becomes short of breath. It may be better to stay in mid stream and float passively to within striking distance of safety, than to immediately strike out aggressively for the bank, only to be swept into a strainer or some other hazard.

The swimmer should plan ahead, swim passively towards safety and use short bursts of aggressive swimming to avoid obstacles and to make it those last few metres to safety. Above all he must remain calm and never give up. (Fig. 15.1).

Eddies

Getting across an eddy line and into the eddy can be very difficult, simply because a swimmer moves comparatively slowly. There are two ways to approach this manoeuvre:

Attack

The swimmer manoeuvres himself to a point a little upstream of the eddy, then turns onto his front facing downstream and aggressively swims across the eddy line , *'eddy fence'*, at a 45° angle. This is essentially a swimmer's version of a break out, *'eddy in'*. The break out can be further helped if the swimmer makes a high overarm stroke with his outside arm just as he crosses the eddy. This lowers his inside shoulder so that his body 'carves' the turn into the eddy, and ensures that the stroke is planted deep in the eddy so as to anchor the turn.

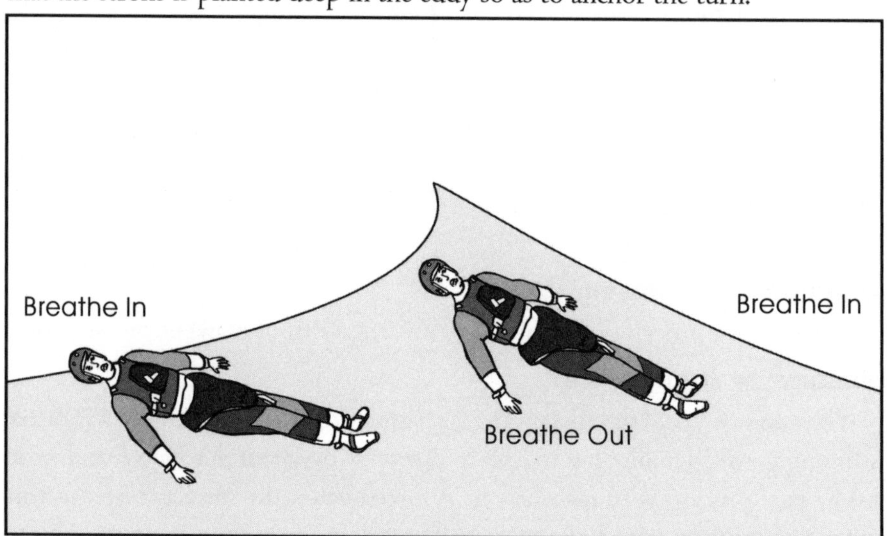

Fig. 15.2 Breathing whilst swimming in waves.

Rotate

The speed of the current may force a swimmer to maintain a ferry angle all the way into the eddy. This is what an open boater calls 'setting in'. The swimmer can help get himself across the eddy line by rolling over and over into the eddy.

Waves

When swimming through a series of waves, a swimmer's head will be on the surface in the troughs and under water in the peaks, (fig. 15.2). The danger is that the swimmer instinctively only tries to breathe in and ends up with lungs bursting with stale air. What he should do is to consciously and deliberately breathe out as he goes through the peaks, (i.e. when his head is under water), so that he can get a lung full of clean air in the troughs.

Equipment

The decision on whether to hang on to boat and paddle, saving everyone a lot of trouble, or ditch them and concentrate on surviving the swim, should be just that: a conscious decision, **not** a panic reaction.

If a paddler is faced with a straight forward swim to the shore or back to the raft, it makes sense for him to hang on to his equipment.

Kayakers

In the kayaker's case, the kayak should be kept downstream so that he can't find himself trapped between 'a rock and a hard place'. Ideally the paddle should be held in the same hand that is holding the boat so that the other arm can be used to swim with.

Open Boaters

The open boater can use the above approach where the prospect of a long swim is not too daunting. If however he has fitted out his open boat as shown in chapter 12, he can grab the free end of the bow or stern throw line, swim to the shore unencumbered and then use the line to swing the boat into the shore.

It is particularly important that open boaters keep their boat downstream when swimming with it. If the boat is broached the pressures are immense. Not only can a swimmer become trapped between the boat and a rock, but it is also possible for the boat to fold around the swimmer. This is known in open boat circles as being 'bear-trapped'.

Rafters

More often than not, it will be best if the swimmer can keep hold of his paddle. None the less, there will be occasions on which being able to swim unhindered makes the difference between getting back to the raft and a nasty swim.

Rescue

For the sake of clarity, I have broken this section down into the following areas:

- Victim Behaviour
- Reaching and Throwing Rescues
- Bank Based Contact Rescues
- Chase Boating For Swimmers
- Chase Boating for Equipment
- Swimmer Rescues
- Dealing With Flipped Raft

Victim Behaviour

Which rescue technique is appropriate in a given situation will depend on, amongst other things, a victim's behaviour. An unconscious or totally unresponsive victim will not be able to hold on to a thrown line, and it would be suicidal for a rescuer to swim out to and make contact with a panic stricken victim.

A victim's behaviour in a water based rescue situation will depend on his state of mind. This can be divided into two broad categories: in control or out of control.

In Control

A person may be totally in control of his faculties and yet behave in an inappropriate way, so we can divide the types of behaviour we might come across into three types:

In Control / Competent

This person is in control, and because he is experienced, and/or well trained, is behaving in a way that is appropriate. Swimming purposefully towards safety or shouting for a throw line are good signs. This is the person who is unlikely to put your life at risk.

In Control / Incompetent

Rescuers should realise that behaviour that might seem inappropriate to a trained boater or rescuer, such as swimming towards a strainer, may be the result of ignorance rather than a loss of control. This person may be doing all the wrong things but is switched on and will probably respond well if given clear instructions.

In Control / Lucky

Even a person who is untrained and inexperienced can make the right decisions and take the right course of action. Whether he is guided by instinct or is just plain lucky matters not, just as long as he keeps doing the right things and making the rescuer's job a lot easier.

Out of Control

People who have lost control of their minds are the ones who pose a very real risk to rescuers. At best they are no assistance and at worst they may actively cause the rescuer harm. In a water based situation, people who lose control may do so in three different ways:

Panic

This is where victims are overwhelmed by anxiety and react aggressively and energetically. Reason goes out of the window as victims try to blindly fight their way out of trouble. Victims may be screaming, thrashing around and wasting valuable time and energy because their efforts lack direction or purpose.

Victims who are panicking pose by far the greatest threat to rescuers. **Contact rescues should be avoided.** It may be possible to calm panicking victims down by talking to them and behaving in a calm, authoritative manner.

Counter Panic

This type of behaviour occurs when victims are overwhelmed by anxiety but react by withdrawing into themselves and becoming totally passive. They are unable to help themselves and do not react to instructions.

Although not actively endangering a rescuer, their inability to assist the rescuer in anyway can hinder rescuers' efforts and force rescuers to use contact rescues. Both of these factors increase the risks involved. Victims of counter panic can sometimes be roused from their withdrawn state. Physically shaking victims and talking loudly to them, ideally calling out their name, may have the desired effect.

Instinctive Drowning Response

Sometimes referred to as Passive Drowning. This will normally only affect victims who are not wearing buoyancy aids. The victim who is unable to swim or float will hold his arms out to the side and try to push down on the water to try and keep his mouth and nose above water. While doing this the victim will be unable to scream or shout as all the effort is going into breathing. An adult will probably last only sixty seconds in this position before going under and drowning, a child only twenty seconds.

IDR victims regard a rescuer as simply a floating object which they can climb onto in order to get out of the water. Such victims are beyond reason and neither know nor care that their actions may drown a rescuer. The best way to deal with such victims is to give them a buoyant object to hold onto. Once they realise that they are not going under and are able to restore a normal breathing pattern they will probably regain control.

Reaching and Throwing Rescues

These rescues involve little if any risk to the rescuer. They work best with a cooperative victim and may work with a panicked or I.D.R. victim.

Reaching Rescues

Rescuers must first of all ensure their own safety by getting a firm hold of the bank, raft or another rescuer before reaching out to the victim. When holding on to another rescuer, it is best to get a firm grip of each other's wrist.

Fig. 15.3 Reaching rescue. Photos: Bob Timms

The length of a rescuer's reach can be extended by using a paddle. If using a single bladed paddle it is best to offer the 'T' grip to the victim. It is easier to get hold of and less likely to injure the victim. If the swimmer is also holding a single bladed paddle the reach can be further extended by hooking the two 'T' grips together. (Fig. 15.4).

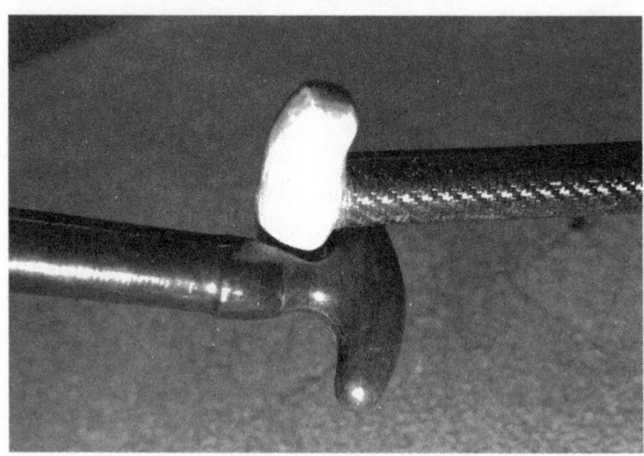

Fig. 15.4 Hooking 'T' grips.

Getting a Victim Back in a Raft

The simplest way is to grasp the swimmer by the shoulder straps of his buoyancy aid, push him down into the water, and then pull him into the raft. The victim's own buoyancy helps to pop him out of the water. As one doesn't want the swimmer to think that the rescuer is trying to drown him, it is important to make clear during the safety briefing that this is normal procedure!

Throw line to Swimmer Rescues

This is probably the commonest form of bank based rescue. The secret of success is regular practice.

This technique usually involves throwing the line to a swimmer from such an angle that, when the line comes tight, the swimmer is pendulumed into a safe eddy or the slower helical flow. There are some notable exceptions which will be covered later.

Positioning

It is worse than useless for a rescuer to throw a rope without giving some thought as to where is the best place to throw a rope from. Such an action would violate two fundamental principles: **The Principle of Personal Safety** and **The Principle of The Victim's Best Interest.**

Fig. 15.5 Rescuer tied off with waist loop using figure of eight on a bight. See: Appendix B

Experienced rescuers are able to make such assessments and decisions in fractions of a second. They may also make a decision in a situation which a less experienced rescuer might find too close to call. Such 'marginal calls' require experience and fine judgment. If in doubt, back off.

Rescuer's Safety

If the bank is very slippery and the rescuer is likely to end up in the water, it would make far more sense to move to a place with a better footing, even if this means that the victim will have a slightly longer swim.

Fig. 15.6 Rescuer tied off on chest harness using clove hitch. See: Appendix B

If the only suitable place does pose this risk, the rescuer will have to be tied off to a suitable anchor. The rescuer must be tied off with a separate line, so that he retains the option of letting go of the end of the throw line should this become necessary.

Victim's Safety

The rescuer must also be sure that when the victim grabs the rope he will be swung into a place of safety and not into somewhere that is even more dangerous than the middle of the river, such as a strainer or undercut bank. (Fig. 15.7).

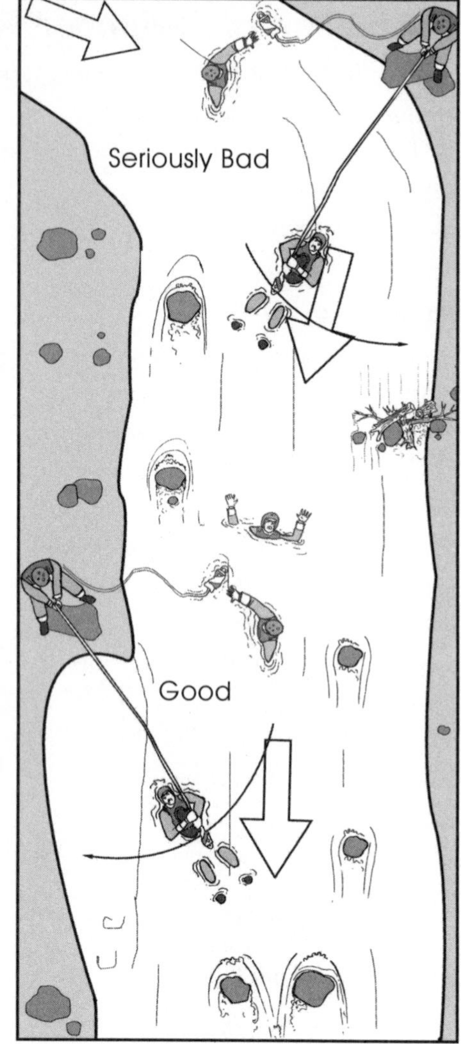

Fig. 15.7 Positioning for a throw line rescue.

Gaining Attention

The rescuer needs to be far enough downstream from the obstacle that is likely to cause a swim, or any waves that will submerge the swimmer, for the swimmer to have come to the surface and recovered his senses enough to see the line. There is no point throwing a line if the swimmer doesn't see it and therefore doesn't hang on to it.

The rescuer should hold the line and bag clearly above his head, shout, "Rope! Rope!" and gain eye contact with the swimmer **before** throwing the line.

Technique

Throwing a line is a hand and eye coordination skill, combined with the ability to track a moving target. In other words it takes a great deal of practice to develop an accurate and reliable throw.

Different circumstances require different techniques. If you have waded out into an eddy and the water is thigh deep you will have to throw **over-arm,** either with an action like an American footballer, or with a bowling action, like a cricketer. If you have to throw under overhanging branches you will have to throw **under-arm.** A **side-arm** throw is difficult to master but can be useful when distance rather than accuracy is the issue.

In all the above the following are useful guidelines:

1. Stand with the opposite foot to your throwing arm forward, i.e. if you are right handed lead with your left foot.

2. Keep your eye on the target the whole time.
3. Follow through, i.e. as you release the bag your hand should be pointing at the target.
4. Do not forget to hold on to your end of the rope but do not wrap the rope around your hand, in case you need to let go in a hurry.
5. Aim to land the rope directly on the swimmer, as in practise you will find that whichever way you aim off will be the wrong way!
6. Try and achieve a low trajectory. This minimises the chances of fouling tree branches or slalom lines and of the wind deflecting the line.

Holding the Line

If the current is not too powerful it is possible for the rescuer to brace against the pull on the line by adopting a stance that will allow him to absorb the shock as the line comes tight.

Standing Brace

(Fig. 15.8). This involves:

- Turning side on to the direction of pull
- Standing with feet apart
- Keeping knees bent to absorb energy and lower the centre of gravity
- Keeping elbows bent to absorb energy
- Holding the loaded line on the upstream side

Fig. 15.8 Standing brace.
Photos: Bob Timms

Sitting Brace

(Fig. 15.9) This involves:

- Facing the direction of pull
- Sitting down as soon as the swimmer grabs the line and **before** the line comes tight
- Sitting with feet apart and braced against a boulder or similar obstruction

Fig. 15.9 Sitting Brace.

- If possible wedging one's bottom against a boulder or similar obstruction
- Keeping knees bent to absorb energy
- Keeping elbows bent to absorb energy
- Holding the loaded line on the upstream side

Shoulder Belay

If the current is very powerful, some form of belay may be necessary. This involves partially wrapping the line around one's body in such a way that the friction makes it easier to hold onto the line, while at the same time allowing one to pay out or let go if necessary.

The advantage of the shoulder belay over other methods is that the line is wrapped around the belayer's body, (fig. 15.10) in such a way that it doesn't interfere with the throwing action.

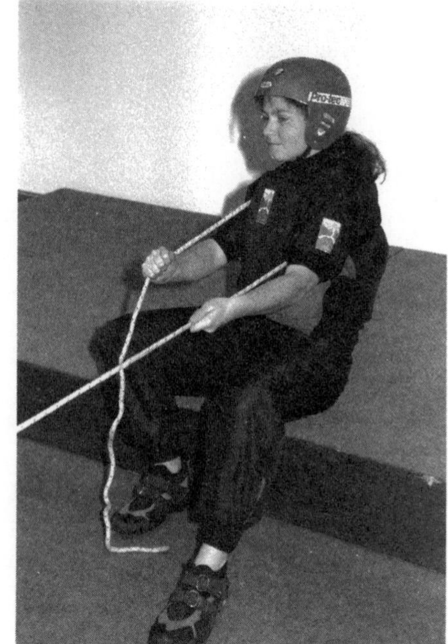

Fig. 15.10 Shoulder belay.

This involves:

- Taking a few metres of line out of the bag
- Holding the bag in the throwing hand
- Wrapping the line around one's back so that it goes from the throwing hand, diagonally across the back, over the opposite shoulder and down to waist height where the clean end is held in the other hand
- Holding the line so that the clean end of the line comes into the hands from the little finger end

As soon as the swimmer grabs the line the belayer sits down, braces with his feet and bottom and takes the strain using the shoulder belay, (fig. 15.10). If the initial strain is considerable it can be further eased by deliberately paying out a little rope.

Receiving the Line

As with any rescue, everything is considerably easier if the victim remains calm, is cooperative and knows what to do.

On seeing that the rescuer is ready to throw a line, the swimmer can indicate that he is ready to receive it **and** make a bigger target by facing the rescuer and spreading his arms out wide. If the rescuer narrowly misses the target, a short burst of aggressive swimming can retrieve the line.

On grabbing the line the swimmer should be on his back facing downstream. The line should be held in both hands and draped over the shoulder that is furthest **away** from the rescuer, (fig. 15.11). This will assist the pendulum by setting the swimmer's body up in a ferry angle, considerably easing the extra strain that would otherwise be caused by the increased drag and water pressure.

Fig. 15.11 Holding on in the flow.
Photos: Bob Timms

As the line comes tight the swimmer looks at his feet which causes his back to curve in such a way that he planes to the surface. Any water that does rush over his head does so in such a way that a pocket of air is created, enabling him to breathe. At the same time there will be a brief moment of instability which he must fight by spreading his legs out wide and kicking out.

Second Throws

The best solution to the problem is to practice so often that you don't miss with your first throw. There are two types of situation we may have to deal with:

1. Where the victim is static, i.e. stranded or held in a stopper, 'hydraulic'.
2. Where the victim is floating downstream and the rescuer has to run down the bank after him.

Static Second Throw

1. Free both hands by standing on the end of the rope.
2. Take in the rope hand over hand and pile it at your feet.
3. Scoop water into the bag to weight it and throw again.

Throwing from Coils

This next section is written for a right handed person. Left handed people simply substitute left for right and vice-versa.

1. With your left hand held palm upwards, trap the end of the rope by curling your little finger over it.

2. Take in the rope with your right hand laying the coils into your left hand. Deliberately drag the rope on the water or ground as this ensures that the coils lay neatly and don't tangle.
3. When you have taken in about half the rope, trap the coils by curling your next two fingers, (ring and middle).
4. Take in the remaining rope laying the coils on your index finger.
5. Separate the two sets of coils, holding the coils nearest the bag in your right hand and those nearest the 'clean end' in your left.
6. Run down the bank and get a little ahead of the swimmer.
7. Throw the coils, leading with the bag end. Keep the end trapped under your little finger.

Non Pendulum Situations

There are four situations where the rescuer is not trying to pendulum the victim to the side:

1. Still or slow moving water.
2. Where the rescuer is moving at the same speed as the victim, i.e. throwing a line from a raft.
3. Where the water is fast flowing all the way to the bank and there are no eddies or helical flow. (This situation is due to the river's bed and sides being very smooth, and would normally be found on a canalised section of river or in a flood drainage channel).
4. Where the thrower is positioned, either by mistake or lack of choice, in such a way that he is parallel, rather than at an angle to the main flow, as is often the case on the outside of a bend. This will hold the swimmer in the current and will probably involve such forces that the thrower is unable to change his position without letting go of the rope.

Situation One and Two

In the first two situations the rescuer simply pulls in the line hand over hand and brings the victim to them. Very little force is involved.

Situation Three

In this situation the water will be moving very fast and the main flow will continue uninterrupted right up to the bank. The forces involved if the swimmer is pendulumed towards the bank and the angles change will be such that either the swimmer or the rescuer will be forced to let go of the line.

Providing the bank is unobstructed, the rescuer can reduce the forces involved by running down the bank at the same speed at which the swimmer is floating and pull him in at right angles to the current.

Situation Four

A second rescuer can change the angle of pull by clipping the throw line with his tape sling and karabiner, then running down the bank, and in the process changing the angles and forces involved, until the swimmer is pulled into the side. (Fig. 15.12)

Fig. 15.12 Second rescuer changes angle of pull with sling and karabiner.

Situation Three and Four (Bank Obstructed)

The following technique would normally be used if there is time to set it up beforehand:

1. Rescuer B clips a second line to Rescuer A's line before it is thrown and moves into position as far down stream of the thrower, (Rescuer A), as he can. (Fig. 15.13).
2. As soon as the swimmer has hold of the throw line, rescuer B pulls his line in as quickly as he can.

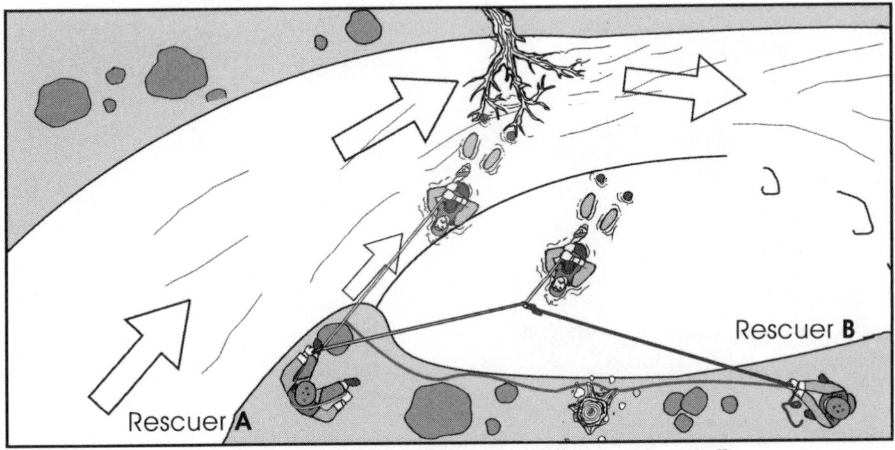

Fig. 15.13 Pre-arranged line used to change angle of pull.

Bank Based Contact Rescues

All the methods illustrated so far depend on the victim being conscious and able to grab hold of a line or paddle. The following methods will also work for retrieving boats, paddles and unconscious or unresponsive swimmers that are drifting in the current.

...'Rescuers must have thoroughly evaluated the risks '...

All involve considerably more risk than reaching or throwing rescues as they involve a rescuer entering the water, therefore considerable judgment must be exercised. Rescuers must have thoroughly evaluated the risks involved, be well practised in the use of these techniques and be confident of a successful outcome.

Handrail

The most important element of this technique is to read the river well. The rescuer needs to find a place downstream of the hazard that is being covered where the main current sets in close to a shallow eddy. (Fig. 15.14).

One end of a line is tied to a suitable anchor and a series of overhand knots on a bight are tied in the other end. The rescuer simply uses the knots to keep hold of the line. The line provides him with enough support to wade out to the edge of the current where he can reach out and grab hold of anything that floats past.

Fig 15.14 Handrail with detail of overhand on the bight. Photos: Bob Timms

Points to note:

1. The line must be anchored in such a position that, should the rescuer lose his footing, he would be pendulumed back into the eddy.
2. The line must be tied off so that only as much as is needed is in the water.
3. The overhand knots should be tied so that the 'bights', (fig. 15.14 insert), are too small to put one's hand through them. The rescuer holds on by grasping the knot rather than by putting his hand through a loop, just in case he needs to let go.
4. Rescuers should only consider using this technique upstream of a stretch of water that they would be prepared to swim if necessary.

'Live Bait' Rescues

This is a two person rescue. Rescuer A is in position ready to jump in the water and swim after a victim or equipment and is attached, via a quick release chest harness, to a line which is belayed by rescuer B.

Positioning

The rescue should be set up where the current will bring the victim or equipment as close as possible to the rescuers. Rescuer B, the belayer, must be positioned so that, when the line comes tight, rescuer A will be pendulumed out of the main flow and into a safe eddy. Ideally the rescue should be set up somewhere where the rescuer would be able to swim unaided to the shore should he become detached from the line.

Fig. 15.15 In position for live bait rescue.

The belayer

In this situation, where the belayer, rescuer B, can sit down with the rope already set up, a waist belay is the preferred method. The rope attached to rescuer A, known as the 'live' rope, is held in rescuer B's upstream hand, passed around his back at waist level and held in the downstream hand **after** it has been wrapped once around his forearm. (Fig. 15.15).

The belayer, (rescuer B), is in a position to take rope in or feed it out as required by rescuer A. Practice is required to ensure that the belayer can do this without letting go of the 'dead' rope at any time.

Entry

Rescuer A, carrying a few loose coils of rope, jumps in when the target has floated as close as it is going to get. The aim is to achieve a low trajectory and a low angle of entry so as to achieve maximum distance and stay on the surface, (a bit like skimming stones). He should hit the water with his belly, with his hands, feet and head raised, so as to keep them on the surface. (Fig. 15.16)

Fig. 15.16 Low trajectory entry.
Photos: Bob Timms

If the target cannot be reached by the leap, the rescuer will have to use front crawl in order to swim fast enough to intercept the target. Therefore, when selecting a position to launch from, care will have to be taken to ensure that the water is deep enough.

With practice, it is possible to become more accurate swimming from an eddy to intercept than leaping. This is particularly the case if the rescuer is wearing swimming aids. (See Chapter 29).

Fig. 15.17 Contact.

Contact

On reaching the victim, rescuer A should turn him on his back and grab him by the shoulder straps of his buoyancy aid. By holding the victim tight against his chest and keeping the victim's head slightly lower than his own, he will ensure that they are both able to breathe when the line comes tight and they plane to the surface and pendulum into the eddy. (Fig. 15.17)

Although in the 'handrail and 'live bait' rescues contact could be made with a swimmer in a state of panic, the risk to rescuers posed by this factor is low. In the case of the handrail rescue, this is because the rescuer is in water that is no more than thigh deep. In the case of the live bait rescue it is because within a second or two, both the rescuer and the victim are swung into a safe eddy where the rescuer can be assisted by the belayer if necessary.

Chase Boating for Swimmers

Rescues of swimmers and their equipment are often made by other boaters, either as it happens, or on more difficult rapids by boaters pre-positioned to cover such eventualities. Rafters running more demanding rivers often use kayakers in this role as extra safety cover. Although less suited to chasing swimmers because of lack of speed and manoeuvrability, rafts do have the distinct advantage of providing a stable platform from which to effect a rescue once contact is made.

Chase boating is a high risk activity. It requires top level boating skills and self-confidence, combined with the ability to make cool, rational decisions and snap judgments. It is vital that team members clearly identify who is prepared and able to take on this role, and who isn't.

Assessing Victim Behaviour

In boater to swimmer rescues, contact with a panic stricken victim poses a very real threat to the rescuer's safety. The rescuer must keep his distance and assess the victim's state of mind by talking to him and observing his reactions before attempting to make physical contact.

...'the assumption must be that he is a homicidal maniac whose only mission in life is to drown you!'...

Until the victim proves otherwise, the assumption must be that he is a homicidal maniac whose only mission in life is to drown **you!** (Principle of Presumed Insanity).

Panic Behaviour

Physical contact with a panic stricken victim should be avoided at all costs. The best a chase boater can do is to keep a safe distance and lure the victim towards safety.

Counter Panic

It may be possible, by talking to and physically shaking a victim, to 'shake him out of it', so he is able to offer some level of cooperation. If not they will need to be treated as unconscious victims.

Instinctive Drowning Response

There are two possible outcomes if a boater allows somebody showing signs of I.D.R. to get hold of the end of his boat:

1. The victim will hold on to the end of the boat, realise he can now float, and passively allow himself to be rescued.
2. The victim will grab hold of the boat and turn into a panicked victim. Therefore the chase boater should not make contact with such a victim unless he is prepared to leave his boat as a float for the victim to hang on to and swim to safety to avoid contact with the victim.

Escorting a Swimmer

Even if the victim's behaviour is 'normal', the chase boater may decide that the difficulty of the water is such that attempting to tow or carry a swimmer is too dangerous. By maintaining station close to a swimmer the chase boater can fulfil a number of useful functions:

Provide Moral Support

The mere presence of another human being is reassuring, even if all he can do is cheer the swimmer on!

Give Directions

The chase boater is able to see and plan much further ahead and is therefore able to tell the swimmer which way to go to avoid hazards and reach safety.

Give Warning

If a hazard is unavoidable, the chase boater can give the swimmer more time to mentally and physically prepare.

Act as a Marker

The chase boater can help bank-based rescuers preparing a rescue by marking the position of the swimmer who might otherwise be hidden from them.

Contact Rescues

Drag

If the distance to safety is short, the swimmer can hold on to the rescuer's stern grab loop and be helped on his way. (Fig. 15.18) Progress is slow and exhausting due to the amount of drag to be overcome.

Fig. 15. 18 Chase boater dragging swimmer.

There is a 'victim mentality' whereby, as soon as contact is made, the victim relaxes and allows things to happen rather than actively contributing to his own rescue. Therefore the rescuer will have to glance over his shoulder to ensure that the swimmer is still swimming vigorously.

Push

Fig. 15. 19 Push. Photos: Bob Timms

This technique is best used in deep water that is not too rough. In rough or shallow water the victim risks being injured. It is particularly useful with exhausted or counter panicked victims who need to be kept under observation.

The victim holds on to the rescuer's bow, keeping it over one shoulder, so that he doesn't get a face full of plastic if the going gets rough.(Fig. 15.19). The victim's legs grip on either side of the boat and the victim is pushed to safety.

Carry

Pros:

- Less drag allows the rescue boat to move faster
- The paddling is less strenuous
- The victim is protected from being battered in shallow rapids

Cons:

- Requires a high skill level on the part of the chase boater
- Requires a cooperative swimmer
- The chase boater's ability to manoeuvre is severely impeded

Interception

If the chase boater is waiting in an eddy for the swimmer, has checked that the section downstream is no problem, and is sure that the swimmer is in control, it is quicker to intercept the swimmer by breaking out below them, (i.e. from downstream). At all other times it is safer to approach a swimmer from upstream. This is because:

1. The chase boater is better able to back off if the swimmer turns out to be in a dangerous state of mind.
2. The chase boater has both the swimmer and his 'future water' in view.

Contact

The chase boater manoeuvres so as to present the back of his boat to the swimmer, with the swimmer on the upstream side. The swimmer pulls himself up the back deck, holding on to the rear of the cockpit rim. He helps the boater by keeping his centre of gravity as low as possible by keeping his head on the rear deck as close to the boater's back as possible. Stability is increased further if the swimmer leaves his legs trailing in the water. (Fig. 15.20).

Fig. 15.20 Carry. Photo: Bob Timms

The untrained swimmer will instinctively try to see what is going on by raising his head and looking over the chase boater's shoulder. The chase boater can counter this by continually talking to the passenger about what is happening, and warning him at the approach of shallows, so that he can lift his legs just enough to avoid them being bumped and scraped.

Unconscious Victims

Dealing with an unconscious victim while chase-boating is both difficult and potentially extremely hazardous. Great care should be taken and if in doubt the rescuer should not attempt the rescue. There are in essence four possible strategies:

- Attach throw line
- Long line
- Escort and swim
- Tow

Attach Throw line

This requires a team effort between a chase boater and a bank based rescuer.

1. The chase boater paddles alongside the victim, until a bank based rescuer can get into a position to throw him a line.

2. He then attaches the line to the victim's buoyancy aid shoulder strap, using a karabiner.
3. The bank based rescuer pulls or pendulums the victim to the shore.

Long Line

For this to work the chase boater has to have a throw line to hand. The best way to carry it while approaching the victim is stuffed down the front of your buoyancy aid.

1. The chase boater comes alongside the victim and attaches the bag end of his throw line to the victim's buoyancy aid shoulder strap.
2. The chase boater paddles downstream of the victim, holding the end of the line in one hand, until the line is fully paid out.
3. The chase boater paddles into an eddy, leaps out of his boat, and braces himself **before** the line comes tight.
4. The victim is pendulumed into the eddy.

Tow

The victim is towed to the side using one of the methods described under 'Chase Boating for Equipment'.

Escort and Swim

The chase boater escorts the unconscious victim until he comes to a relatively safe section of river where he is prepared to get into the water, abandon his boat and perform a swimmer rescue. This is described later in this chapter.

The chase-boater should only use the last two techniques when he is **certain** that there are no downstream hazards, and that he can tow the victim to the side **before** the current carries him out of this zone of relatively safe water.

Chase-Boating for Equipment

When chase-boating for equipment the risks involved are nearly as high as when going after swimmers, but much harder to justify. If in doubt, leave it!

...'If in doubt, leave it!'...

Paddles

If faced with both paddle and boat, it is probably best to deal with the paddle first. Firstly, they are much quicker to deal with and secondly, they are easier to lose sight of.

The Pick-Up

When collecting a paddle, it is best to aim to arrive alongside the paddle at one end and pick it up by a blade or the 'T' grip. The classic mistake is for the chase boater to aim for the middle of the loom, run over the paddle and then struggle to retrieve the paddle from under his boat. Having retrieved the paddle, the chase boater can either throw or carry the paddle to the shore.

Throwing

When the paddle is being thrown at or, in a series of throws, towards the bank, it is best to throw it like a javelin. If however the thrower is expecting someone to catch the paddle it is best to throw it sideways on, so that the catcher is presented with the loom.

Fig. 15.21 Throwing paddles so that they can be caught.

Parallel Carry

This is simple enough in theory but requires some practice. The chase boater's own paddle is held as normally as possible and the recovered paddle is held parallel to and alongside it. People with small hands may not be able to use this technique.

Fig. 15.22 Paddling with two sets of blades.

Open Boat Carry

The paddle is stuffed under the bow buoyancy bag, so that it is securely wedged between the buoyancy bag and the hull, or between the buoyancy bag and the cord that holds the bag in place.

Samurai Carry

Useful for single blade paddles. The paddle is stuffed down the back of the boater's buoyancy aid so that it sticks out above his head, like the pennant of a samurai horseman.

Boats

Getting a boat to shore is fraught with danger. The chase boater must wait for a favourable stretch of water and be prepared to back off at any time.

Getting a boat to shore is difficult enough; keeping it there is even harder. It is therefore essential that, on reaching the shore, the person who has lost his boat must run down the bank and offer assistance. Ideally, another member of the party would get out on the other shore and offer assistance should the boat be landed on the other bank.

If help is not immediately at hand, the chase boater may be able to use a tape sling to tether the boat to a convenient branch or exposed root until the boat's owner arrives.

There are three main ways of getting a boat to the shore:

Nudge

The chase boater pushes the boat towards the shore using the bow of his boat, keeping the abandoned boat at a ferry angle (45°) to the main flow.

The main advantage of this method is that the rescuer is not physically attached to a waterlogged boat that could drag him to his death, and is able to back off, at any time.

On low to medium volume, relatively narrow rivers, this is **the** technique to use.

Flip and Shove

If the current is going to take the boat within range of a large eddy, it can be flipped the right way up and given a good shove into the eddy. (Providing of course the boat is properly equipped with buoyancy bags).

Long Line

The above methods are ineffective when tackling open boats. The chase boater grabs the downstream throw line or, if swim lines (as described in chapter 12) are not fitted, clips one to the downstream end of the boat. He then paddles downstream, holding the line in one hand. By paddling downstream he ensures that the line is not pulled tight. When the line is fully extended he maintains his distance from the boat until the current carries the convoy within range of a suitable eddy. At this point he breaks out ahead of the open canoe, leaps out of his boat and uses the line to pendulum the boat into the eddy.

Tow

Towing a boat on fast moving or white water is a very hazardous activity. If the boat becomes snagged or is carried into a hazard and the chase boater is unable to immediately release the tow line, he will be dragged or pendulumed into the hazard. For this reason I would suggest the following guidelines:

1. On creeks and narrow technical rivers, chase boaters should not tow at all. They should use other techniques or wait for the boat to become lodged on one of the many obstacles.
2. On high volume, wide rivers, chase boaters should only use towing systems that are fitted to the boat itself. That way, if the system fails to release, the rescuer can bale out and take his chances as an unattached swimmer.

Waist belt tow systems are designed for use on placid water and are not suitable for use on fast moving or white water. No matter how well designed the release mechanism, the chase-boater will only be able to get at it if he is able to lean back, exposing his face to the river bed in the process. If the chase-boater is forced to lean forward or, as in the case of a fatality on a grade II section of the River Dee, the belt rides up under his buoyancy aid, he will be unable to release it.

Boat Based Tow Systems

These should be designed so that they are easy to attach and even easier to release. The release system must work whether the tow line is being subjected to a massive load or a very gentle one. The length of the tow line needs to be such that the bow of the boat being towed is close behind the stern of the boat that is towing.

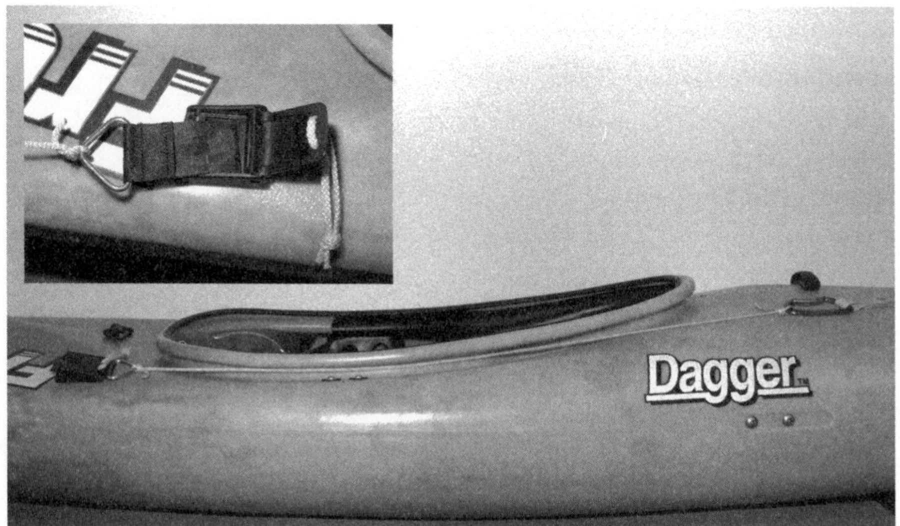

Fig. 15.23 The 'Buddy Line'. A commercially available tow system. The quick release swivels so that when towing it faces the opposite way to when it is not in use. Photo: Bob Timms

Improvised Tows

For all the reasons given above **my advice is not to use these.** There are a couple of systems that are occasionally used by some paddlers. Guidelines are precisely that, guidelines; "for the strict obedience of fools and the guidance of the wise." Providing the person using them is **aware** of the hazards involved and has **judged** the method to be suitable in **that particular situation**, exceptions can be made.

The only justification for an improvised system is that it is **rarely used.** If you find yourself regularly using such a system, you should invest in a proper boat mounted system.

Fig. 15.24 Home made tow system.
Photo: Loel Collins

Sling Tow

The chase boater attaches a tape sling to the boat with a karabiner and drapes the sling over his arm so that it is held in the crook of his elbow.

Pros:

- Easy to release

Cons:

- Uncomfortable
- Interferes with paddling technique

Chest Harness Tow

The boat is either attached directly to the cow's tail of the harness, or, better still, a sling and karabiner are used to extend the tow to a more suitable distance.

Pros:

- Quick to set up
- Doesn't interfere with paddling as much as sling tow

Cons:

- The attachment point of a chest harness is high up on the boater's back. This means that if there is a lot of resistance when towing, the boater is pulled back onto the rear deck of his boat making it difficult to paddle effectively.

- Chest harnesses are designed to release under pressure. The chase boater may decide to release the tow in anticipation of the need to increase speed to avoid a hazard downstream. It may be that the towed boat provides enough resistance to slow the boater down, but not enough to release the chest harness. In these circumstances, the only way that the chase boater can be sure of the 'quick release' working, is if he pulls the toggle and then reaches behind his back and pulls the cow's tail hard enough to feed the belt through the system! **Far too complex!**

Painter Tow

With open boats an easily releasable towing system can be improvised using one of the painters of the boat being recovered. The painter is wrapped around a thwart to create friction and then the boater simply kneels on the end of the rope. If it becomes necessary to release the tow, the boater simply unweights the relevant knee.

Quick Release Hitch

Another alternative is to make the painter fast to a thwart using a quick release version of the clove hitch.

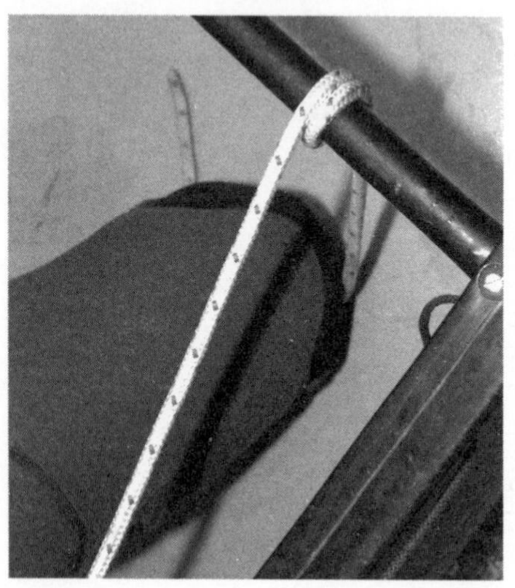

Fig. 15.24 Painter tow. Photos: Bob Timms

Fig. 15.25 Quick release hitch.

Swimmer Rescues

Personally, I believe that it is hard for a boater or rafter to justify the risks involved in swimming out to rescue a victim unless:

1. The victims are either unconscious, counter panicked, exhausted or hypothermic, i.e. unable to help themselves or grab hold of a line.

2. The stretch of water is straight forward and there is ample time to get a victim to shore before the next set of rapids or hazards.
3. The rescuer is a very strong swimmer.

Making Contact

The rescuer should approach from upstream so that it is more difficult for the victim to 'rush' him. The victim's type of behaviour must be assessed and if he is in a state of panic contact must be avoided at all costs.

Fig. 15.26 Swimmer to swimmer rescue.

If the victim is conscious he should be instructed to turn on his back facing downstream, i.e. away from the rescuer. If he complies, is unconscious or counter-panicked the rescuer can grab hold of the buoyancy aid shoulder strap that is furthest from the shore he is headed towards, (which sets the victim up in a ferry angle), and tow him in using back or side-stroke. (Fig. 15.26). If the victim is not wearing rafting or boating safety equipment the rescuer will have to grab a collar, loose clothing, or a bunch of the victim's hair at the nape of the neck.

Defensive Tactics

Avoidance

The first line of defence is for the rescuer to swim, on his back, away from the victim. He needs to remain close enough to talk to the victim and try to calm him down, but far enough away to avoid being grabbed by the victim. If the struggling victim is making any progress through the water in his efforts to grab the rescuer, the rescuer may be able to lure him towards safety.

Fending Off

A panicking victim is trying desperately to grab hold of a floating object, any floating object; it is particularly serious if that object happens to be you! The victim will be totally unaware of anything below the water. By swimming on his back away from the victim, the rescuer has a second line of defence if the victim manages to close the gap. He can fend the victim off by placing a foot on the victim's chest and pushing him away.

Releasing a Grip

Despite the rescuer's best efforts, a panic stricken victim may be able to get hold of him. There are a number of effective ways of releasing a grip. However, most of them require regular practice if they are to be remembered and used effectively under pressure.

I will therefore only describe one method that is simple and easy to perform. The rescuer grabs hold of the victim's thumb and bends it back the way it shouldn't go!

Dealing With a Flipped Raft

by Paul O'Sullivan

When a raft flips the guide's first priority is to try and retain contact with the raft. This is usually achieved by holding onto the outside line on the raft. Should the guide lose contact with the raft, then he or she needs to get back to it as soon as possible. It is only from the raft that the guide can begin to stabilise the situation and help the crew. Thus if safety kayakers are available their first priority must be to rescue the guide.

Once back in touch with the upturned raft the guide needs to get onto it. Various options are available here depending upon the construction of the raft and any aids that might have been pre-placed. Options include: -

1. Using the drain holes/lacing from the self-draining floor as finger holds. Long arms and strong fingers are an advantage here.
2. Tape handles may have been constructed using two drain holes and a short length of webbing. These provide a firm hand hold and eliminate any risk of finger entrapment in method one above.
3. On big volume rivers, lines are sometimes tensioned across the bottom of the raft either between a D-ring on each side of the boat or between the drain holes/ lacing on the floor. These provide a hand line to help the guide onto the boat.
4. The guide may clip their flip-line onto a D-ring on one side of the raft and throw the other end over the upturned boat. They can then make their way to the other side of the boat and use the flip line as a hand line onto the upturned boat. Sometimes flip bags are pre-attached onto each side of the boat which can be used in a similar way.

Whichever method is used it needs to be pre-practised. Climbing onto an upturned raft in white water is not just a matter of strength but involves technique and timing.

Once on the upturned raft the guide has a number of jobs to do rapidly.

Count heads - are any of the crew missing?

Decide whether to re-flip the raft or not? Factors affecting this decision include:-

1. How easy is it to re-flip the raft? A boat loaded for a multi-day trip will require more than one person to re-flip it and indeed may have to be paddled into an eddy before attempting the manoeuvre.
2. How deep/difficult/cold the river is? If the crew are in a difficult/cold or rocky section of the river it may well be best to get all the crew onto the upturned raft so that they are out of the water and then paddle the boat to easier water before attempting to re-flip.

3. Is anybody missing? In an ideal world once the guide gets onto the upturned boat they will look around to see the crew all holding onto the outside line on the raft and making their way along the line to either end to allow the guide to re-flip. If only! Crew members may be under the raft. This in itself is not disastrous as there will be air inside the upturned raft, but anyone under the boat is at a greater risk of colliding with underwater obstacles and the whole experience is rather disconcerting for the uninitiated. Guides should brief the crew that should this happen they are to reach out to the outside line and then swim to the outside of the boat.

The guide's decision on what to do, should they suspect that a crew member is under the boat, will depend upon how long it will take to re-flip the raft. In a small to medium sized unloaded boat, I would argue that it is best to re-flip the raft straight away, thus releasing the crew from under the boat. Should the boat be loaded, or the guide decide it best to get the crew onto the upturned raft and paddle it upside down, the guide will have to swim under the upturned boat and check for any crew trapped there. In very shallow rivers this can be a bruising experience!

The other occasion when a guide may have to swim under the raft to release crew is when having made a decision to re-flip the raft quickly, the guide finds that this is not possible due to a crew member being under the raft and holding onto a tube or footstep, thereby preventing the raft from being re-flipped. Again this will involve the guide going under the raft to recover the crew member before continuing.

Re-flipping

As with climbing onto upturned rafts there are a number of methods of re-flipping rafts depending upon the size of the boat and whether it is loaded for a multi-day trip.

1. Small, narrow rafts can be flipped by the guide hooking the T-piece of their paddle under the outside line on the opposite side of the boat from the one they are standing on. Lean back and pull on the paddle whilst at the same time pushing down with your legs on the nearside tube.
2. Perhaps the most standard method for unloaded boats is for the guide to carry a 'flip line' approximately 2-3 metres *(6-9 feet)* long with a karabiner on one end. This is clipped onto the 'outside line' halfway along one side of the raft whilst the guide stands on the opposite side. Similar to the method above the guide leans back on the line whilst pushing down with legs and feet. By 'climbing' hand over hand on the line as the boat lifts the guide can maintain the load on the line. If properly timed, waves on the river can be used to make the job much easier.
3. Rafts loaded for multi-day journeys at best will require a number of people to re-flip them. To aid this a length of rope is sometimes pre-attached between two D-rings on one side of the raft and then tied off. Once flipped this can be released to form a U-shaped 'flip line' allowing for 3-4 people to get a hold and re-flip the raft. If this is not possible then the raft may need to be paddled upside down to the shore or a suitable eddy, where it is carefully unloaded before being re-flipped.

Chapter 16
Stoppers

There are basically two stopper, '*hole or hydraulic*', rescue situations:

1. A boater or a raft held in a stopper. This is not necessarily a serious situation because, more often than not, if the boater bales out or a rafter falls overboard, he will, being less buoyant than his craft, be flushed out by the undertow.
2. A swimmer held in a stopper, '*hydraulic*'. This is by definition a serious matter.

Boaters

Self Rescue

By spending a lot of time playing in 'tame' stoppers, '*holes*', boaters develop the skills which will enable them to paddle their way out of trouble. More importantly, it will build up the experience which will enable them to judge whether a stopper is runnable or not.

When caught in a stopper a boater will usually be turned sideways and held firmly in the slot. If the boater does nothing, the water flowing down the face of the wave will capsize him. In a powerful stopper the recirculating water will roll the boat and boater over and over like a roller blind.

Staying Upright

The boater prevents a capsize by lifting the upstream edge with his knee, so that the water flows under the hull of the boat and if necessary leaning onto his paddle for support on the downstream side, (fig. 2.14, page 19), using a low or high brace. In some stoppers the best support will be found by placing the paddle on the surface of the boil line. On others the best support will be gained by reaching down into the less aerated water in the undertow.

How the boater stays upright is often dictated by the angle of the face of the stopper. The steeper the angle the more use will have to be made of the paddle.

Feeding Out

As soon as control is regained the boater must gently unweight the paddle so that the boat is kept upright by a mixture of balance and edge control. Once the weight is off the paddle, the boater can slice it forward or backward so that he

---

Safety and rescue training. Practising how to try and get over a strainer as a swimmer. Lower Oertz, Austria.
Photos: Paul O'Sullivan.

Fig. 16.1 Powering along to the outwash at the end of the stopper. Photo: Bob Timms

can put in a series of power strokes, (fig. 16.1), to drive the boat along the stopper. By doing this he can reach a point where there is a weakness, some outflow *(outwash)*, which will allow him to escape.

When moving forwards the boater can use a low or high brace in between power strokes, depending on the shape of the stopper. However, the low brace sets the boater up for a more powerful forward power stroke. (Fig. 16.1). When reversing, he must use a low brace or he will be unable to use the powerful muscles in his trunk in the reverse power stroke.

The layout of the stopper will dictate which techniques are used and on which side strokes will need to be performed. It is therefore essential that we strive to become equally proficient on both sides.

...'proficient on both sides.'...

In a 'frowning' stopper that feeds towards the centre, rather than out to the outflow at one or each end, it will be hard work to make it to the weakness. There are three ways to increase efficiency:

1. Make best use of edge control and balance so that all of the paddle power can go into moving the boat along the stopper rather than keeping the boat upright.
2. Deliberately move the boat in the opposite direction to the weakness you are trying to get to so that when you change direction you can get a run along the length of the stopper and build up enough speed to break through to the outflow.
3. Many stoppers 'pulse', that is to say that they change their shape and holding characteristics in a cyclical, predictable manner. By timing your run at the weakness to coincide with the best part of this cycle you can maximise your chances of breaking free.

Top: A vertical pin on the Leah River, Tasmania, Australia..
Bottom: Kayak on a two point broach. Northern Italy.
Photos: Chris Sladden

Endering Out - Not for Big Stoppers!

Though not an option in 'traditional' open boats, this is an option for specialist white water open boats as well as closed deck CIs and kayaks.

If the boater hasn't quite made it clear of the stopper and it is clear that he is going to be sucked back in, he can deliberately drive the bow or stern deep into the face of the stopper. The boat can be made to literally stand on it's end. The idea is to get the end of the boat down in the undertow so that it is pushed clean through the stopper and into the outflow.

If the stopper is too powerful or the boater's boat control inadequate, the boat may perform a complete loop, (go end over end), and end up back in the slot again. The following techniques can help prevent this:

Bow Enders

1. As the boat begins to stand on end, the boater stands upright on his footrest and leans back against the rear deck. This keeps his centre of gravity directly over the bow of the boat as opposed to having the weight of his own body overbalance him, so that he falls back into the slot.

Stern Enders or 'Tailees'

These only work on small stoppers.

1. As the stern digs in and the bow of the boat lifts towards the sky, the boater throws his weight forward so that his forehead is touching the deck. This will adjust his centre of gravity.
2. At the same time he digs his paddle as deep as he can into the undertow and uses it to help pull him through the stopper. The support thus gained also enables him to apply pressure with the opposite knee to twist the boat through a few degrees and spill water off the back deck.

Boater to Boater Rescue

These rescues don't work in serious stoppers and are only likely to be used when guiding or coaching novices on easy rivers. They should only be attempted if the rescuer is considerably more skilled than the victim and is convinced that he can **easily** get himself out of the stopper concerned. If the length of the towback *(backwash)* is more than half a boat length they are definitely out of the question.

Bumping Out

This technique involves another paddler deliberately positioning himself so that he is upstream and parallel to the victim who is stuck in the stopper. The 'rescuer' then drops into the stopper and 'bumps' the victim out. This is a dangerous technique that is far more likely to cause an injury than any stopper where it might work. **Dont do it!**

Bow Rescue

This rescue will work in any situation where bumping out will work, and as it involves far less risk of injury, should, in my opinion be used instead of it.

The rescue boater approaches from downstream and, keeping most of his boat on the downstream side of the boil line, he positions his bow so that the victim can get hold of the grab loop. The victim can use the rescuer's bow for support while the rescuer reverse paddles out of the stopper.

In a weak stopper, the rescuer may be able to simply pull the victim and his boat over the boil line and out of the stopper. More often he will have to reverse paddle at a ferry angle to drag the victim along the stopper to a weakness where the outflow will push the victim out.

Bank Based Rescue

Reach

It is sometimes the case that the weakness at the end of the stopper that the boater is trying to get out of, is close to the bank or a rock that the rescuer can easily get to. The rescuer can simply get hold of the end 'grab' loop and pull the boat and boater out of the stopper.

Throw

If a boater is able to maintain a stable upright position but is unable to paddle out of the stopper, it is best to throw him a line **before** he subsequently bails out. (See swimmer rescues for further details).

Rafts

The big problem when a raft is held in a stopper is that if anyone falls in and is flushed out by the undertow, he rapidly loses contact with the raft. Though problematic enough for experienced rafters, it poses a much more serious problem for a commercial raft guide whose clients will have received a safety briefing but no real training.

Self Rescue

Rafts rely primarily on their buoyancy to keep them upright and feed them out of a stopper but there is a considerable amount that can be done to help.

Staying Upright

A raft will flip in a big enough stopper so it is crucial to 'high side', i.e. to get everyone onto the side that is lifting. In the case of a stopper, that is the downstream side away from the face of the stopper. The weight of the crew will then act as a counterbalance to counteract the weight of the water trying to push the downstream side of the raft down into the undertow.

Feeding Out

The raft can be encouraged towards the outflow of a stopper in two ways:

Trimming

By high siding, the balance of the boat is maintained. The trim of the raft can be changed by shifting some of the crew forwards or backwards. If the weight is shifted towards the back, the raft will tend to move forwards and vice versa.

Paddling

If the raft is not being thrown around too violently, the raft guide and selected members of the crew can paddle the raft along the stopper.

Line Rescues

A line is thrown to the raft, either from the bank or from another raft. Depending on circumstances, the raft can either be pulled directly downstream over the boil line or along the slot to the end where it is most likely to be fed out by the outflow.

Raft Flipped and Held in Stopper

If this happens the crew will usually be flushed through the stopper or catapulted clear. As with any raft flip, (see Chapter Fifteen), the raft guide's first task is to count heads and make sure that nobody is trapped underneath. If someone is missing, the only thing he can do is to try and get back onto the raft, assuming that he can, and cut through the bottom of it to find the customer.

Swimmer Rescues

Any swimmer caught in a recirculating stopper is in a life threatening situation. Time is limited. Rescues will have to be set up and effected quickly. This means that the simpler they are, the better.

The chances of a successful rescue are further enhanced if the rescuers and the victim are already familiar with, and practised in, a range of stopper rescue techniques. This means that while one method is being tried, other ones can be prepared by other members of the team.

Self Rescue

Some stoppers are so turbulent that a swimmer may become totally disorientated. Even in this situation he should try to remain calm and feel around. Something might turn up: a buoyant object that can be held onto, the river bed that can be kicked off from, a throw line to hold on to.

Many stoppers **can** be coped with, and will allow the swimmer who remains calm and maintains a positive mental attitude to help himself. We should remember that a towback which is flowing at only two to three miles an hour is going far faster than people can swim. Therefore, many deep recirculating stoppers that will hold a swimmer are not necessarily very turbulent, but will still be powerful enough to put a swimmer through 'the rinse cycle'; (pushed down under the water by the undertow, floating up to the surface upstream of the boil line and being sucked back into the slot by the backtow). A panicked victim will waste precious oxygen and energy by trying to swim against the backtow, even after it should have become obvious that it is moving faster than he can swim. If an initial attempt to swim across the boil line has failed, the swimmer should swim at right angles to the towback so as to try and reach a bank or a break in the stopper where the current is flowing through and will flush him out.

As soon as the swimmer gets to the surface he needs to get some air, shake the water from his eyes and ears and get his bearings. He may only need to swim a few strokes to get to an outflow that will flush him clear of the stopper. A rescuer may be about to throw him a line. There may be an overhanging tree branch he can hold onto. Who knows? Not the victim, **unless he is looking for the breaks.**

Getting Down

An alternative way to try and get out of a recirculating stopper is for the swimmer to deliberately swim as far as possible into the face of the green water that is flowing into the slot, (fig. 16.2). If he can penetrate deeply enough into the downward flowing water, he may be pushed along the bottom in the undertow, past the boil line and out of the clutches of the stopper. There is a risk of being snagged on some obstruction on the river bed, so it is best if the swimmer tucks up into a ball to minimise this risk.

Fig. 16.2 Getting down in a deep re-circulating stopper, 'hydraulic.

The important thing here is **not** to try and 'duck dive' towards the river bed. The secret is to penetrate the down flowing water horizontally so that the swimmer is pushed to the bottom by the power of the water.

The Buoyancy Aid (PFD) Controversy

There is a theory that a swimmer being recirculated in a stopper should, if all else fails, take off his buoyancy aid, *(Personal Flotation Device)*. The idea is that, being less buoyant, he may now be able to stay down in the undertow long enough to get past the boil line and be swept out of the stopper.

Most experts agree that this is not a good idea. It should only be considered if all other forms of self rescue have failed and there is no prospect of being rescued by people on the bank. This is because:

1. If the swimmer has had time to consider this option, it is because he has survived this long by getting a breath of air each time he surfaces. If he takes his buoyancy aid off and **isn't** flushed out of the stopper, he may no longer have enough buoyancy to reach the surface and get a breath of air!
2. The only way to guarantee that a swimmer is no longer buoyant is to fill his lungs with water!
3. There is a high probability that an exhausted swimmer, swept out of a stopper minus his buoyancy aid, will drown in the rapids down-stream.

Body Surfing

By holding his body in a position similar to that of a free-fall parachutist, while facing upstream it is possible for a swimmer to body surf a stopper and maintain a stable position. This means that, instead of being helplessly put through the rinse cycle, he is in a position to breathe and get his bearings. Even if a swimmer can't get out of the stopper, he can buy time for rescuers to set up and effect a rescue.

If he spots a break in the stopper where the water is flowing out, he can surf across to it by simply tilting and angling his body. If he tilts and angles to the right, he will move to his right, (river left) and vice-versa.

Bank Based Rescues

The following bank based rescues have the advantage of involving little if any risk to the rescuers. They are listed in order of their simplicity and the speed with which they can be effected. A well trained team would organise themselves so that the more complex rescues were being set up at the same time as the simple ones were being tried. That way, by the time it became clear that one method wasn't going to work, other members of the team would be in position and ready to try another.

Reach

On narrow creeks and boulder choked rivers, stoppers may only be a few metres in width. The most effective rescue may be as simple as reaching out to the swimmer with a paddle or a canoe pole. The rescuer must ensure his own safety by keeping a hold of something on the bank or holding onto another rescuer. When offering support it is best to grasp each other's wrist, rather than hold hands.

Throw

A well aimed throw line is another quick and simple rescue technique. However, when throwing a line to a recirculating swimmer, the following points should be borne in mind:

Timing

The temptation when throwing a line to a recirculating swimmer is to throw it the instant he bursts to the surface. The rescuer should remember that at that precise instant the swimmer's only concern is to get a breath of fresh air. The line needs to be thrown after the swimmer has had time to get his bearings but before he is fed back into the slot.

Excess Rope

A swimmer in a stopper may be tumbling violently when in the slot or under water. There is always a danger, in such a situation that the rope may become wrapped around the victim's neck.

...'remove any excess rope before throwing the line'...

To reduce the chances of this happening the rescuer should estimate how much rope will be needed and remove any excess from the throw bag **before throwing the line.**

Float-Boat

The rescuer clips the bag end of a throw line to one end of his boat and piles the line into the boat. Whilst hanging on to the other end of the line he pushes

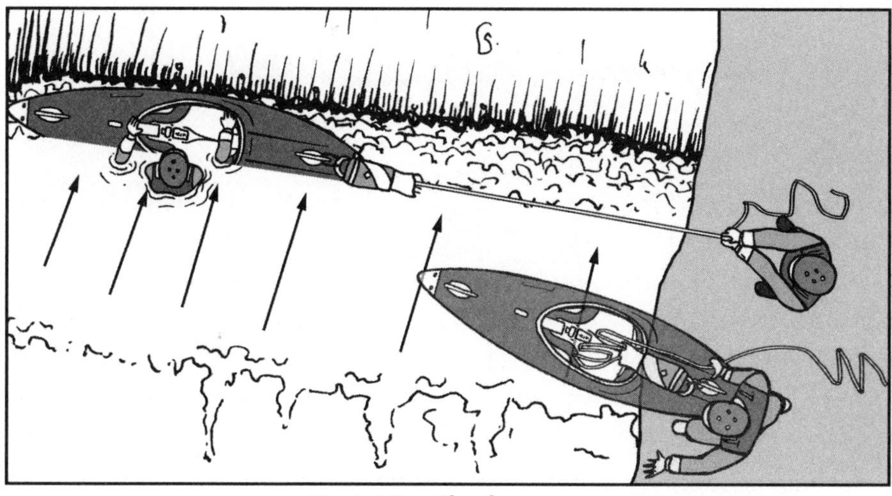

Fig. 16.3 Float boat rescue.

the boat out into the current so that it is fed into the part of the stopper where the victim is recirculating. Depending on the geography of the location, this is sometimes best achieved by feeding the boat into the slot by pushing it out into the towback and sometimes by pushing it out into the current upstream of the stopper. When the swimmer grabs hold of the boat, the boat is dragged out of the stopper bringing the swimmer with it. (Fig. 16.3).

This method can be used by one rescuer but is a little easier if two are involved. One holds the line while the other pushes the boat out.

Pros

The advantage of this method is that, even if a victim is panicking to the point where he neither sees nor reacts to a thrown line, a drowning person will instinctively cling on to a large buoyant object.

Cons

The disadvantage is that in a turbulent stopper the boat may be thrown around violently. This introduces the possibility of the victim being injured. Therefore, in the case of a particularly violent, pulsing stopper, rescuers may have to rule out this form of rescue.

Tag-Line

This method requires a rescuer on each bank. Either two bags are clipped together to make a bright floating object, or even better, a spare buoyancy aid is tied to the rope. The rope is then tensioned so that the float is suspended above the water where the swimmer is expected to surface. As he surfaces the float is lowered right in front of his eyes. (Fig. 16.4).

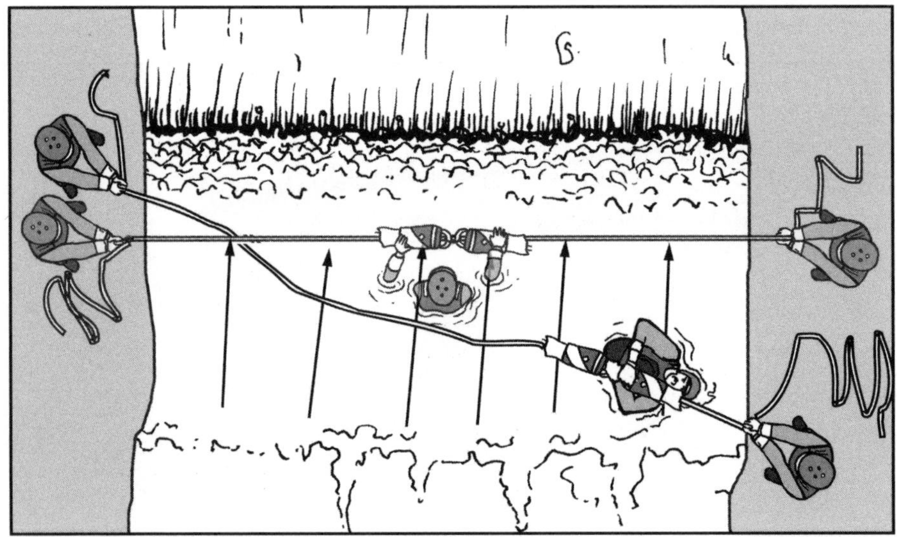

Fig. 16.4 A tag line used in a stopper rescue.

When the swimmer grabs the float, either:

1. Both rescuers move down the bank at the same speed and pull the victim over the boil line and out of the towback. Or:
2. One rescuer pays out line while the other pulls the swimmer towards a weakness in the stopper which will flush him through.

In either case neither rescuer should let go of the line. That way if the victim lets go the rescuers are already set up to try again.

Pros

- Difficult for swimmer to ignore the float
- No risk of injury to rescuers or victim

Cons

- Time consuming to set up
- Communication can be a major problem
- May not be practicable if banks are heavily vegetated or too far apart

Turn Off the Water

May take a little time but on many dam release rivers it can be arranged.

Contact Rescues

If victims are unconscious or counter panicked, they are not going to hold on to the line. Therefore someone will have to go out and make contact with them.

Or will they? These techniques are potentially very risky and the topography and the hydrology of each stopper is different. The rescuers involved must carefully assess both the risks involved and the likelihood of a successful outcome before committing themselves to such a course of action.

At the risk of sounding callous, I must point out that there is no point in indulging in heroics if the victim has been in there so long that he is almost certainly dead. It may be that the role of the leader in this situation is to stop people following their hearts rather than their heads and risking a multiple tragedy.

The following rescues are listed in the order of **increasing risk** to the rescuer.

Four Point Tethered Raft

This rescue is remarkably simple in theory but difficult to control in practice. This is because it involves **five** groups of people, probably out of voice contact, working as a coordinated team.

One line is attached to each 'corner' of the raft. The upstream lines are used to pull the raft over the boil line to where the swimmer is surfacing. The down-stream lines are used to stop the raft being fed into the slot by the recirculating water. If person power is a problem, the leader should allocate more rescuers to the downstream lines than the upstream lines. **All** the lines must be kept taut at all times, so as to ensure that the raft doesn't build up any momentum and become hard to control. (Fig. 16.5).

It is best to have two rescuers in the raft, one to concentrate on dealing with the swimmer and one to fine tune the positioning of the raft with a paddle, and liaise with the teams controlling the lines.

This is the safest contact method and it will work in most weir, *(low head dam)*, situations. It is **not a viable option above grade III,** ***(class III)***.

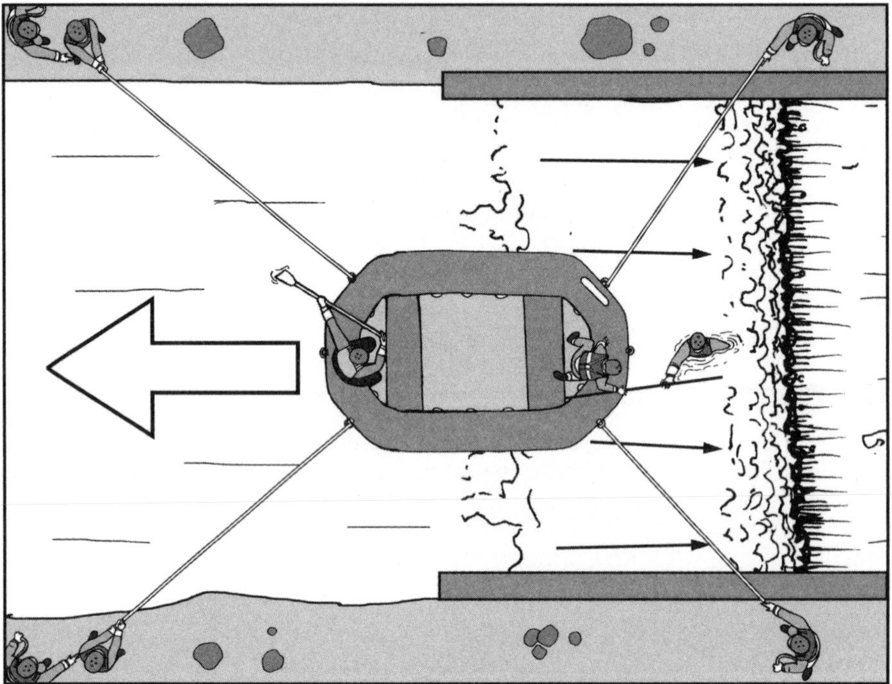

Fig. 16.5 Four point tethered raft rescue.

Live-Bait

This is essentially the same as the live bait rescue for swimmers. The difference is that, instead of one rescuer waist belaying, it is better to have two or more rescuers holding the rope tug-of-war fashion, ready to pull the swimmer/rescuer and victim out.

Moving water and ropes are always a dangerous mix. This is particularly true in a stopper where there is more potential for the line to get wrapped around some part of the rescuer's body. Those controlling the line will need to let out as little line as possible, and hold it as high as they can to keep as much of it out of the water as possible.

Pros: It is quick to set up and little coordination is needed.

Cons: It is a very high risk option for the rescuer and is only an option where the victim is close to the bank.

Tethered Boater

Other than deciding that a rescue is too risky, this is the only option left if:

1. The victim is unconscious or unresponsive.
2. There is no raft available.
3. The victim is being re-circulated too far from the bank for a live bait rescue.
4. There is still a reasonable possibility of a successful outcome.

The rescue boater is attached via a long line to a group of rescuers on the bank. Their task is to ensure that the rope is kept taught once he crosses the boil line so that he isn't sucked into the slot. As soon as contact is made, they pull the rescue boater and victim back across the boil line and into the shore.

Line or Lines?

After considerable experimentation with this technique in Austria, it was found that it is best to attach a single line to the boater's chest harness. A line fed through the stern grab handle and attached to a quick-release towing system did make it easier to control the angle of the boat to the current. However, it was found that this was more than made up for by the extra time needed to set it up and the possibilities of entanglements and confusion.

Ray Goodwin, Lower Tryweryn, North Wales

I was getting a new exhaust fitted to the car. From behind the garage came the scream, "There's a child in the river."

I ran around behind the garage. The child was being cycled around in a deep re-circulating stopper. He kept reappearing four metres down stream of the weir face before being towed back in. The river doubled in width below the weir and a powerful eddy fed back in from each side. The child was still conscious. I had no rescue kit with me.

I yelled at the garage mechanic to get me a rope, anything! He returned minutes later with a hose pipe. I went out on the concrete, coiling the hose for a throw. The child surfaced again but was now unconscious and not breathing. A throw was useless.

A bowline secured the hose around my waist. My instructions to the people on the bank were simple; "Once I dive on to the child, don't wait to see if I've got him, just pull me out!" The weir was a shallow 'V', so I could wade out along the lip above the stopper. My last thought before I dived in was a fervent hope that there was no plastic push joint in the hose.

I clutched the child to my chest as we were slammed to the bottom. We were being pulled against the kick of the stopper. In a desperate attempt to reach air I let go of the child with one hand, and I have a vivid memory of him being pulled away from me, my other hand embedded in his tee shirt.

We broke surface in the eddy. The pullers held me against the concrete apron while I put two breaths in him. Then on reaching the bank another six breaths and he started.

Chapter 17
Pins and Entrapments

This chapter deals with any situation where paddlers are trapped, in or out of a boat or raft. These include:

- Stranded victims
- Broaches
- Vertical Pins
- Foot entrapments
- Strainers
- A swimmer trapped under a raft

Each entrapment situation that we may be confronted with will be different, but the way each of them is dealt with follows a basic pattern.

1. Assess the situation.
2. Stabilise the situation.
3. Extract the victim.

Only if the victim is extracted unharmed or he has been treated and evacuated to hospital would we then consider how to recover any equipment. (These elements are dealt with in Parts Three and Four).

Assessing the Situation

Rescuers need to ask themselves:

1. What hazard does the entrapment pose for rescuers?
2. Is the situation stable or unstable?
3. Are the water levels rising, falling, or stable?
4. What time of day is it? This will affect water levels on glacier fed rivers and the onset of darkness will make rescues more difficult and hazardous.
3. Are there any dangers downstream that the victims or rescuers need to be aware of/protected from?
4. What is the quickest and acceptably safe way of getting into a position to be able to rescue the victim.

Danger to Rescuers

An assessment of the potential dangers faced by rescuers is something that should be done in any rescue situation. It may only take a few seconds but it must be done.

Stable or Unstable?

Any situation where victims are trapped in cold water or in an exposed position will have to be dealt with reasonably quickly because of the onset of hypothermia.

However, if victims are in a situation where they have no difficulty breathing, rescuers can afford to take more time over the planning stage of the rescue.

In many cases, the victim may have already decided that the situation he is in is relatively stable. A victim stranded on a rock or a boater held in a vertical pin may decide that it is far safer to wait to be rescued than to swim for it. (Fig. 17.1).

On the other hand, a victim who is unable to breathe or having difficulty breathing needs to be dealt with in a matter of minutes.

Downstream Hazards

It is vital to consider these and arrange some protection or back up. It is no use freeing a trapped victim, only to see him carried by the current into an even worse hazard. Even if there are no significant hazards downstream a means of getting the freed victim to the side must be in place as the victim will probably be exhausted and unable to swim effectively.

Access Techniques

Boating, rafting, swimming, wading, nothing should be ruled out. If the victim is unable to breathe the quickest method will be the best. However, in most situations the technique used should be the one that involves the least risk to the rescuers. The following approaches are listed in order of priority:

- Self rescue
- Access from the bank
- Access by boat
- Access by wading
- Access by swimming

Chapter Twenty Nine explores a variety of alternative or more complex techniques that may need to be employed in situations where the above mentioned, quick and simple techniques are judged to be too hazardous or not practicable.

Stabilising the Situation

The aim is to ensure that the victim can breathe and that the situation does not deteriorate further. The solution must be quick and simple. The fancier the rope tricks, the longer it takes, the more likely it is that you will be dealing with a body. It must be borne in mind that there are occasions where extracting the victim is so easy, that it is the quickest and simplest method that stabilises the situation.

The methods used for stabilising the situation can be grouped into three areas:

- Direct contact
- Line pulls
- Snag lines

...'The solution must be quick and simple.'...

Direct Contact

It is often the case that the very obstacle that has caused the problem, or the eddy that forms downstream of it, provides a means for rescuers to gain access to the victim. The victim's buddy can simply break out, *'eddy in'*, behind the obstacle, climb on to it, grab a hold of the victim and support him so that he can keep his head above water.

Line Pulls

In a situation such as the one described above where it is difficult to maintain such a position, or the rescuer needs to be freed up to perform other duties, a line can be attached to the victim and tied off.

In many situations, where it is not possible to make direct contact with the victim, a line can be lowered, thrown or floated to them. The victim is then able to simply hold onto the line for support or clip it into a chest harness or shoulder strap. The victim will probably be holding onto something to keep his head above water. This means that he will have to attach the line one handed, so this is one situation where it may be a good idea to tie a loop in the end of the line and even have a karabiner already attached.

If a rescuer can get close to the victim it may be possible to attach a line to him directly, or by using an improvised paddle hook. (See Chapter Fourteen).

Snag Lines

If a victim is trapped in midstream and is in need of support a snag line may be the only viable option. A line is held across the river and dragged upstream until it snags across the victim's waist or across his chest and under his armpits. The line is then pulled tight enough to support the victim. (Fig. 17.1). If there are suitable anchor points available, one or both ends of the line can be tied off if the rescuers need to be freed up for the extraction phase.

Fig. 17.1 A snag line supporting the victim of a foot entrapment. Photo: Bob Timms.

A broached victim may be able to pass a loop of rope over his head and shoulders so that the rescuer can pull on both ends of the line and support the victim's upper body, allowing him to keep his head out of the water.

Extracting the Victim

The technique used to free a victim will depend on the exact circumstances of the entrapment. Stabilising the situation may have bought some time but the rescuers will still need to come up with a solution quickly. Cold water, the force of the current and fear will be sapping the victim's energy reserves and morale.

This is definitely a time for lateral thinking. A victim may be freed by using one or a combination of the following approaches:

- Pulling the victim in the right direction
- Freeing the boat and in the process the victim
- Cutting any webbing or line that is holding the victim.
- Cutting the boat or raft so as to relieve pressure or free the victim
- Removing the obstacle that is causing the problem

It is absolutely vital that rescuers have planned for what will happen to the victim once he is freed. It would be extremely bad form if a victim, who was freed from an entrapment, was allowed to float off into an even more dangerous hazard!

Specific Entrapment Situations

Stranded Victims

By definition these are relatively stable situations. The victims are only stranded because they have decided that it is unnecessarily risky to swim or climb out of their predicament unaided.

The quickest and simplest solutions will involve the same techniques as used to rescue a swimmer. The difference being that everything can be set up before the victim is committed. A line can be got to the victims and set up for a pendulum before they enter the water. The victims can be fetched by a raft or chase boaters and climb on board in relative safety.

Tensioned Diagonal

This is a useful method for moving people across a fast current in a controlled and precise manner. It is particularly useful for getting a rescuer into the eddy behind an obstruction in a high risk environment where free swimming and boating are not an option. It is also particularly useful for evacuating a large number of people in a quick and controlled manner. As it has a large number of different applications it is **discussed in detail in Chapter Twenty Nine.**

In essence it consists of tensioning a line across a river at an **angle of forty five degrees or less to the main flow**. The stranded paddlers then work their way along the rope to safety.

Read Chapter 29 as this technique needs to be thoroughly understood.

Broaches

In a single point broach, where the boat or raft is caught sideways onto a single boulder it is often relatively easy for a rescuer to access the victim via the eddy that forms behind the obstruction. In a two point broach, where the boat is held at each end and the paddler is trapped in the middle it may well be quicker and simpler to lift one of the ends over the obstruction to free the boat and paddler. If the pressure is such that the rescuer is unable to do this, another option is to cut off the end of the boat or puncture the end tube of the raft to achieve the same effect.

Once the situation has been stabilised by whatever means, the victim needs to be extracted. Different craft will have different considerations.

Open Boats

When open boats are broached the pressures involved are enormous and often result in the boat being badly damaged. Therefore, moving the boat is seldom the quickest or easiest option. Fortunately, as there is no deck the boater is less likely to be trapped by the structure of the boat. He is much more likely to be caught up in webbing or line. If the boater is unable to cut the line himself, a rescuer will have to do the job for him.

Rafts

When rafts wrap themselves around an obstacle, the forces involved are even greater than in an open boat. If 'high siding' the raft, (see Chapter Two), has kept the raft upright but the raft is wrapped, the raft guide will need to evacuate the raft and account for all the crew. Although the obstacle itself and the eddy formed by it will provide temporary refuge, the crew will need to be evacuated to the shore. The options for doing this are as for dealing with stranded victims.

There are two possibilities for entrapment, either:

1. Someone gets a foot caught in a twisted foot strap or in the gutter wedged between the side and floor tube.

Or:

2. When trying to 'high side' the raft, a crew member falls between the raft and the boulder.

In the first case, unless the raft can be moved quickly and easily, the best solution will be to puncture the floor of the raft. If, in the case of a twisted foot strap, the loss of pressure is insufficient, a way will have to be found to cut it. If a rescuer supports the victim, he may be able to cut the strap himself. Depending on exactly how the raft is broached it may be possible to get at the strap from the eddy, by cutting a small hole through the floor of the raft.

If there is even the slightest suspicion that someone is caught between the raft and the obstruction, the raft guide will have no option but to cut a hole in the floor of the raft, or even cut the raft in half. **Immediately!**

Kayaks

If a kayaker lifts his upstream edge and leans onto the obstruction, he will probably be able to work his way off the broach unaided. If the upstream edge catches and the boat is rolled over so that the spraydeck is collapsed by the force of the water it will wrap. Due to the development of the keyhole cockpit the kayaker will still probably be able to exit the kayak providing he is quick about it.

Assuming that the victim is trapped and the situation stabilised, there are several possibilities for extricating the victim. The simplest solution is often to pull the victim towards the rear of the kayak so that his body straightens out and he slides out of the cockpit. If this is done by attaching a line to the victim, the rescuers have already put in place the means to pendulum him to the shore.

Other solutions include cutting the boat up or freeing the boat by pulling or pushing it in the direction that the current favours. **Great care must be taken that attempting this solution does not worsen the situation by increasing the pressure on the victim's legs, or cause the boat to lodge itself in a position that makes things even worse.**

Vertical Pins

Vertical pins, (see photo on page 161), are almost exclusively the province of kayaks and closed deck C1s. With modern footrest designs and keyhole cockpits the boaters are rarely unable to exit the boat. They may bark their shins on the way out but they can almost always get out if they choose to. This is not true of older designs and, in an incident on the Conwy Falls, a kayaker faced with the choice of drowning or allowing the force of the water to force him out, chose the latter. The result was a broken femur and a dislocated knee but a live paddler!

A boater who waits for rescue in this situation has usually decided that the swim is not an attractive option. The rescuer's main concern is to get a line to the boater so that he can reach the bank safely. If it is possible to set up a line in such a way that he can effect a more controlled exit so much the better.

In creek boating, the volume of water can be so low that it is possible to thread the clean end of a line through the stern end grab. The rescuers then pull on the doubled line and, when the boat is free let go of the clean end. The end of the line feeds back through the end grab and the boater is free to continue his run.

Foot Entrapments

Foot entrapments are extremely dangerous. People who lose their footing when wading or find themselves swimming in fast shallow water, must swim on their back and keep their feet and hands on the surface!

Hand Rail

If a foot entrapment occurs fairly close to the bank and the current is not too powerful, a rescuer may be able to use a handrail, (see Chapter Fifteen), to gain enough support to stay on his feet and wade out to the victim. Once contact is made, the victim will be able to use the tensioned line to support himself while the rescuer frees the trapped limb.

Snag Line

More usually, the only way to stabilise the victim will be by using a snag line. Once the victim is snagged, it may be possible to free him by simply using the snag line to pull him upstream. (Fig. 17.1).

Rescue Swimmer

If the snag line isn't sufficient to free the trapped victim, it does at least provide him with support. If one end of the line is tied off, a rescuer, who should be a strong swimmer, can use the snag line as a tensioned diagonal, (see Chapter 29), to gain access to the victim. Once in position, the rescuer can use the eddy created by the victim and support from the line to try and get in to a position to help the victim free his trapped limb. This rescue should only be attempted if the stretch of water downstream of the entrapment is a straight forward swim, or sufficient safety cover is in place to collect the victim **and** the rescuer.

Fig. 17.2 Swimmer helping victim, having used the snag line as a tensioned diagonal. Photo: Bob Timms

Two Line Loop

With this method it is possible to either simply change the direction of pull that can be applied with a snag line, and a greater force applied by creating leverage on the tensioned rope, (see Chapter 28); or the snag line can be cinched around the victim's body.

1. The victim is stabilised with a snag line.
2. A second line is thrown across the river, upstream of the victim and clipped to the snag line.
3. The line is pulled at a ninety degree angle to the snag line to change the direction of pull.
4. As a last resort, the line is pulled at a shallower angle so that the snag line is cinched around the victim's body and pulled towards the bank.

If, having completed stage three, the victim is in an unstable position and is in the process of drowning, I would move on to stage four. However, if the victim was in a relatively stable position and there was time to reorganise I would advise using the Two Line Cinch instead.

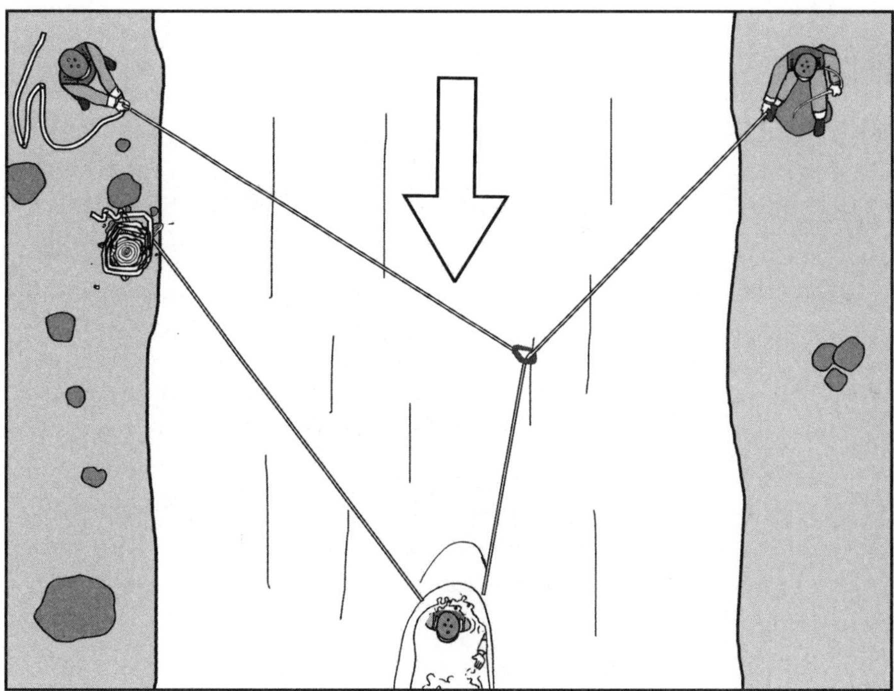

Fig. 17.3 Two line loop used to create a vector pull.

Two Line Cinch

This is an ingenuous method of getting a rescue line securely around a trapped paddler's waist in such a way that a more directional pull may be attempted without the risk of losing contact with the victim. It gives the rescuers a greater degree of control than a Two Line Loop.

It works best with throw bags that have a fairly firm layer of foam sewn into the body of the bag, so that the bag is relatively stiff. If foam padded bags are used, the bag limits how tight the 'cinch' can become and acts as a padded waist belt, affording the victim a greater degree of comfort and safety.

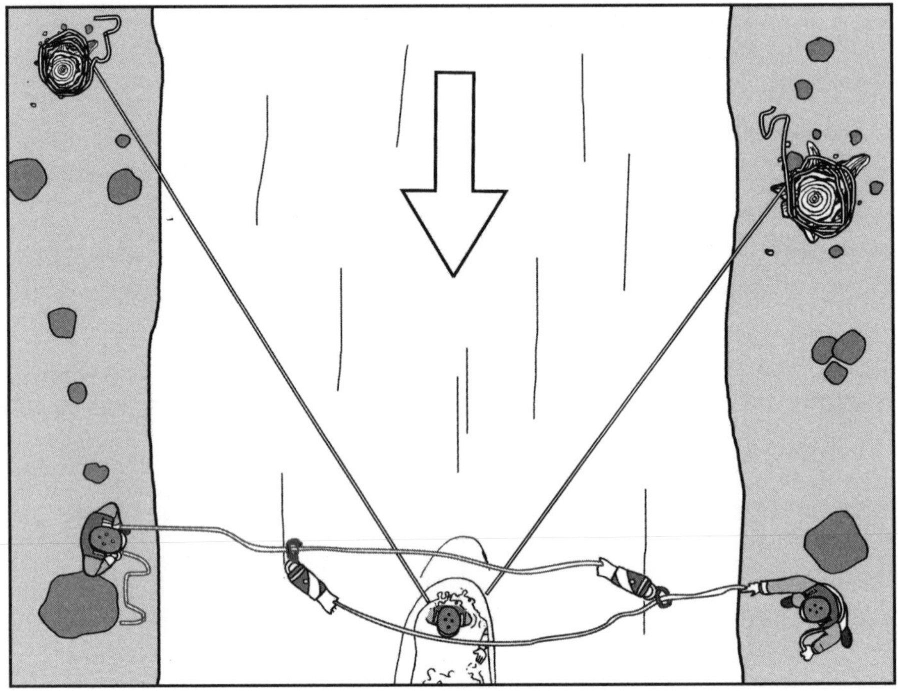

Fig. 17.4 Two line cinch being worked into place.

1. Throw two lines across the river; one from each side, one upstream and one downstream of the victim. (Note that in fig. 17.4 the victim is already stabilised with a snag line).
2. The bags are then either clipped to the other rope using a karabiner, or better still, the clean end is threaded through the handle of the other line.
3. The lines are then pulled tight forming an enclosed loop around the victim's body.
4. If necessary, one of the lines can be thrown to the other bank so that both lines can pull in the same direction.

Two Point Tethered Rescuer

This rescue, sometimes known as a 'V' lower, involves holding a rescuer in the current using one line from each bank. (Fig 17.5) The rescuer is attached via a chest harness.

By creating an eddy with his own body, the rescuer takes some of the pressure off the victim. Once in place just upstream of the victim the rescuer may also be able to help the victim remove the foot, or hand from the entrapment.

Signals

It is vital to establish a set of signals to ensure that the tethered rescuer's (A) wishes are clearly understood. If possible, it is a good idea to have a rescuer (B) stand downstream of the rescuer A so that he can see his face and keep eye contact. This rescuer then relays the signals to the rescuers (C and D) who are handling the lines.

In a small team where the leader has to become physically involved in the rescue, this is the best job for him to take on. This is because he is in the best position to see everything and is the least physically involved in the rescue.

Two Point Tethered Raft

Similar to the rescue described above except that a raft is lowered with a team of rescuers in it. The advantage over the tethered rescuer is that the rescuers can work from a stable platform and do not need to enter the water. The disadvantage is that the raft doesn't form a deep eddy and therefore most of the force of the current is still pressing on the victim.

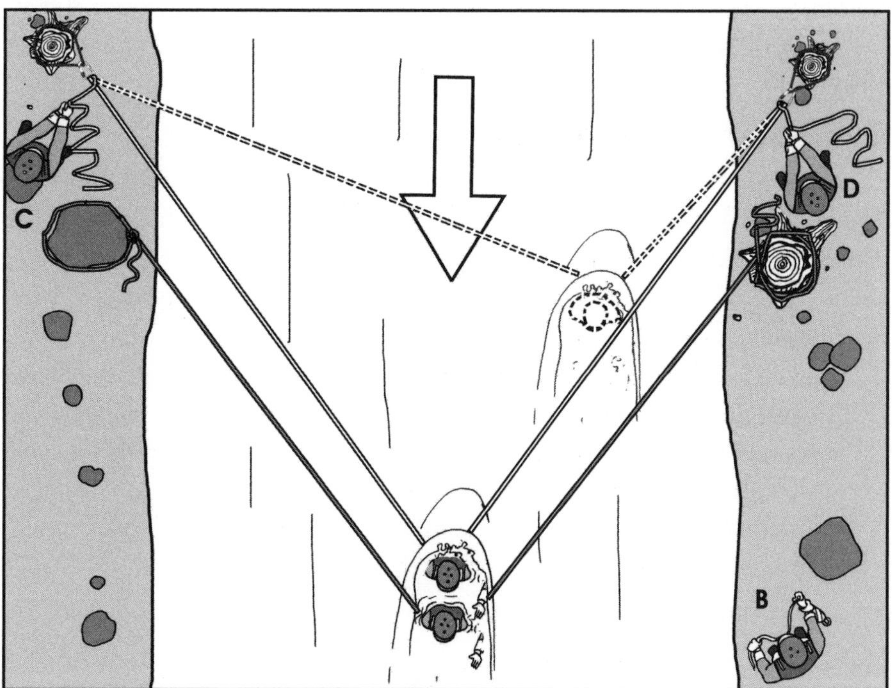

Fig. 17.5 A two point tethered lower, in this example Italian, 'Munter' hitches are used to control the rate at which the ropes are let out. See Chapters 28 and 29.

Raft Team

Ideally the team would consist of three rescuers, two to assist the victim and one to use a paddle to fine tune the raft's position and co-ordinate with the team on the bank.

Strainers

The techniques described for foot entrapments can be used in strainer rescues. However it should be borne in mind that any technique that involves rescuers being upstream of the strainer **puts the rescuer at extreme risk**.

If at all possible it is far better for rescuers to approach the victim from the downstream side of the strainer, either climbing over the obstruction or cutting their way through it.

Two Point Tethered Raft

Providing it is correctly trimmed, the shallow draught of a raft allows it to be easily positioned in the eddy below an obstruction. This makes it a very useful technique for getting at a victim from the downstream side of a strainer.

If an approach from upstream is the only solution, a tethered raft offers a stable platform and, provided it is properly controlled, the least dangerous solution. A pair of canoes can be lashed together and used in reasonable conditions, though a bridle will have to be made to keep the towing point low and stable. See Chapter 29.

Swimmer Trapped Under Raft

It sometime happens that a person, having fallen out of a raft, is then run over by it. More often than not the swimmer simply swims or pushes off the underside of the raft until he is clear. If however, the victim is disorientated, panicked or counter panicked, he may become trapped. There are two ways to get the victim out from under the raft:

1. If it is obvious where the victim is, because his buoyant body is pressing up against the floor of the raft, the raft guide can force the victim towards the outside of the raft. This is done by stepping on the floor of the raft above and slightly to one side of the victim.
2. If the above doesn't work or the victim's position under the raft isn't clear, a hole will have to be cut through the floor of the raft.

Chapter 18
Protecting a Rapid

If, on inspecting a rapid, it becomes obvious that there is a reasonable possibility of members of the group blowing their line, it makes sense to have the means of effecting a rescue in place before the event. On easier rapids this may be necessary to protect less skilful or experienced members of the party. On harder rapids it is part and parcel of running the river. In Chapters 6 and 7 we looked at how to scout a rapid, and how to identify hazards and assess the risks involved. In this chapter we need to look at how best to lessen the consequences of mistakes and consequently lower the risk.

Guidelines

When deciding how best to deploy the person power we have available, one should bear in mind the following guidelines:

- Provide a back up wherever possible
- Try not to rely on one method
- Have the means available to cover both banks
- Stay flexible
- The Principal of Most Usefulness

Back Up

If someone goes for a swim, and the swim is serious enough to warrant protection, we have to allow for human error. If the rescuer misses with a throw line we need to have another rescuer in a position to take over.

Multiple Methods

Whenever possible it makes sense to cover a potential rescue situation with more than one method of effecting a rescue. In fig. 18.1 a stopper is the hazard. The consequence of not tackling it correctly is a trashing followed by a long swim. The other members of the team are covering the situation by having one rescuer standing by with a throw line and the other in position as a chase boater.

Both Banks

If one bank is inaccessible or the eddies are all on one side of the river, it is easy to end up with all the rescuers positioned on one side of the river. If something unforeseen happens on the other side of the river, there is no one in a position to deal with it. In fig. 18.1 there are only three members in the team, and therefore only two available to provide cover. The chase boater could have positioned himself in the large eddy on river left but deliberately positioned himself in the smaller eddy on river right. There are two reasons for doing this:

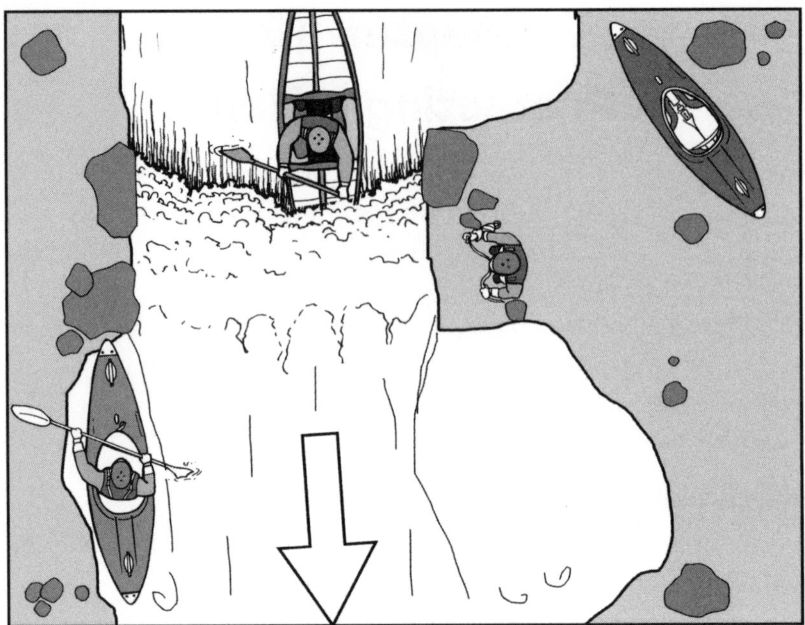

Fig. 18.1 Making the most of available resources.

1. There is the possibility of getting tangled in the throw line if he breaks in, *(eddies out)*, from river left.
2. If anything should happen that requires a bank based rescuer to be on river right, he can get out of his boat and deal with it.

Flexibility

When planning a line down a rapid, making best use of the cover available can be built into the plan. In fig. 18.2 rescuer B is in position with a handrail to recover equipment or swimmers and is also able to quickly move upstream to help anyone who gets into trouble in the strainer.

Rescuer A is ready to throw a line to a swimmer but prepared to move up or downstream to assist as necessary.

The rescue boater C is positioned as far upstream as is useful. It is easy enough for a chase boater to move downstream to cover an incident but difficult if not impossible to quickly move upstream.

Usefulness

In accordance with the Principle of Most Usefulness, rescuer B is positioned where he is most likely to be of use despite the fact that the strainer is a serious hazard. This is because the team have decided that this is an unlikely event given the line to be followed and the way the water is flowing. None the less there is a contingency plan for rescuer B to quickly get to the strainer should the unlikely event occur.

Organisation and Communication

It is vital that every one knows who is coordinating the rescue cover and exactly what their job is. To avoid confusion, when inspecting a rapid and discussing a feature, or a hazards in midstream, it may help to throw a stone at it to ensure that everyone is talking about the same feature.

Good briefings, prior training and/or experience of working together, combined with clear effective signals can speed the process up. (See Chapters 9 and 10). This is important. After all, we are there to paddle, not mess about on the bank longer than is necessary.

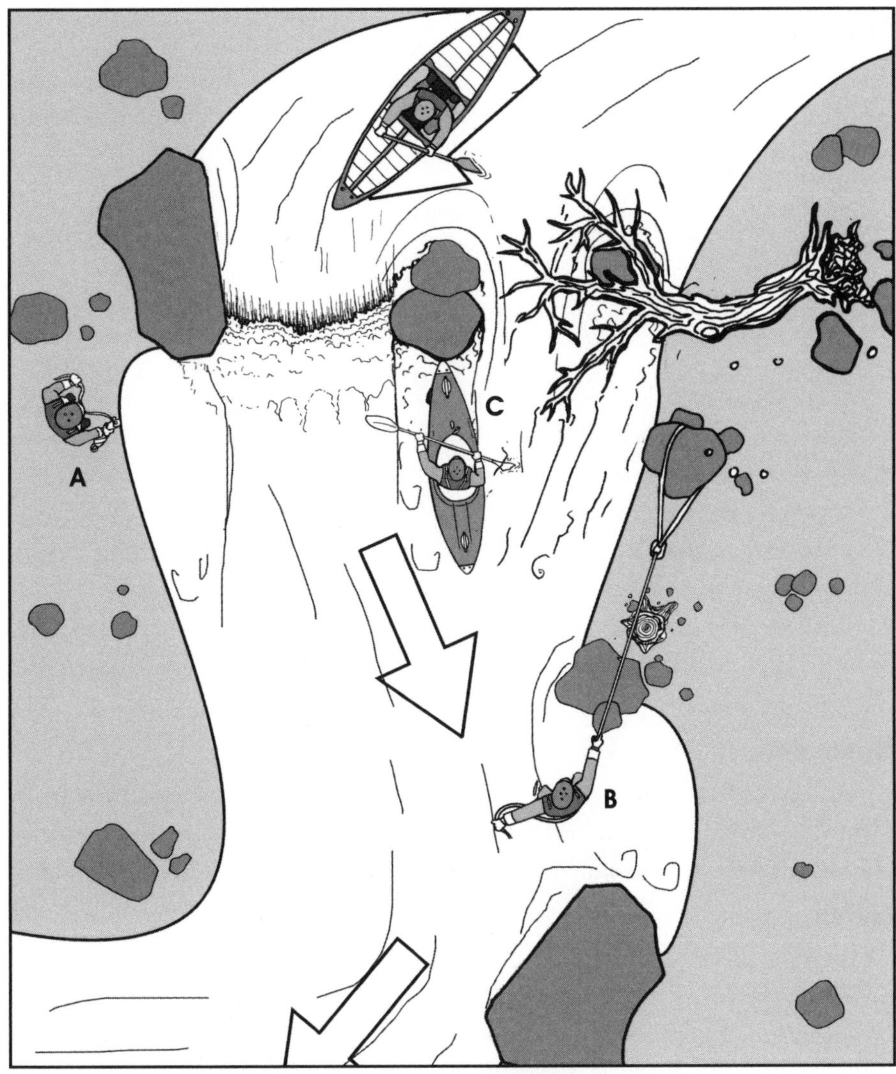

Fig. 18.2 Using back up and being in the most useful place.

Chapter 19
Incident Management

When a mishap first occurs in a white water situation, either the victim or a nearby person will have to do something to retrieve or at least stabilise the situation. The situation is often retrieved so quickly that the only team organisation needed is to recover the equipment. However, if the initial action is only able to stabilise the situation and buy time, the team will be faced with a rescue that will require effective management.

Roles

It is essential that team members are clear as to what their roles are in the event of a rescue. Whether in a formally structured rescue team or an informal group of friends we can identify the following roles:

- Leader
- Specialist
- Gofer
- Rescuers

Leader

If at all possible leaders should take a 'hands off' approach. They should literally take a step back, tuck their hands in their buoyancy aid, and see the whole picture. As soon as rescuers become physically involved in a rescue they, quite rightly, become 'focused' on the task, or the individual they are helping. This means that they will probably not realise that there is no back up down-stream, or that no one has been sent to call an ambulance.

With small teams of boaters, the lack of numbers means that the leader has to be in on the action. In this case the leader should take on the task that requires the least involvement.

Specialist

Different people in the team will have different skills that may need to be identified. They may be trained first-aiders, have climbing and rope skills, or be particularly strong and confident swimmers, willing to be involved in 'wet' rescues.

Gofer

It is a good idea to appoint someone whose role is to try and make sure that the rescuers have all the equipment or people they need. If this person has no other specific task, he also has an overview, which enables him to anticipate rescuers needs and make up the shortfall before it occurs. With complex rescues or recoveries, it makes sense to establish an equipment dump. All the spare equipment that rescuers have but don't anticipate using to complete their allotted task is left here for the gofer.

Rescuers

This should be everyone else in the team. Some will be less experienced, skilled or confident than others but anyone can help out by pulling a rope or keeping an eye out upstream for floating hazards or other paddlers.

Sequence of Events

Most rescues will involve a sequence of events that will be something like the one outlined below:

1. Assess the situation.
2. Stabilise the situation.
3. Reassess the situation.
4. Decide on a plan of action.
5. Communicate plan to team.
6. Allocate tasks and ensure everyone is clear what their task involves.
7. Execute the plan.
8. Review incident to learn lessons and improve future performance.

The Plan of Action

The plan of action will typically be broken into a number of phases. These are:

1. Get victim safely to shore. If victim OK, carry on with trip.

If not:

2. If injured, administer first aid
3. Evacuate injured
4. Recover equipment
5. Evacuate team members and equipment

If there are plenty of rescuers available, a team leader who is able to keep the whole picture in view will try and have more than one of these events happening at the same time.

A Scenario

Imagine the following:

The scene is that a member of a two raft team was catapulted out of a raft, took a bad swim and finally ends up stranded on a rock in mid stream. It is obvious, even from a distance that the victim is in pain and has badly hurt his lower leg.

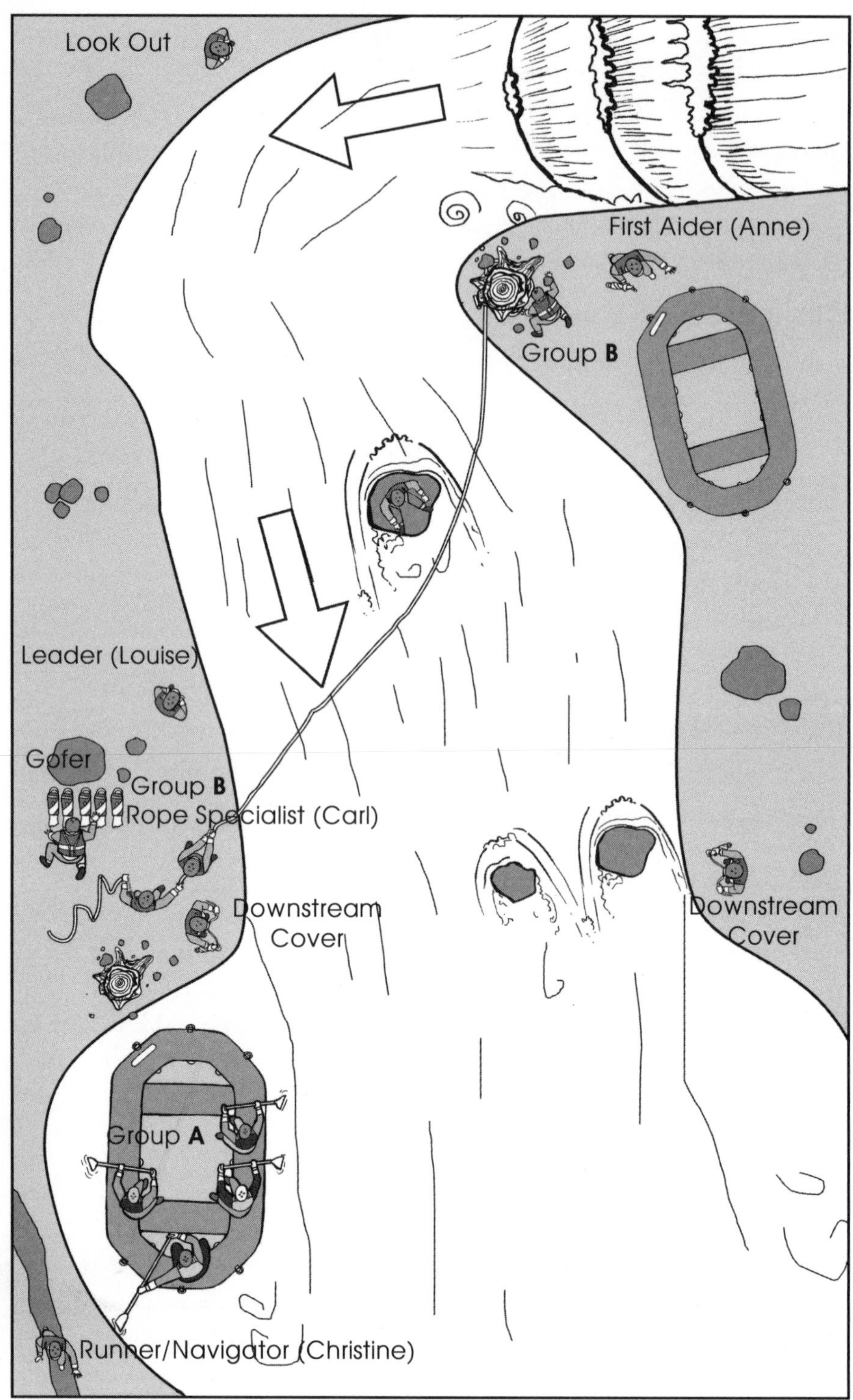

Fig. 19.1 A rescue scenario.

Phase One

The **leader, Louise**, quickly assesses the situation, formulates a plan of action and delegates the following tasks to the fourteen people she has available.

Carl, (specialist), the other raft guide is tasked to set up a tensioned diagonal to access the boulder. Three **rescuers** are tasked to work under his direction.

Jane, who has quite a lot of rafting experience, is promoted to **raft guide** and is tasked to ferry rescuers back and forth across the quiet stretch of river below the rapid as required. She is allocated three other **rescuers** to crew the raft and is also charged with using the raft as a chase boat should anyone fall in during the rescue.

Pete is appointed **gofer** and establishes a central equipment dump.

Christine, who is a ranking orienteer, **(specialist),** is sent to the nearest road to await the ambulance that she has already summoned by mobile phone.

Eric is posted as upstream lookout. His task is to warn any other paddlers that the rapid is obstructed with lines and that they should not run it till the rescue is complete.

The **two remaining rescuers** are positioned, one on each bank, below the scene of the rescue, ready to throw a line to anyone who might accidentally end up in the water.

Once every one is briefed they get on with the first phase of the rescue plan. (Fig. 19.1).

Phase Two

As soon as the tensioned diagonal is set up, **Louise** splits **Carl's** team in two.

Anne, who is a trained first-aider, **(specialist),** is sent down the tensioned diagonal accompanied by one of the other rescuers. Her task is to treat the victim's injuries and evacuate him from the rock.

Eric and the other rescuer are now tasked with building a Stretcher with which to carry the injured victim to the road.

Phase Three

As soon as the victim is safely on the bank, **Louise** sends the two rescuers who were standing by with throw lines to dismantle the tensioned diagonal. This done, everyone is ferried to the same side of the river. The whole group help in the evacuation to the road. They take it in turns to carry the stretcher and change places frequently as it is a tiring job. **Anne**, the first aider stays at the head of the stretcher and monitors the victim the whole time.

Phase Four.

Once the casualty is handed over to the ambulance crew, **Louise** has to think about whether to evacuate the whole team by road or carry on with the trip.

If she had allowed herself to become an actively involved rescuer with a specific task, Louise would not have been able to be forward planning. There would probably have been oversights and mistakes. There would certainly have been a great deal of time wasted when one step was completed before anyone thought about the next step.

With smaller teams the approach is still valid. However, there will obviously have to be compromises due to the lack of numbers.

Signals

Dealing with a rescue and coordinating rescuers requires different signals from those used when running a river. In addition, we may receive help from, or offer help to, other paddlers or even professional rescue teams. I therefore propose to introduce the **standard** signals that are taught on Rescue Three International™ Swift Water Technician courses. This is because these courses have become the *de-facto* internationally recognised standard for rescue teams and raft guides.

Hand Signals

The following signals should be made with clear deliberate movements:

Distress/Need Assistance

One hand extended above head

Okay

Two hands forming an 'O' or one hand on head

Move, Swim, or Move Boat

Two hands extending above head then pointing left/right

Break In, That Direction

Two hands extending above head, wave arms, then point left/right

Need Medical Kit and Help

Both arms crossed in front of chest

Whistle Signals

Stop or Attention!

One blast

Upstream

Two blasts

Downstream

Three blasts

Emergency

Three blasts repeated

PART

CARE OF VICTIMS

III

A special thanks to Chris Sladden, paddler and Doctor of Medicine, for proof reading and advice in this section.

Chapter 20
Principles of Care

A number of the principles that apply to rescue also apply to the care of the injured or ill. These are:

Principle of Personal Safety

"Rescuers should not take unnecessary or unjustified risks."

Potential rescuers are of no use to the victim or anyone else if they become victims themselves.

Principle of The Victim's Best Interest

"No action or treatment by the rescuer/first aider should place victims in more danger than they were already in."

Principle of Simplicity

"Keep it simple, keep it fast."

In most rescue situations, time is of the essence. The simpler a solution, the quicker it can be put into practice.

Principle of Immediate and Temporary Care

"The rescuer/first aider's job is to treat victims' injuries and get them to qualified medical attention as soon as possible."

Principle of Limited Competence

"First aiders must work within the limits of their training."

If first aiders attempt a treatment that is beyond the scope of what they have been trained to do, and this treatment is subsequently found to have contributed to the victim's death, they would be deemed negligent.

Top photos: Boat pinned in a siphon on the Rio Santa Maria, Mexico. It was impossible to arrange anchors so that the boat could be pulled back up at the correct angle.
Bottom left: Success came five and a half hours later. A line was attached to the bow, and the kayak was pulled down through the siphon.
Bottom right: Simon Drinkwater somewhat the worse for wear but happy to be out of the trapped boat.
Photos: Lara Tipper

Chapter 21
First Aid

In my view, anyone who regularly participates in risk sports owes it to themselves, and their friends, to regularly attend first aid training courses.

If you haven't, **get yourself on a first aid course ASAP!**

This is a subject that would require a separate book to do it justice and the chapter is written on the assumption that the reader already has a basic knowledge of first aid. I would recommend the following two books:

First Aid Manual

The authorised manual of : St. John's Ambulance, St. Andrew's Ambulance Association and The British Red Cross.

ISBN 0-86318-978-4

Medicine for Mountaineers (and Other Wilderness Activities)

(Particularly useful for those operating in remote locations).

ISBN 0-89886-331-7

Aims

The aims of the chapter are as follows:

1. To suggest an accident procedure.
2. To offer some guidelines aimed specifically at the water based first aider.
3. To discuss some issues that affect first aiders in a white water situation.
4. To look at how we can adapt our kit to improvise in a first aid situation.

Accident Procedure

When approaching an injured or distressed person it is important that the first aider remains calm and thinks logically. This may be easier said than done when the adrenaline is pumping, so it is important to have a system that will ensure that nothing is forgotten and that the priorities are taken care of in the right order.

If a first aider is suddenly confronted with a situation, he should physically take a step back to help trigger the ability to mentally step back. Given the luxury of some prior warning, the first aider should stop a short distance away from the victim, compose himself and survey the scene.

Rescue and Emergency Care™, suggest the following pneumonic to remember the sequence of priorities when dealing with an accident:

Before and after heavy rain on the Haffus in South Wales.
Photos: Chris Sladden

Assess	The situation
	Safety
	The level of consciousness of the victim
Breathing	Check airway, (see Issues)
	Assess normality of breathing
Circulation	Check pulse
	Look for bleeding
Deformity	Casualty examination
	Signs of fractures, shock, internal injuries
Emotion	Reassurance and continuing care
	Emotional wellbeing of patient

If we work our way methodically through the sequence, we won't miss out anything vital. The sequence works in terms of both **order** and **priority**.

For example, the safety of the rescuer comes first; but unless he takes time to assess the situation he cannot make a judgment on safety. If a victim is clutching a badly bleeding arm and screaming for help, it is obvious that he is fully conscious and breathing. Therefore the fact that the rescuer is going to deal with the bleeding arm, fits in nicely with our sequence of checks and priorities.

If at any time the first aider gets confused, he should finish off what he was doing and then start from the top again, A,B,C,D and E.

The Situation

Taking the time to survey the scene allows the first aider to try and work out how the accident happened. The **history** of the accident is an important factor in assessing safety and diagnosing possible injuries. If the victim fell ten feet onto his head, one can suspect head and neck injuries!

It is important to find out how many people were involved. There might be someone missing. Someone might have been swept downstream by the current or simply wandered off looking for help.

Safety

The first aider needs to prevent a second accident. The priorities are as follows:

1. The first aider
2. Other rescuers
3. Bystanders
4. The Victim

Our ability to help the victim will be seriously impaired if the first aider is injured or he ends up having to treat several other victims.

Whenever possible it is best to examine the casualty and treat injuries before moving him. If the casualty is in a dangerous position, it may be necessary to move him first.

Guidelines for Outdoor First Aid

- Do not rush
- Delegate if possible
- Never step over the casualty
- Treat from the downhill side
- Try to compose the casualty
- Keep talking, even if the casualty is unconscious
- Never leave the casualty - unless safety considerations require it, or you are the only person who can go for help
- Never lose body or eye contact with the casualty
- Prevent heat loss
- Take account of weather conditions

Do Not Rush!

A few seconds spent composing one's self, surveying the scene or deciding on the correct course of action is time well spent. Getting it right will more than make up for any time used up in this way.

Delegate if Possible

Ideally, the leader should not be directly involved in administering first aid as he needs to be coordinating all the other things that are going on.

Once contact has been made, whoever has been assigned the role of first aider needs to closely monitor the airway and vital signs, and reassure the casualty. Therefore the first aider should delegate as much of the treatment as possible to other rescuers so that he can remain at the casualty's head.

Never Step Over the Casualty

Rescuers should get in the habit of walking around the casualty. Time and time again one sees rescuers tread on an already painful injury.

Treat from the Downhill Side

It is disconcerting, to say the least, if a casualty rolls down the slope into the river.

Try to Compose the Casualty

It is difficult to sufficiently stress the importance of the victim's morale when it comes to fighting the onset of shock and hypothermia. By not rushing and by appearing calm, the first aider can do a lot to reassure and calm a casualty. Speaking calmly, both to the victim and other rescuers is important. Rescuers need to be very careful what they say within the casualty's hearing. Phrases like: "He's done for!" are generally considered to be unhelpful.

Keep Talking

It is important to remember that even a totally unresponsive unconscious casualty may be able to hear what a rescuer is saying. Many casualties who have recovered from a deep coma report that one of the things that kept them going was the calm reassuring voice of the rescuer. If this voice suddenly stops, and it is the victim's only way of knowing that he is being looked after, it will be very distressing. If the casualty's name is known, use it when addressing him.

Never Leave the Casualty

In a white water situation, it may be some time before help arrives or the casualty can be evacuated to the nearest road. The casualty will have formed a reassuring bond with whoever first started treating him. It is important that this person stays with the victim and monitors his progress even if another more experienced first aider takes over responsibility for the casualty's treatment. The casualty does not need the stress of losing someone he has come to trust, and having to rebuild a new relationship.

Never Lose Body or Eye Contact

Just as a calm friendly voice is reassuring, body and eye contact is important. Once the first aider first lays hands on the casualty, he should try not to lose physical contact. When treatment has been completed and the first aider is monitoring, he should hold the victim's hand, talk constantly and maintain eye contact throughout.

Prevent Heat Loss

In all but the warmest of climates hypothermia is a concern. (See Chapter 3, Hazards). Any one who is injured is far more likely to succumb to hypothermia. **This cannot be stressed enough!**

Take Account of Weather Conditions

This is linked to the above point. Weather conditions and their effect on a casualty and the rest of the party will play a major role in deciding on a plan of action.

Issues

Cervical Spine and Airway

Airway always takes precedence over cervical (neck) spine injuries. In other words, even if the first aider suspects neck injuries, if the victim is not breathing, the airway must be opened. None the less, the first aider should quickly assess the possibility of 'C' spine injuries before opening the airway.

If the history of the accident, signs such as bruising or swelling, or pain in that area suggests that 'C' spine injuries are a possibility, care should be taken not to do any unnecessary damage. This is why first aiders are now taught to open the airway using two fingers on the forehead and the chin. (See: Chapter 22, Resuscitation). This ensures that the airway is opened with the minimum of force. The first aider should also take care to stabilise the head and ensure that the 'C' spine is only tilted back and not twisted, rotated, or moved form side to side.

Jaw Thrust

This is an alternative way of opening the airway that keeps the head stable and can be used when 'C' spine injuries are suspected.

1. Kneel at the casualty's head looking down the length of his body.
2. Place your thumbs on his chin and your fingers on the corner of his jawbone.
3. Gently but firmly lift his jaw up and forward.

Helmets

If there is no need to remove the helmet it is best left on to provide protection and warmth. However, if an airway needs to be established or resuscitation started it should be **carefully** removed.

Casualty's Dignity

It is important that we remember that we are dealing with a sensitive human being and to consider feelings and dignity at all times. If the first aider needs to examine an injury in a potentially embarrassing location, there is no need for the rest of the team to stand there gawking. (Although it is a good idea to have a witness of the same sex as the casualty present).

We should try not to treat the casualty as a 'body'. It is far better to ask a casualty to move or adjust his clothing than to manhandle him unnecessarily.

Consent

This is an important issue, both from the point of view of the casualty's dignity and in terms of possible legal repercussions. If a person tells a first aider not to touch them, then that is the end of the matter. To continue an examination or treatment would constitute assault.

The best way to address this issue is for the first aider to talk to the casualty the whole time and tell him what he is going to do next. If the casualty does not object, consent is implied.

Monitoring Vital Signs

If first aiders keep a record of the casualty's progress it can save vital time when he receives expert medical attention. This is because monitoring has already taken place and information on which to base decisions has already been gathered. An examination will give a doctor a great deal of information but a record of a series of checks tells us whether the patient is stable, deteriorating or improving.

If for example, a patient is going deeper into shock and the examination has revealed no obvious reason why this should happen, we must suspect internal injuries.

A surgeon may be able to decide to prepare for an exploratory operation even before the casualty arrives at the hospital on the basis of the first aiders' observations.

In order to help us diagnose what is abnormal, it is vital that we practise monitoring the vital signs of as many 'normal' people as we can. We need to be confident in our ability to do this. The vital signs are:

- Level of Consciousness
- Breathing
- Pulse
- Temperature
- Colour

(Blood pressure is also an important vital sign but most first aiders will not have the means to monitor this).

A record card can be improvised, or better still, kept in the first aid kit. The vital signs should be monitored and recorded every five minutes.

Level of Consciousness

The pseudonym AVPU helps us remember the four levels that we can differentiate in a first aid situation.

Alert	Normal behaviour given the circumstances.
Vocal	The victim is less than fully conscious but responds to direct questions.
Pain	The victim is deeply unconscious but responds to pain
Unresponsive	The victim is totally unresponsive.

Breathing

With an unconscious victim the airway should be checked, even if the victim is breathing. There may be debris or blood in the mouth that needs to be cleared. Very often, the act of checking and clearing the airway is all that is needed for an unconscious victim to start breathing unaided.

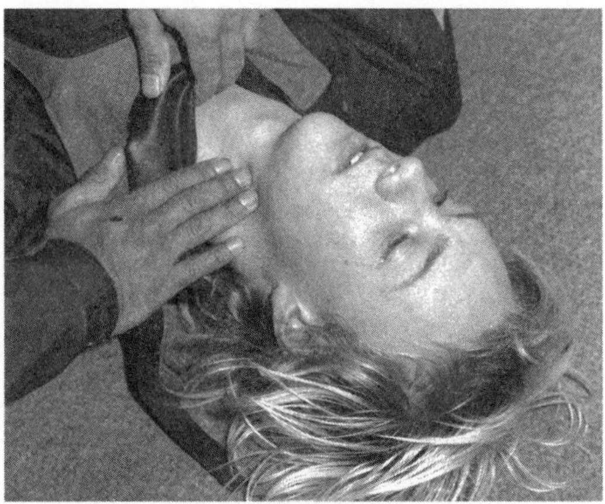

Fig. 21.1 Taking the neck pulse.
Photo: Bob Timms

Even if a person is alert and is obviously breathing, it is important to check out how normal his breathing is. A normal range is twelve to fifteen breaths a minute. This will help us diagnose other, possibly hidden injuries. Painful or irregular breathing could indicate chest injuries. A significantly faster breathing rate than usual, (more than 20 breaths a minute), is one of the signs of shock.

We can **listen , look and feel** for breathing. Listen for sounds of breathing by putting our ear close to the victim's mouth. Look to see the chest or abdomen rise and fall. Feel the casualty's breath on our ear and put a hand on his abdomen to feel the movement of the upper belly/chest.

Pulse

Cold, restrictive clothing and wrist seals can make a wrist pulse very difficult to detect. Therefore the best way to take a pulse in an outdoor situation is take the neck pulse. (Fig. 21.1). The tips of two or three fingers are placed on the Adam's Apple and then slid gently but firmly to the side, until they slide into a groove between the Adam's Apple and the first large set of neck muscles. Here the finger tips will push the artery against the large muscle and the first aider is able to feel the pulse. A normal adult pulse rate is between sixty and a hundred beats a minute. If there is a pulse it can tell us a great deal:

- A fast weak pulse, (over 100 beats a minute), is a sign of shock
- A slow, bounding pulse is a sign of head injuries
- A slow weak pulse is one of the signs of hypothermia

Temperature

In a windy, wet environment it is very difficult to accurately gauge someone's temperature. Normal thermometers don't work very well in these conditions and the use of a rectal thermometer is impractical. In such conditions the history of the accident and other signs will be of more use.

Sign	Probably Indicates
• Cold and Sweaty	• Shock
• Hot and Sweaty	• Fever, Infection
• Unusual Warmth	• Heat Exhaustion
• Coolness	• Hypothermia

Colour

A healthy underlying skin tone is a sign that oxygen is reaching all parts of the body as it should. We should look for changes in skin colour especially in the face. This is especially useful in detecting the onset of shock.

Skin Type	Changes To
• Caucasian (White)	• Pale, Ash Grey
• African/Asians (Black)	• Dull Ash Grey
• Chinese	• Pale Grey

We should also look at the inside of the lips and cheek for changes in the normal pink/red colouring. Blueness of the lips, (cyanosis), is a serious sign which indicates a low level of oxygen in the blood. It indicates that attention to the airway and pulse is necessary or that hypothermia is setting in.

Treatment Issues

Being in a white water environment and dressed in outlandish garb raises a number of issues that affect treatment.

Breathing

If a casualty's breathing has stopped or is impaired, it may help to remove his helmet and loosen or even remove his buoyancy aid, *(PFD)*. Tight fitting neck seals of dry tops may be cut for the same reasons.

However, I would advise trying not to do this unless it is really necessary. Apart from the issue of damaging a friend's expensive equipment, we must never forget the nature of the environment we are in. There are two issues here:

1. When the time comes to move a casualty he will need to be wearing personal protective equipment, just as the rescuers will. On or within ten metres of the water's edge this means helmets and buoyancy aids.
2. Any injured person is far more susceptible to the onset of hypothermia. Removing or reducing the efficiency of clothing can only make this worse.

Bleeding

From a first aid point of view, the problem with clothing that is designed to keep water out is that it is very good at keeping blood in. This can hide major blood loss from a first aider. The blood will pool, and the first aider may be able to feel liquid, like water in a bag.

Running water will make it harder to stop wounds bleeding by washing away the blood that is clotting. Therefore it is important to keep casualties out of the water. If the wound is minor or it is decided that the easiest way to evacuate is by continuing the journey, the dressing should be 'waterproofed' by using electricians' insulating tape or a combination of a piece of polythene and electricians' tape.

Unconsciousness

People who are less than 'Alert' on the AVPU scale are deemed to be unconscious in terms of

Fig. 21.2 Preparing to roll the casualty.

Fig. 21.3 The Safe Airway Position, SAP. The airway is maintained and fluids drain from the mouth. The neck and head are supported throughout the roll and the knee is used as a lever. Photos: Bob Timms

treatment. The main worry is that they cannot protect their own airway due to the loss of their choking reflex.

They should be placed in the Safe Airway Position. (Fig. 21.2 and 3). From a medical standpoint, people who are less than completely conscious are in a state of unconsciousness. Forty percent of unconscious victims who die might have been saved if their airways had been protected. The S.A.P. does this by putting casualties in a position that ensures they cannot swallow their own tongue and that any fluids drain out of their mouths rather than into the back of their throat.

Ideally, casualties should be monitored at five minute intervals and the first aider ready to intervene with resuscitation at any time. Heat loss from the casualty is even more of an issue with unconscious casualties.

Shock

This is a condition where insufficient oxygen is reaching the vital tissues of the body, due to a lack of **effective** circulating blood volume. It is a serious sign that the body is not coping and can be thought of as the phase before death. Faced with more than one casualty, a first aider must decide who is in most urgent need of evacuation to expert attention; the casualty in shock is the priority.

Cause

The cause of shock is a loss of body fluids arising from:

- External bleeding

- Internal bleeding
- Burns weeping
- Dehydration
- Diarrhoea
- Septic shock, caused by severe infections

Signs and Symptoms

- Cold, pale, ('pale as death') sweaty, (clammy) skin
- Rising pulse, usually climbing to over one hundred beats a minute
- Rising breathing rate, usually climbing to over 20 breaths a minute
- Fear, anxiety and restlessness

Treatment

- A,B,C
- Treat injuries
- Reassure
- Monitor vital signs
- Raise legs to concentrate blood supply where it is needed
- Prevent heat loss
- Evacuate as quickly as possible

If the casualty is not evacuated the outlook is bleak!

Limitations of Treatment

First aiders must always work within the limits of their training. In a situation where help is a long way off it helps to remember that a casualty surgeon, who does not have access to specialist equipment, could do little more than a trained first aider in most situations.

First aiders should not be tempted to carry out medical or surgical procedures in which they have had no training. If they do, and a post-mortem indicates that the bungled procedure contributed to the casualty's death, they are in serious trouble.

Remote Medicine

The exception to the above comment is if the first aider is told to carry out such a procedure under the direction of a medical practitioner. Due to the increased use of radios and mobile phones, specialist casualty surgeons are becoming increasingly adept at 'remote medicine'. The potential for remote treatment is another reason why it is important to become practised in the monitoring of vital signs. The doctor will only have your observations to go on.

Remote Locations

There are some issues that arise if evacuation to expert medical treatment will take several hours or even days.

Pain Relief

The general rule when expert medical help is close at hand is to relieve pain by treating the injury but not to give pain killing drugs, (analgesics). This is because they will mask signs and symptoms and hinder diagnosis when the victim arrives at a hospital. However, the relief of pain is an important part of the treatment of shock. If help is a long way off there is no doubt that the use of suitable analgesics may improve the casualty's prospects.

There are also a number of legal problems involved with the administration of even mild analgesics. My advice is that when paddling in remote areas, people should carry their own analgesics. They should also consult their own personal physician as to which ones to take. (Not least because some analgesics cannot be safely taken in combination with other medicines. Paddlers should therefore seek advice on all the medicines that they may decide to take on such trips).

Analgesics can be divided into three types:

Mild e.g. aspirin, ibroprufen
Moderate e.g. codeine combined with paracetamol
Strong e.g. morphine and its derivatives

Strong analgesics have a tendency to depress respiration and should therefore not be taken by casualties with head injuries.

Aspirin and ibroprufen should not be taken by anyone suffering from a stomach disorder.

Asthma can be aggravated by a number of analgesics, especially aspirin. People who are known to have asthma should not be given aspirin based pain killers.

Certain mixtures of drugs can cause serious complications. Therefore it is essential to know if a patient is already on medication.

Giving Fluids

Once again the general advice is not to give fluids if expert medical attention is close at hand. The main reason is that with anyone who is less than fully conscious, first aiders need to be careful to safeguard their airway. Allowing victims to drink may induce vomiting. If vomit gets into the lungs it can cause irreparable harm. (Vomiting is also a possible side effect of strong analgesics).

If help is a long way off the gains in terms of treating shock more than outweigh the risks. Casualties who are conscious enough should be encouraged to take small sips of water at body temperature, little and often.

People expeditioning in extremely remote locations should consider getting a doctor to join the team, or getting paramedic training, and carrying the equipment needed for giving fluids intravenously. There are, however, great difficulties in terms of storage as the solutions used have to be pre-packed, sterile and kept within certain temperature ranges.

Another option, in remote locations, is to administer fluids through the rectum. The advantages are:

1. The fluid is delivered directly to the part of the body at which fluids are absorbed.
2. Although the fluid used, (re-hydration fluids or slightly salted water), should be as clean as possible, it doesn't have to be sterile.

Reducing Dislocations

Dislocated shoulders are one of the injuries we are likely to come across in a paddling situation. The general first aid advice is that if it doesn't pop back in of it's own accord it should be immobilised and dealt with in hospital. This is because, although it is true that the sooner a dislocation is dealt with the easier it is to reduce it, (put it back in its socket), if it is reduced badly, nerves can be trapped and long term damage done.

That said, in terms of outcome, a reduced joint is nearly always better than a long standing unreduced joint. On a remote trip where the only feasible way out is to carry on paddling, immobilisation may not be an option. If this has occurred before and the casualty knows how to deal with it the first aider can help reduce it under the casualty's direction. Whichever approach is used, it should be the casualty's decision whether to attempt to reduce the dislocation or not.

The principle of reducing a dislocation is to exert a very slow and continuous pull to tease out the muscle spasm. The following approach is the least risky:

1. If the decision is made, the sooner it is attempted the easier it will be.
2. The casualty should take the strongest painkiller available, preferably one that also acts as a muscle relaxant.
3. The casualty should lie down somewhere where his arm can hang down, (a boulder or steep edged river bank).
4. A helmet or bag is tied to the affected arm and stones loaded into it until it weighs about two kilos, (4.4 pounds), or three kilos for a large patient.
5. The weight is slowly increased to about double. If this causes pain the weight is reduced.
6. The casualty is left alone so that gravity can do the work as the casualty's muscles relax. The patient should feel a 'clunk' as the shoulder relocates.

After the attempt, whether it is successful or not, the casualty's wrist pulse should be checked to ensure that no major blood vessels have been trapped. If no pulse can be found the arm will have to be moved till it can. Another important sign to look out for is a colour change, (this occurs very quickly). If the arm appears white and 'dead' a major blood vessel has probably been trapped.

Conclusion

All the publications on 'wilderness medicine' that I have read agree that unless a hospital is reasonably close, a dislocation should be reduced. They go on to say that the chances of doing further harm are small. The advantages are:

- Pain relief is usually dramatic
- the risk of circulatory or neural damage is **reduced**
- Immobilisation of the joint is easier
- Transportation of the victim is easier

After the reduction the joint should be immobilised. On return to civilisation a doctor and a physiotherapist should be consulted.

First Aid Kits

Most first aid treatment of traumatic injuries is relatively simple:

- Bleeding is treated by applying a sterile dressing and pressure and elevation
- Fractures are immobilised in the position that the victim finds most comfortable
- Burns are treated by cooling with cold water for at least ten minutes and then covering with a sterile dressing

There are obviously lots of complications and exceptions but everything else is basically a variation on the theme.

What most people call first aid kits can be divided into two parts:

Medicine Chest

Tender loving care and longer term treatment.

First Aid Kit

Immediate temporary care of traumatic injuries.

First aid kits need only contain the following items:

- Sterile Dressings - for stopping bleeding
- Band aids for small wounds
- Non stick sterile dressings - burns or the first layer on a wound
- Triangular bandages - for bandaging or immobilising fractures
- Conforming (crepe) bandages - bandaging or immobilising fractures

There should be two kits in any party in case the boat that is lost is the one containing the first aid kit.

Improvisation

Much of the materials and equipment used by white water paddlers can be adapted for first aid purposes.

Gaffer Tape

Also known as Duct Tape, is found in most boaters' repair kits. It is great for immobilising fractures or water proofing dressings. In my opinion it is better than purpose made straps.

Electrician's Tape

Great for taping a broken finger to a sound one, covering rubbing points on fingers to prevent them blistering, and waterproofing small dressings.

Foam

The closed cell foam in camping mats and buoyancy aids can be used as padding, or by folding it, as a splint. (Fig. 21.4).

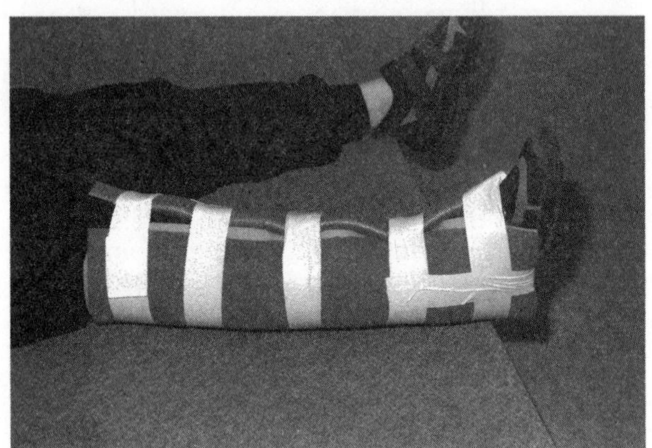

Fig. 21.4 Camper mat and duct tape leg splint.
Photo: Bob Timms

Neck Brace

If a person has sustained head injuries one should suspect neck injuries. The first aider should feel for any irregularities along the spine and try not to move the neck unnecessarily. If the patient must be moved it should be ideally on a rigid stretcher and with a 'collar' fitted. If necessary a collar can be improvised by removing the slab buoyancy from a buoyancy aid, (PFD), carving it to the right shape, and taping it in place with some 'gaffer' tape from the repair kit. The fit of the collar should be checked by trying it out on someone else who is of similar build to the casualty.

Polythene Bags

Although not sterile, a clean sheet of polythene makes a good non-stick burn dressing. 'Cling Film', the stuff used to wrap sandwiches, is sterile if it is fresh off the roll.

Polythene bags are also useful for waterproofing dressings.

Driftwood or spare paddles

Driftwood can be cut into suitable lengths, padded with foam and used as rigid splints.

Nylon Tape

The tape slings and lengths carried for rescue and recovery purposes can be pressed into service as straps for immobilising fractures.

Chapter 22
Resuscitation

The protocols taught by first aiders are put together by an international committee of physicians, whose advice is based on statistics. These show that the vast majority of incidents involving Basic Life Support concern heart attack victims in an urban situation. In any situation where the heart has stopped and full CPR, (Cardio Pulmonary Resuscitation), is needed there is very little chance of the first aider restarting the heart, and **in the case of a diseased heart,** none at all. The first aider acts as a machine that mechanically ventilates the lungs, and compresses the heart so as to pump oxygenated blood around the body. This keeps the vital tissues oxygenated until a defibrillator can be used to electrically stop the fibrillation, (the fibres of the heart muscle contracting in an unsynchronised way), and electrically 'kick start' the heart. In most cases, by giving Basic Life Support, first aiders merely bridge the gap between someone collapsing and the arrival of expert medical attention. Thankfully, new protocols introduced in April 1997, distinguish between suspected heart attack victims and the victims of trauma or drowning. Although the odds are still stacked against them, the victims are often young, fit and have healthy hearts. Therefore, unlike with heart attack victims, resuscitation can occasionally succeed, even without a defibrillator.

Basic Life Support Protocol

As always the first priority is to assess for danger. That done the victim's level of consciousness is assessed. Anyone dealing with an unconscious casualty, whatever the cause, should clear and open the victim's airway, (fig. 22.1), and check for breathing. It is suggested that the first aider should look , listen and feel for ten seconds before deciding that breathing is absent.

One Rescuer

The protocol is complicated by the fact that there is a different procedure for victims of drowning or trauma than there is for suspected heart attack victims, (anyone who has stopped breathing for reasons other than drowning or traumatic accident). These differences only apply if the first aider is the only person who can go and summon help. The differences are:

Unconscious/Not Breathing - Drowning or Trauma

- Give 2 breaths
- Check for pulse

Pulse Present

- 10 breaths of rescue breathing
- Go for help
- Return and reassess

No Pulse

- Give CPR for 1 minute
- Phone, radio, or go for help
- Return and reassess

Unconscious/Not Breathing - Other (Suspect Heart Attack)

- Phone, radio, or go for help
- Return and reassess

Multiple Rescuers

When there is more than one rescuer involved there is no need for decisions on when one should go for help. The first aider gets on with the resuscitation while someone else goes for help.

Rescue Breathing

When we breathe in and out at a normal rate we only use a small amount of the oxygen in each lung full of air. This leaves more than enough for the casualty's needs during rescue breathing. Breaths should be given at a rate of about ten per minute, (one every six seconds), and the pulse should be checked after every ten breaths.

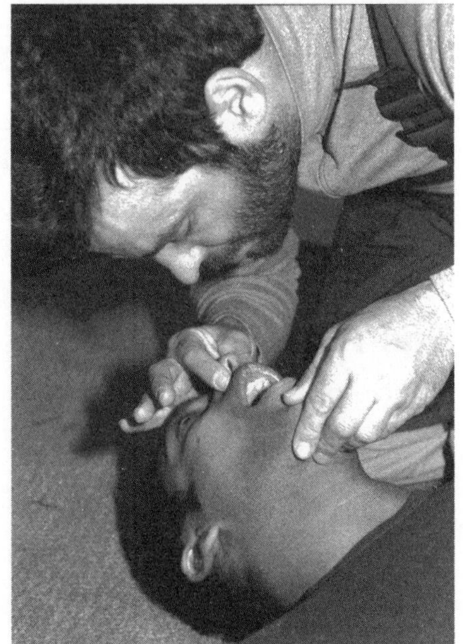

Fig. 22.1 Preparing to give rescue breathing. Photo: Bob Timms

Mouth to Mouth Ventilation

1. With the casualty lying flat on his back, if possible, look inside and remove any obvious obstructions from the casualty's mouth. Leave well fitting dentures in place but remove any that are broken or displaced.
2. Open the airway by placing two fingers under the casualty's chin and lifting the jaw, while at the same time putting the fingers of the other hand on his forehead and tilting the head back. Take

care to keep the neck in line if there is any reason to suspect injury to the cervical spine.

3. Close the casualty's nose by pinching it between your finger and thumb. Take a full breath and place your lips around his mouth, making a good seal. (Fig. 22.1)
4. Blow slowly and steadily into the casualty's mouth until you see his chest rise. It should take about 2 seconds for a full inflation.
5. Remove your lips and allow the chest to fall fully.

Chest Does Not Rise

If you cannot get breaths into the casualty's lungs, check that:

- The casualty's head is tilted far enough back
- You have remembered to pinch the casualty's nose
- You have a firm seal around the casualty's mouth
- The airway is not obstructed by blood, vomit or a foreign body

Clearing Obstructions

These measures should only be taken if one is certain that there is an obstruction, because the other possible causes of the chest not rising have been eliminated. Providing the jaw is relaxed, open the casualty's mouth, and looking for the obstruction, carefully sweep a finger around inside the mouth. If this fails because there is a blockage in the throat, turn the victim on his side and slap him firmly between the shoulder blades. If after five slaps the obstruction has not shifted, turn the victim back on his back, kneel astride him and give him up to five abdominal thrusts:

Put the heel of one hand below the ribcage, cover it with the other hand, then press sharply inwards and upwards. If this fails, alternate five slaps and five thrusts.

Use of Masks

The risk of infection through performing rescue breathing is negligible and rescuers who do not have a mask or face shield should not hesitate to give help in this way. Nevertheless there are a number of advantages to using these devices.

Face Shields

These consist of a simple sheet of plastic with a valve through which the rescuer ventilates the casualty. (Fig. 22.2) The shield simply acts as a barrier. Although the risk of infection through contact with saliva is minute, contact with saliva, blood or vomit is far from pleasant. Though not as useful or effective as a proper mask, face shields pack so small that it is feasible to carry one in a pocket.

These shields are also extremely useful for dealing with sucking chest wounds as the shield can be placed on the wound the 'wrong' way round. The one way valve then allows air that is collapsing the lung out of the chest cavity but does not allow air in.

Masks

As well as being a more efficient barrier, a proper face mask makes it easier to make a seal around the casualty's mouth than a shield. This is particularly true if the casualty's mouth is damaged.

Fig 22.2 Face shield, (left), and face mask. Photos: Bob Timms

Mouth to Nose

Mouth to nose is just as efficient for getting air into a casualty's lungs. However, it can be more difficult for the air to be exhaled than in mouth to mouth. If a casualty's mouth is damaged and a mask is not available it will work well enough.

Cardio Pulmonary Resuscitation (CPR)

Cardio Pulmonary Resuscitation consists of rescue breathing combined with chest compressions. The casualty is given two breaths of air to oxygenate the blood, followed by fifteen chest compressions to pump the oxygenated blood around the system so that it reaches the vital organs.

Chest Compression

Although more difficult, it is possible to perform rescue breathing with the casualty in a variety of positions. Chest compressions can only be performed effectively if the casualty is lying on his back on a firm surface. It is essential to remove the victim's buoyancy aid or the foam will absorb much of the pressure being exerted by the rescuer. It can also make it difficult to achieve a full release.

1. Kneel beside the casualty and using your index and middle finger find one of the lowest ribs. Slide your fingers along until you find the point where the lower ribs meet. Place your middle finger on this point and your index finger on the breastbone above.
2. Place the heel of your other hand on the casualty's chest and slide it down the breastbone until it reaches your index finger. This is the point at which pressure is applied.
3. Place the heel of your first hand on top of the other hand and interlock the fingers.

4. Lean over the casualty, and with your arms straight press down vertically to depress the breastbone about 4-5 centimetres, (2 inches). Release the pressure without removing your hands but ensuring that you allow the rib cage to fully expand, (this allows the heart to expand, sucking in more blood).
5. Repeat the compressions, aiming at a rate of about 100 compressions a minute.

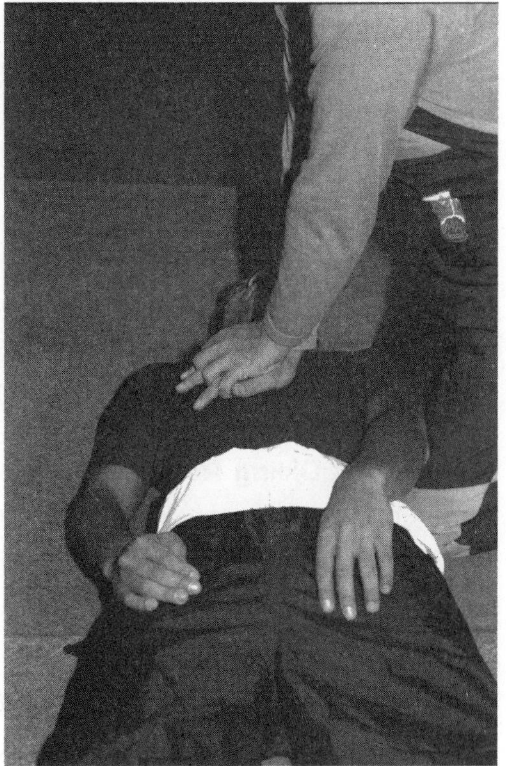

Fig. 22.3 Chest compressions.
Photo: Bob Timms

Full CPR

1. Ventilations and compressions are combined at a ratio of 2 breaths to 15 compressions.
2. Check for breathing and pulse if and when the victim shows any sign of improvement, such as a more normal colour returning.
3. If more than one first aider is present, one should rest and one perform CPR, swapping over frequently. It is possible to work as a pair and work at a ratio of 1 breath to 5 compressions. However, coordination is difficult and it is no more effective.

Drowning

In a white water environment we are more likely to have to intervene in a drowning situation. The internationally taught protocol does work but it is best if we understand what we are dealing with and how it differs from the statistical norm.

To be technically correct, drowning is what occurs if the victim doesn't survive. If the victim does survive the medical term for what occurs is 'near drowning'. The reason why many people do survive near drownings is that the human body is capable of a number of remarkable 'reflexes'.

Dry Drowning

The vast majority of both drowning and near drowning victims have little water in their lungs. In a last desperate attempt to survive, the human body will cause muscles in the throat to spasm and block the airway. The victims do not so much drown as suffocate. Blowing air into the victim's lungs, (rescue breathing), will of itself open the casualty's air passage.

Water in the Stomach

Due to the effects of dry drowning most of the water that the victim swallows goes into the stomach. During or after resuscitation, rescuers should not attempt to squeeze or in any other way force the water out. The danger is that this water is accidentally aspirated into the lungs.

Mammalian Diving Reflex (MDR)

This reflex usually occurs in very cold water and mostly affects children and fit young adults. As well as the throat constricting, the victim's heart beat slows down to an imperceptible one beat a minute or less. The majority of the cardio vascular system is shut down and what little oxygen there is in the bloodstream is diverted to the vital organs, in particular the brain.

The norm is that permanent brain damage occurs to the brain after the casualty has stopped breathing for four minutes. There have been rare instances of people who have been submerged in icy water for three hours, being resuscitated and making a complete recovery. The norm for rescue teams is to assume that a person submerged in cold water has a chance of survival for up to one hour. (Often referred to as the 'golden' hour).

Secondary Drowning

Anyone who has been the victim of a near drowning, **must** be admitted to hospital for tests and observation as soon as possible. This is the case even if the victim feels fine and is convinced that he has fully recovered.

The human body deals with any water that does get into the lungs by absorbing it into the bloodstream. This leads to dangerous, often lethal, complications, chief amongst which are:

1. Chemical imbalances in the bloodstream which can cause vital organs to malfunction.
2. Water seeping back into the lungs, (usually while the victim is asleep).
3. Swelling and subsequent blocking of the air passages caused by the lung tissue being irritated by water.
4. The possibility of pneumonia developing extremely rapidly, (it can happen in two hours!)

White Water Issues

There are a number of factors that affect white water paddlers where resuscitation is involved, that are not tackled on standard first aid courses. These are:

- The effect of the elements
- The effects of cold water immersion in a near drowning situation
- The decisions faced by rescuers who may be several hours or even days away from expert medical assistance

Vital Signs

The effects of cold on a casualty's body and the effects of wind, rain or noise in a white water environment, conspire to make checking for breathing and pulse more difficult. Rescue and Emergency Care™ suggest that we take about fifteen seconds over checking for signs of breathing and ten seconds over checking for a pulse.

Dry Drowning

Whereas it is not possible to carry out chest compressions until the victim can be laid out on a firm surface on the river bank, it is possible to perform rescue breathing whilst in a raft, an open canoe or wading in the shallows. In such a situation it will do no harm to open the airway, give two breaths and then head for the shore.

Mammalian Diving Reflex

Many people worry about the fact that they may not be able to find a pulse and commence CPR, when because of MDR, the heart is still beating, albeit very slowly. It is true that if chest compressions are performed on a heart that is beating, it may well disturb the heart's rhythm and cause it to fibrillate. However, if despite our best efforts we are unable to find a pulse, the advice currently available is that we commence CPR. It is important when performing CPR on a victim who has been pulled out of very cold water to check frequently for a pulse.

Remoteness

If someone's heart stops beating it is extremely unlikely that it can be restarted without specialist medical attention. Anyone who has a cardiac arrest in a remote situation is unlikely to survive despite the best efforts of first aiders. This does not mean that we should not attempt basic life support. Rescue breathing is often successful and CPR may succeed. We might get lucky and help may arrive sooner than expected or from an unexpected quarter. It is also important to try for the future mental well being of the rescuers.

The normal advice given to first aiders is to carry on performing CPR until expert medical help arrives or the first aider is too exhausted to continue. There are two reasons why a decision to stop CPR could be made:

1. The safety of the rest of the party is threatened, e.g. by the onset of hypothermia or approaching darkness.
2. CPR is not keeping the victim alive.

Legally, only a Doctor of Medicine can **declare** a person dead. However, as laymen we may have to make the **reasonable assumption** that someone is dead.

It would be reasonable to assume death if:

1. The victim has sustained injuries that are incompatible with life. To give an extreme example, if someone's head was severed it would be reasonable to assume that he was dead.

Or:

2. There was a complete absence of signs of life. This would mean:
    - No breathing - for a prolonged period
    - No pulse - for a prolonged period
    - Completely dilated pupils and, 'glassy' eyes
    - No reaction of the eyes to a light source

In a wilderness situation where there is no prospect of help arriving within a reasonable time, most sources seem to agree that CPR should be stopped if there is no sign of life after thirty minutes.

Key Points

1. Most victims who survive a near drowning still have a heart beat.
2. If the throat has constricted, the act of opening the airway by removing any debris, tilting the head back and giving the first breath or two of rescue breathing is the action that is most likely to save the casualty's life.

If you are ever unlucky enough to come across a resuscitation situation you must be mentally prepared for the fact that the odds are against the victim. This means that the odds are that the victim will die. If he does it will not be your fault! Anything you do will give the victim more of a chance than he would have otherwise had.

Practice

Like a good deal of first aid, it isn't what you know that saves lives; it's what you do. Rescue breathing and CPR are skills, and skills need to be practised if they are to remain effective. Keep your resuscitation skills up to date and organise 'top up sessions' using the practice mannequins.

...'Keep your resuscitation skills up to date'...

Chapter 23
Moving Casualties

When deciding how and whether to evacuate or even move a casualty there are a number of important considerations:

1. Is it necessary to move the casualty at all?
2. What are the nature of the injuries?
3. What resources are available?
4. How far does the casualty have to be transported?
5. Over what sort of terrain?

Guidelines

The following guidelines may help:

- Don't move the casualty without good reason
- Unless in imminent danger - assess casualty first
- Stop bleeding and immobilise fractures before moving
- Use most efficient method time allows
- Plan movement
- Leadership / teamwork
- Communication - with casualty - with team
- Keep monitoring casualty
- Involve the casualty as much as possible
- Be gentle but firm

To Move or Not to Move

If the emergency services can get to and stabilise the casualty with their specialist equipment and skills, there may be no point moving the casualty at all.

...'Don't move the casualty without good reason'...

Possible reasons for moving a casualty are:

Immediate Danger

The casualty is in immediate danger, e.g. of being washed away or sliding down a slippery bank. This is the one case in which it may be necessary to move a casualty before he has been examined.

Shelter from the Elements

Except on remote rivers where the nearest road is some way off, or dense forest would make a helicopter evacuation dangerous, this is the most likely reason for moving a casualty. If a casualty's injuries have been treated and his condition is stable the greatest threat is posed by the onset of hypothermia. Therefore moving a casualty a short distance to a sheltered, comfortable spot is well worth the effort.

In a hot climate we may need to move a casualty to a cool shady spot.

Casualty Assessment

Apart from the need to identify and treat injuries, a proper casualty examination will enable rescuers to make decisions about how to move the casualty. This is because we can divide serious injuries into two types:

1. Injuries which require urgent surgical intervention if the casualty is to survive. Speed of evacuation is the priority.
2. Injuries which have been stabilised or are by their nature stable but which could deteriorate if the casualty is badly handled. Careful casualty handling is the priority.

The question is whether we "stay and play, or load and go"?

Speed

Injuries that would come into this category include:

- Serious head injuries
- Internal injuries
- Chest injuries where the lung or lungs are damaged
- Any injuries where the casualty is going deeper into shock

Care

Injuries that would come into this category include:

- Spinal injuries (back), (suspected or diagnosed)
- Spinal injuries (neck), (suspected or diagnosed)
- Any major fracture, such as a pelvis or femur, including those where shock is present but not worsening

Stabilising the Casualty

Any treatment that stops bleeding, prevents further damage occurring and relieves pain should be carried out before moving a casualty. The aim is to stabilise the casualty's condition so that he doesn't continue to deteriorate during transport.

Moving the Casualty

The detail of how the casualty is moved will be dictated by the nature and location of the injuries, the number of rescuers available and the type of terrain. If the injury is to the spine, only a rigid stretcher is appropriate, even though this will entail waiting for one to arrive, or spending some time manufacturing one. If the injury does not involve the casualty's legs and speed is of the essence, it may be best if he walks out.

Plan Movement

Whoever is going to coordinate moving a casualty should take time out to plan while the casualty is being stabilised. This is true even if the distance involved is only a few metres. In the case of a full evacuation, rescuers should be delegated to scout and mark a route.

Leadership/Teamwork

When evacuating an injured person, it is essential that there is a plan and that every one knows what it is. Once again, everyone must know:

1. Who their boss is.
2. What their job is.

This is definitely a situation where most people, not least the patient, will be reassured by a decisive/formal leadership style.

If a long stretcher carry is necessary, the leader must not allow any of the rescuers to perform heroics. If there are enough rescuers, the people performing the carry should change over frequently; alternatively the team should rest frequently.

Communication

Teamwork is only possible if the task is clearly understood and timing is coordinated. Instructions to other members of the team should be clear and concise. Team members should acknowledge that they have understood **or** make it clear that they have not understood.

It is equally important to communicate with the casualty. Apart from simply reassuring him and letting him know what is going on, it offers him the opportunity to be of assistance or provide valuable feedback.

Monitoring

Whoever first established a rapport with the victim should stay at the victim's head and monitor his progress throughout the evacuation. With seriously injured people, vital signs should be monitored every five minutes. This is not as much of a nuisance as it sounds as the rescuers carrying the stretcher will need to rest frequently. None the less, such frequent monitoring may not be practical. The first aider may have to settle for frequently monitoring the airway and recording the other signs regularly, but at greater intervals, perhaps every ten or fifteen minutes.

Involve the Casualty

Casualties should be encouraged to do as much of the moving as possible for themselves. Why risk a back strain lifting a casualty onto a stretcher when he can get on it himself? Another reason is that the casualty can feel which is the least painful way to move.

A combination approach is often best. The first aider may say to the casualty: "If I support your injured leg, do you think you can get yourself onto the stretcher?"

Handling

When handling the casualty the rescuers must be gentle but firm. The casualty will not be best pleased if he is dropped because someone didn't get a good grip, even if it was because they were worried it might hurt him. Equally, his sense of well being will not be enhanced if he believes himself to be at the mercy of a bunch of clumsy sadists.

Carrying Techniques

All of the following techniques could result in a back injury to the rescuer if they are carried out incorrectly or inappropriately. Anyone with a history of back injuries should inform the leader so that he can be delegated to perform an equally important task that does not involve lifting. As a general rule, single person carries should only be attempted on casualties that are lighter than the rescuer. All lifts must be coordinated and the coordinator must ensure that everyone has bent knees and a straight back before giving the order to lift. (Fig. 23.8).

Walking Wounded

Depending on the nature of the injuries it may be possible for casualties to walk. It is worth asking casualties if they think they can walk. Injured people will often fall prey to 'victim mentality' and just do as they are told. It may not occur to them to offer to walk. A rescuer can be placed on either side of a victim, providing or ready to provide support if necessary.

Dragging

If a rescuer or even a couple of rescuers need to move a heavy casualty, this may be their only option. That said, dragging a person carefully will cause him far less pain and damage than carrying him badly. Providing the ground is not too rough it supports the casualty and keeps the spine straight.

Fig. 23.1 One person drag. Note how the neck is supported.

One Person Drag

The rescuer gets down on hands and knees with his knees either side of the casualty. The victim clasps his hands around the back of the rescuer's neck and the rescuer crawls forward, dragging the casualty with him. If the casualty is unable to hold on, the rescuer will need to tie his hands together. (Fig. 23.1).

If neck injuries are suspected the rescuer will have to support the back of the neck/head as best he can with one hand.

Three Person Drag

One rescuer supports and protects the neck. The other two grab a buoyancy aid, *(PFD)*, shoulder strap each and pull evenly.

Seat Carries

These are particularly useful with conscious casualties who have lower limb injuries.

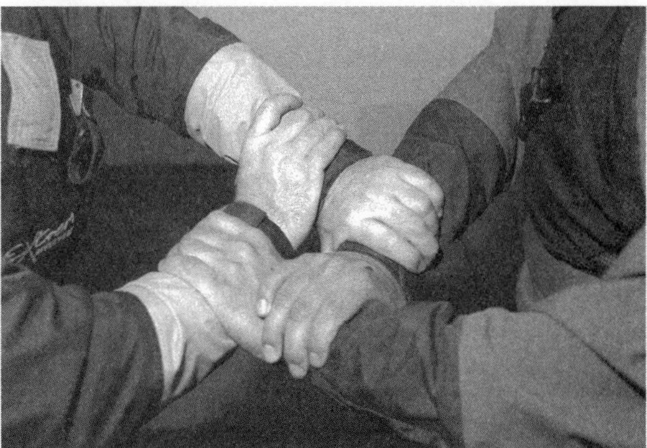

Fig. 23.2 Four handed seat.
Photos: Bob Timms

Four Hand Seat

Two rescuers grip each others hands as shown in fig. 23.2 to make a seat. The casualty sits on the seat with an arm over each of the rescuers' shoulders. Quick, simple, and suitable for a short carry.

Bosun's Chair

A pole or paddle is supported by nylon tape slings supported over two rescuers' shoulders. This provides a sturdy seat leaving the rescuer's hands free to support the casualty. (Fig. 23.3). A better choice if longer distances are involved.

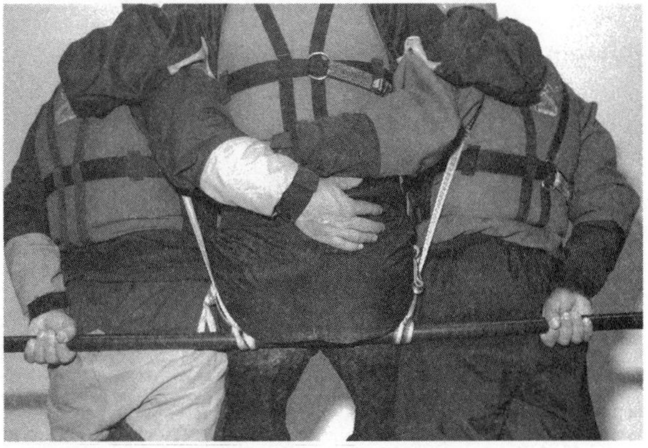

Fig. 23.3 Bosun's chair.

Fireman's Lift

The fireman's lift is not particularly comfortable for the victim but is very effective. It is a good choice if the casualty needs to be moved urgently over

Fig. 23.4 Fireman's lift, note the squat and straight back for the lift.

terrain where dragging is not feasible or the injuries do not require careful handling. (Fig 23.4)

Split Rope Carries

First of all, the rope used must be coiled using a method that mountaineers call a 'classic' coil. A full arms span length of rope is measured and coiled. The action is repeated until all the rope is coiled. The coil is then tied off as shown in fig. 23.5. The size of coil thus formed is perfect for a single person carry. For a double person carry the coils are longer. The rope will have to be padded for the casualty's comfort.

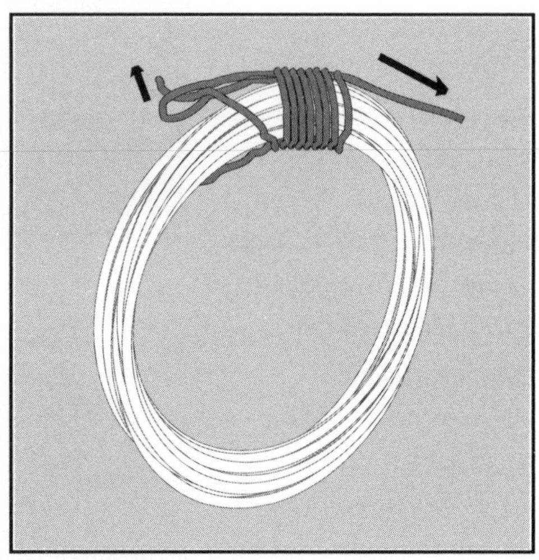

Fig. 23.5 Mountaineer's coil.

Single Person Carry

The coils of rope are split into two and the casualty puts one leg through each of the two sets of coils. The rescuer then carries the casualty using the coils as if they were rucksack straps. (Fig. 23.6).

Two Person Carry

The coils are once again split into two. This time, each of the two rescuers wears one set of coils over one shoulder. The casualty is then carried as if he were sitting on a swing. (Fig. 23.7).

Fig. 23.6 Single person carry.

Fig. 23.7 Two person carry. Photos: Bob Timms

Litters

Litters are **quick** and **simple** to make but do not provide the same splinting effect as a rigid stretcher. They would be ideal for a hypothermia victim but useless for a victim with spinal injuries or a broken femur. Camping mats or buoyancy aids should then be used to pad and insulate the litter.

Biwi Bag Litter

Items required to make this litter:

- One 2x1 metre polythene bivouac bag
- Six half fist sized pebbles
- Six short pieces of cord

The pebbles are inserted into the bag so that there is one in each corner and one half way down each side of the bag. The pebbles are given a couple of twists so that the nearby polythene is wrapped around them. The string is used to tie the bag so that the pebbles remain in place, forming a kind of handle. (Fig. 23.8).

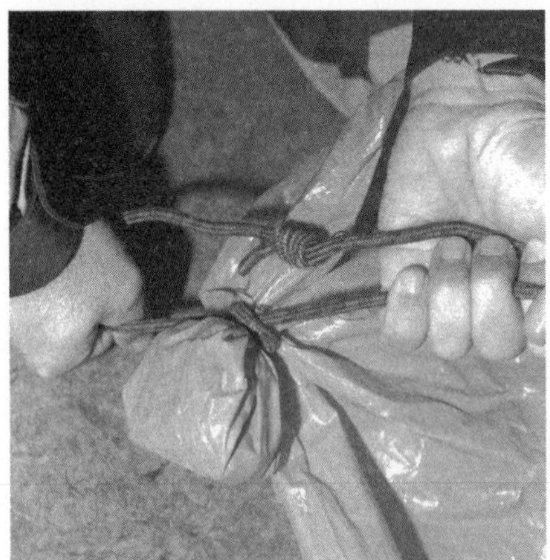

Fig. 23.8 Bivvi bag litter. Note the correct lifting technique.

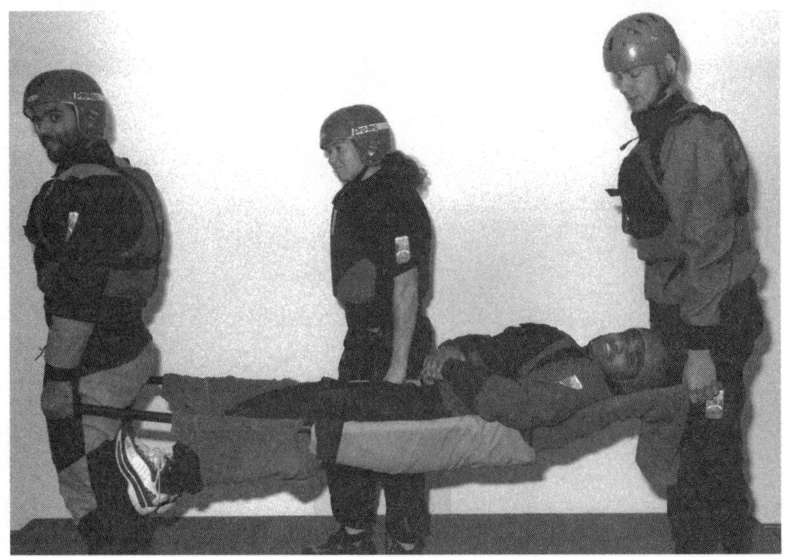

Fig. 23.9 Pole and jacket litter.

Pole and Jacket Litter

Items required to make this litter:

- Two poles (The two halves of a sectioned open canoe pole are ideal)
- Four or five jackets or cagoules

The arms of the jackets are turned inside out so that they are inside the jacket and the poles fed through them. (Fig. 23.9)

Rigid Stretchers

The best rigid stretchers are those that are purpose made. However it is possible to make a rigid stretcher by constructing a framework of poles using 'square lashings' to hold the structure together.

If carrying a casualty any distance on a stretcher, it is important to follow these guidelines:

1. Ensure that the casualty is well padded and insulated.
2. Ensure that the casualty is securely fastened to the stretcher with a series of straps. The casualty should be so well secured that, if he were to vomit, it would be possible to protect his airway by turning the stretcher on its side without the casualty falling out of the stretcher. (Fig. 23.10).
3. Monitor the casualty at all times.

Unconscious Casualties

When paramedics prepare to evacuate an unconscious casualty, they may decide to intubate the patient, i.e. protect the casualty's airway by inserting a tube down it. This option is not available to first aiders who have not been specifically trained to do this.

The other approach is to load the casualty onto the stretcher in the Safe Airway Position, (SAP). Plenty of padding, (air bags can be useful here), and strapping will have to be used to keep the casualty securely in position.

Spinal Injuries

If spinal injuries are suspected it is best not to move the casualty at all if possible. However, if hazards or the presence of other, life threatening injuries dictate that movement is necessary, rescuers should not hesitate.

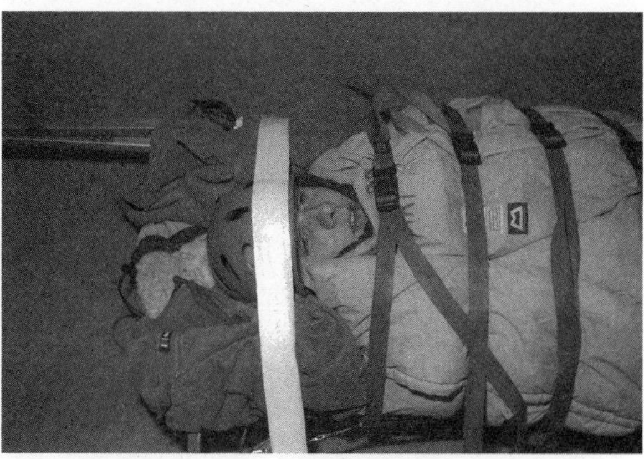

Fig. 23.10 A well secured casualty.

When moving a person with suspected spinal injuries the aim is

Fig. 23.11 Spinal log roll.
Photos: Bob Timms

to keep the whole of the spine, including the neck in a straight line. Bending or twisting must be avoided. Tilting the head far enough back to open an airway should not do any further harm provided care is taken to avoid any sideways movement or twisting. The jaw thrust is a better option for opening the airway in this situation. If possible a collar should be used to protect the casualty's neck. If not his head should be immobilised using plenty of padding.

A casualty with spinal injuries is normally left lying on his back. However, if the casualty is unconscious and there isn't the means to intubate him, he will have to be placed in a slightly modified Safe Airway Position. As much padding as possible is used to prop the casualty up in such a way that his spine is kept in as straight a line as possible.

Spinal Log Roll

This is a useful technique if a casualty needs to be turned over, to inspect or treat other injuries.

1. The first aider, who will coordinate the roll, holds the casualty's head firmly between his hands.
2. As many people as possible kneel down to one side of the casualty. They then lean across the casualty and grab a hold of his clothing.
3. On the first aider's instruction every one pulls steadily on the casualty so that he rolls over towards them. (Fig. 23.11).

Table of Knees

This is a good technique for loading a person with suspected spinal injuries onto a stretcher.

1. With the casualty on his back the first aider holds the casualty's head.
2. Three or four rescuers, (group A), kneel along side the casualty with one knee up and one knee down. (Note that rescuers have the same knee up).

Top left: *Huw Evans just before his paddles snapped on the first drop.*
Top right: *Belayed rescuer connects a line to his vertically pinned boat, (second drop).*
Bottom: *2:1 Pig rig being used to haul the boat out. Swallow Falls, River Llugwy, N. Wales.*
Photos: Ray Goodwin

3. Three or four other rescuers kneel along side the victim on the opposite side, (group B).
4. All the rescuers feed their hands under the natural hollows of the casualty's body or get hold of his clothing. It is best if rescuers who are on the same side alternate hands, this makes it easier to coordinate the lift as one can feel when the people on either side are starting to lift.
5. On the first aider's instruction the casualty is lifted and rested on the 'table of knees' formed by group A. (Fig. 23.12).
6. Group B get out of the way while the stretcher is placed beside the victim.
7. Group B get as close to the victim as possible and reach across the stretcher to hold the casualty.
8. On the first aider's instruction the casualty is lowered onto the stretcher.

Lower Leg Injuries

With upper limb injuries, the casualty will nearly always hold the injured limb in the position of most comfort. With lower limb injuries the casualty may not be able to do this unaided. A first aider may need to straighten an injured leg to reduce pain and prevent further injury or to make it physically possible to load the casualty onto a stretcher.

Fig. 23.12 Table of knees.
Photo: Bob Timms

The first aider will need to get a firm hold and apply traction whilst straightening the limb into it's anatomically normal position. One of the easiest ways to splint a leg is to strap it to the good leg. However, if the casualty is unconscious it will make it easier to load the casualty onto the stretcher in the SAP if the leg is splinted and kept separate from the other leg.

Top: The first paddler has the perfect line but the second is held in a deep recirculating stopper from which he could not escape un-aided. River Golo, Corsica.
Photos: Chris Sladden
Bottom: Bank inspection on the Zambezi River, Zimbabwe.
Photo: Alan Fox/Palm

Chapter 24
Post Traumatic Stress

In recent years there has been a growing acceptance that members of emergency services who come face to face with horrific accidents can become **overwhelmed** by the psychological stresses involved. If suitable steps are not taken to help these people deal with these stresses a condition that is now known as Post Traumatic Stress Disorder can develop.

What is not so well recognised is the fact that anyone involved in an accident can find themselves in this position. This includes:

- Victims
- Rescuers, (whether members of the party or outsiders)
- Anyone who witnessed the accident or its aftermath

...' Post Traumatic Stress Disorder can only occur following a traumatic event. Most survivors, although initially affected, do not develop PTSD.'...

Sources of Stress

The sources of the stresses involved can be divided into those caused by the accident itself and those that are hidden.

Accident Stresses

These can be caused by a number or combination of factors:

- The sights, sound or smells associated with the accident
- The fact that the casualty may die
- The sheer physical effort required
- A feeling of helplessness induced by the enormity of the task or the inadequacy of the resources
- Enforced periods of inactivity such as when waiting for the first aider to do his bit or awaiting the arrival of the emergency services

Hidden Stresses

These can range enormously, from the fact that the rescuer is already burdened with sufficient stresses from his everyday life, to his perceptions as to what can and can't be reasonably achieved by the rescuers. Possibilities are:

- Personal, financial or legal problems at home
- Pressures of work
- The rescuer being already weakened by illness or fatigue
- Unrealistic optimism on the possibility of a successful outcome

- A perception that the rescuer failed because he was not up to the task
- A perception that the rescue failed because other members of the team were not up to the task

Normal Reactions

Everyone who has to deal with, or is the victim of a bad accident will react to the stresses of the situation. These reactions are normal and should be recognised as such. Recognising and accepting these reactions as normal is an important part of dealing with the aftermath of a traumatic situation.

Immediate Reactions

These can be divided into emotional reactions, thinking (cognitive) difficulties and physical (physiological) signs and symptoms.

Emotional Reactions

These may include all or any of the following:

- Anxiety
- Apprehension
- Hopelessness and despair
- Doubting one's own abilities

Many people also experience 'disassociation'. This is a defence mechanism where people block out their emotions and only allows the logical part of their brain to surface. It is a useful defensive tactic that many professional rescuers consciously develop.

Disassociation cannot be kept up indefinitely. As soon as the emergency is dealt with, emotions must be allowed to run their course.

Thinking Difficulties

Typical amongst these would be difficulty making decisions, difficulty concentrating and forgetting where one has just put something.

Physical Signs and Symptoms

The physical signs and symptoms usually fade away within a day or two but the underlying emotional cause cannot be ignored. The following are often reported:

- A pounding sensation in the heart
- Nausea
- Headaches
- Muscles trembling
- Sweating profusely

- Cramps
- Chills
- Muffled hearing
- TATT, (Tired All The Time)

Delayed Reactions

Delayed reactions may occur a few hours or many years after a traumatic event. Once again this is perfectly normal and most people are able to work through these reactions. Reactions may be inward, that is suffered by the individual, or outward, that is directed at other people.

Inward

Inward reactions may include:

- Feelings of guilt
- Apathy
- Depression
- Nightmares
- Insomnia
- Headache
- Loss of appetite
- Nausea

Outward

Outward reactions may include:

- Irritability
- A tendency to 'flare up' easily
- Anger

Abnormal Reactions

Abnormal reactions can take various forms, ranging from an immediate and complete mental breakdown, the signs of which are usually clear for all to see, to PTSD which can easily go undiagnosed. Superficially the victim may appear to be coping.

Post Traumatic Stress Disorder

If an individual is unprepared, unsupported and unable to work through the normal reactions to traumatic stress PTSD may develop.

Diagnosis

The table in fig. 24.1 shows the criteria that are most widely used for the diagnosis of PTSD. These were developed by the American Psychiatric Association and are from their Diagnostic and Statistical Manual, (DSM-IV).

A. Exposure to a traumatic event in which both the following were present:

i. The person experienced, witnessed or was confronted with an event(s) that involved actual or threatened death, serious injury or a threat to physical integrity.
ii. The person's response involved intense fear, helplessness or horror.

B. The event is persistently experienced in one (or more) of the following ways:

i. Recurrent and intrusive distressing recollections of the event, including images, thoughts or perceptions. Note: In young children, repetitive play may occur in which themes or aspects of the trauma are expressed.
ii. Recurrent distressing dreams of the event. Note: In children, there may be frightening dreams without recognisable content.
iii. Acting or feeling as if the traumatic event were recurring (includes a sense of reliving the experience, illusions, hallucinations and dissociative flashback episodes, including those that occur on awakening or when intoxicated). Note: In young children, trauma-specific re-enactment may occur.
iv. Intense psychological distress at exposure to internal or external cues that symbolise or resemble an aspect of the traumatic event.
v. Physiological reactivity on exposure to internal or external cues that symbolise or resemble an aspect of the traumatic event.

C. Persistent avoidance of stimuli associated with the trauma and numbing of general responsiveness (not present before) as indicated by three (or more) of the following:

i. Efforts to avoid thoughts, feelings or conversations associated with the trauma.
ii. Efforts to avoid activities, places or people that arouse recollections of the trauma.
iii. Inability to recall an important aspect of the trauma.
iv. Markedly diminished interest in participation in significant activities.
v. Feeling of detachment or estrangement from others.
vi. Restricted range of affection (e.g. unable to have loving feelings).
vii. Sense of foreshortened future (e.g. does not expect to have a career, marriage, children or normal life span).

D. Persistent symptoms of increased arousal (not present before the trauma), as indicated by two (or more) of the following:

i. Difficulty in falling or staying asleep.
ii. Irritability or outbursts of anger.
iii. Difficulty in concentrating.
iv. Hypervigilance.
v. Exaggerated startle response.

E. Duration of the disturbance is more than one month.

F. The disturbance causes clinically significant distress or impairment in social, occupational or other important aspects of function.

Fig. 24.1 DSM-1V diagnostic criteria for post traumatic stress.

The criteria that must be met are split into the following areas:

Exposure to an Abnormally Stressful Situation

It is important to realise that one doesn't have to be the victim of an accident to be a victim of PTSD.

Re-experiencing Symptoms

These are sometimes known as intrusive symptoms. The person experiencing them is unable to control when, where or in what form he is forced to relive the experience.

Avoidance Symptoms

It is usually the victim's family and friends who are more aware of and likely to complain about these.

Increased Arousal

The soldier's illustration of a startle response is the person who dives for cover when a car backfires. Another form of increased arousal is that the victim's family complain of how irritable the victim has become.

Duration

As mentioned earlier, most people show some stress related symptoms at some time after a traumatic incident. For PTSD to be diagnosed these symptoms have to persist for over a month.

Some Degree of Disability

It is quite possible for someone to exhibit many of the symptoms and still continue to function as before. The thinking is that if there is no loss of function or disability then the person cannot be thought of as having a serious psychological disorder.

Treatment

Once PTSD is diagnosed, treatment becomes the province of specialists. The role of friends, team members, leaders and family is at the preventative stage.

Prevention

Preventing what is a perfectly normal reaction to a traumatic situation from **developing into** Post Traumatic Stress Disorder can be approached in two phases:

1. Preparation that can take place before a traumatic accident occurs.
2. Team strategies can be developed for supporting each other in the immediate aftermath of such an event.

Preparation

This can take the form of appropriate training and mental preparation.

Training

Some of the most crippling symptoms that rescuers experience are those of helplessness and inadequacy if they are unable to help in a given situation. This is often followed by a sense of guilt.

If we train and maintain our paddling, safety and rescue, and first aid skills, we are better prepared in a number of ways:

1. We are better able to offer assistance in the event of a traumatic accident.
2. We will, if the training is good, have a more realistic appreciation of what is and isn't possible.

We are therefore less likely to blame ourselves if intervention is not successful or not possible.

Mental Preparation

We need to prepare ourselves for the possibility that we may have to deal with a traumatic event in the future. We need to think about, discuss with friends and in groups at training sessions the possibility that we may have to face up to traumatic situations.

Topics that might be considered are:

1. The fact that accidents do happen. That even if we conform to accepted safe practice we are involved in a risk sport.
2. The possibility that even if we are well trained and equipped, a rescue situation may develop that is beyond our resources to deal with.
2. The fact that even if a first aider does everything that is possible, people might still die.
3. The fact that if a surgeon has no access to an operating theatre, or a paramedic to specialist equipment, they can do little more than a first aider can.
4. The possibility that we may see a friend, loved one or client we are responsible for who is badly injured or dead.

The very fact that these possibilities have been acknowledged and explored will lessen their impact should we be unfortunate enough to be faced with such situations.

Team Strategies

There are a number of steps that we can take as a group of paddlers, to lessen the impact of, and work through, traumatic stress.

Supportive Environment

It is important to develop a team approach to confronting problems. We need to foster an atmosphere where team members are able to discuss their emotions.

In other words we need to drop this macho, 'I don't like to talk about it' stuff and admit that we are only human.

Each member of the team should have the well being of the rest of the team as their main priority.

During the Trauma

Whilst we are actually dealing with an accident there are some preventative steps that we can take if we have thought about the matter before hand.

The Leader

The leader can help protect everyone concerned in a number of ways. By standing back from the incident and keeping the whole picture in view the leader will be able to organise the rescue more efficiently. This will lessen the effect of traumatic stress in three ways:

1. The incident will be dealt with more quickly which will benefit both the victims and the rescuers.
2. The leader can ensure that everyone has a job to do. This will help prevent feelings of helplessness and inadequacy.
3. The leader will be able to create time to keep every one informed which will also help with feelings of helplessness.

Team Members

Team members need to accept the fact that they may not be the best person to deal with a particular situation. For example it may be that the person who has been delegated to administer first aid is too emotionally involved with the accident victim. The rescuer concerned should ask the leader to delegate the first aid to someone else and be given another, equally vital job.

If a supportive atmosphere has been cultivated, the rest of the team will not see this as a weakness but as a show of strength of character. It takes strength to admit that you are not the best person for the job. The easy option would be to muddle on and hope for the best.

The Victim

The psychological well being of the victim is dealt with in the chapter on first aid.

Debriefing

Everyone involved in a traumatic experience should realise that 'stress overload' is almost inevitable if the accumulated emotions are not shared with others. This can be approached as individuals; it only takes someone who is a sympathetic listener to help an individual work through the emotions involved.

Full time rescue teams are increasingly developing more structured approaches to 'psychological debriefing', which we would do well to adopt in the event of a traumatic accident. A typical approach would be as follows:

Exercise

Within twenty four hours the whole team takes part in some form of strenuous physical exercise. This helps flush out various fatigue and stress related poisons that can build up in our bodies. It also relaxes the muscles and in itself provides a form of emotional outlet.

Emotional Debrief

Within one to three days, the whole team takes part in a group debrief. This is not a technical debrief. Everyone who was present at the traumatic event should take the opportunity to describe their feelings and emotional reactions to the event. Everyone present should be encouraged to share their emotions honestly and without embarrassment in a supportive and non judgmental atmosphere.

The debrief should take place without alcohol being consumed as mind altering drugs of any kind will lessen the effectiveness of the session.

After these two sessions everyone involved should eat and rest well.

Technical Debrief

Only after the emotional and physical well being of the team has been assured should any technical debrief take place. After a period of ten to fourteen days has elapsed, it is possible to analyse an incident and learn from the inevitable mistakes without the people involved feeling emotional and defensive.

Dealing with the Press

The press can become a major source of stress in themselves. Most large organisations have a laid down procedure which they adopt in the event of a serious incident. The following steps could be adopted by any group of people:

1. Appoint a 'Press Officer'.
2. Prepare a 'Press Release'.

The Press Officer

Ideally this will be someone who was not directly involved in the incident. That way the person concerned only has to deal with the stress of dealing with the press. This will make it easier for him to think clearly and calmly.

Another advantage is that if the 'Press Officer' is asked for the gory details that are not included in the prepared statement, he can in all honesty reply that he doesn't know and cannot give any further details at this time.

The Press Release

If reporters are told nothing at all, they will simply make something up and attribute it to 'local sources'. Worse still, they may harass people who were involved in the incident or their relatives.

It is far better to give them something to be going on with. The advantage of issuing a press release is that the bare facts of the situation can be outlined in black and white. This effectively denies the less responsible members of the media the opportunity to write works of fiction.

Seeking Professional Help

If an incident has been particularly traumatic, it may well be worth considering the use of professional counsellors to help with group and individual debriefs. Families, friends and team members can help individuals by simply being available and good listeners.

However, if an individual's reactions go beyond what is normal or show signs of developing into Post Traumatic Stress Disorder it is essential that he seeks professional help.

PART

ACCESS AND RECOVERY

IV

Chapter 25
Principles of Recovery

Recovery is about retrieving equipment.

Principle of Least Risk

"Rescuers should not take unnecessary or unjustified risks."

Time is less of an issue in recovery situations and the only lives at risk are those of the people attempting the recovery. The strategy used should be the least risky rather than the quickest.

Principle of Clear Communication

"Misunderstandings must be avoided at all costs."

Signals, instructions and briefings must be simple, clear and concise. Do not make assumptions; repeat signals to confirm understanding.

If necessary, question to check understanding.

Do a 'dry run' to check that everyone **really** understands.

Principle of Using Natural Forces

"Gravity and water rule!"

Try to work with these forces rather than against them whenever possible.

Principle of Diminishing Returns

"Use as little mechanical advantage as you can get away with."

With each extra pulley added to a pulley system, the percentage of force gained that is lost to friction increases, as does the time it takes to set it up and operate it.

Chapter 26
Specialist Equipment

As discussed earlier in the book, the vast majority of rescue and kayak recovery situations can be easily dealt with if each member of the team carries a throw bag, a knife, a 2.4 metre (8 foot) sling and two karabiners. However, there are a number of situations in which more specialist equipment may be required:

1. The forces exerted on a broached raft or open canoe can be so great that pulleys are required to gain sufficient mechanical advantage.
2. Kayakers paddling in very small groups may need to employ mechanical advantage to make up for lack of numbers.
3. In steep sided gorges, or other places where access may be only possible from above, the ropes we use for throw lines are totally inadequate.

Groups covered by situations 1 and 2 should consider carrying the following additional equipment:

- Two pulleys
- A **few** extra screwgate karabiners, (one per person in a small group and one between two people in a large group)
- Three 'prussik loops' or specialist rope jamming/camming devices
- Two or more lengths of nylon tape
- A 45 metre (150 foot) 'static' caving or canyoning rope

It is best to have more than one set of specialist equipment between the team in case the boat carrying the gear is the one that gets into trouble.

In situations where difficult vertical access problems are envisaged, the team should also consider adding:

- A 45 metre (150 foot) 'dynamic' climbing rope
- A climbing or caving harness
- A 'figure of eight' descender

Too much equipment can become a hazard in itself, weighing down our boats and getting in the way. Unlike rescue teams, paddlers running white water need to adopt a minimalist approach.

Static versus Dynamic Ropes

There are two different types of rope designed for different purposes.

Static Ropes

Static ropes are designed for use in situations where the loads they will bear are increased slowly and are more or less constant. They are constructed in such a way that there is very little stretch. This makes them far more suitable for hauling, lowering and tensioning than dynamic ropes.

Throw lines

All throw line ropes are static, however, due to the fact that they are required to float they are generally made out of polypropylene. This is a material that is not as strong as other static ropes and has the disadvantages of a low melting point and a tendency to abrade easily. For anything that involves rescuers being suspended over a big drop they are unsuitable. Kevlar or spectra cored ropes are as strong as caving ropes, but still have the disadvantage of a polypropylene sheath with it's low melting point.

If throw lines are used in a dire emergency for such purposes it is worth wetting the ropes as a precautionary measure.

Caving ropes sink in water, making them unsuitable for many water based situations.

Caving or Mountain Rescue Ropes

These are designed expressly for abseiling, (*rappelling*), lowering and hoisting. They are stronger, more abrasion resistant and heat resistant than polypropylene floating ropes. They are therefore the rope of choice in many recovery or vertical access situations. These ropes vary in size from 9-12 mm. (Fig. 26.1).

Canyoning Ropes

A recent development is the arrival on the scene of ropes specifically designed for the activity of 'canyoning'. This is the descent of mountain streams by abseiling and climbing down waterfalls, stream beds and gorges. These ropes are usually 9.5 mm in diameter and combine all the advantages of caving ropes with the ability to float. **This combination of qualities makes canyoning ropes ideal for recovery and vertical access in a water environment.**

Unfortunately these ropes are too stiff for use as throw lines.

Dynamic Ropes

These are nylon ropes that are designed for use by rock climbers and mountaineers. They are designed for situations in which a rope can be suddenly shock loaded as would happen if a climber fell some distance before the rope came tight. The rope is constructed in such a way that it stretches and absorbs energy. This means that much of the energy created by a falling climber is absorbed by the rope, rather than putting a massive and sudden load on the climber and the anchors that the rope is tied off to. A dynamic rope can stretch up to a third of its original length before it would break.

These qualities make dynamic ropes the first choice where a rope is being used as an additional safety back up, in a situation where a slip or a rope system failure could result in a serious fall. The fact that much energy has to be wasted taking up the stretch in the rope means that it is not particularly suitable for most recovery purposes.

These ropes also sink, which means that they are unsuitable for most white water rescue situations.

Full Weight Ropes

Full weight ropes are designed to be used as a single rope and are what should be used in most rescue and recovery situations. They come in a variety of diameters from 9.8 to 11 mm; 9.8 mm ropes are lighter, smaller and almost as strong as 11 mm ropes. Their disadvantages are that they are more expensive and wear out quicker than their heavier counterparts. Full weight ropes have the symbol I over I on them.

Half Ropes

Half ropes are 9 mm or less in diameter and have the symbol of I over 2. As the name implies they should only be used in pairs. Those with a rock climbing background will know how and where to use them. Those without should stick to full weight ropes.

	Polyprop. throw line	Spectra core throw line Poly. sheath	Canyon	Caving	Caving
Diameter	10 mm	10 mm	9.5 mm	10.5 mm	11 mm
Type	Static	Static	Static	Static	Static
Static Strength	1000 kg	1900 kg	1950 kg	2700 kg	3000 kg
Strength fig. 8 knot	??	??	??	1950 kg	2050 kg
Pros	cheap floats handles well non stretch	strong floats handles well non stretch	strong abrasion resistant non stretch	very strong abrasion resistant non stretch	very strong abrasion resistant non stretch
Cons	low melt point abrades easy	low melt point abrades easy	stiff	stiff sinks	stiff sinks

Fig. 26.1 Table of comparison of rope strengths and qualities.

Nylon Tapes

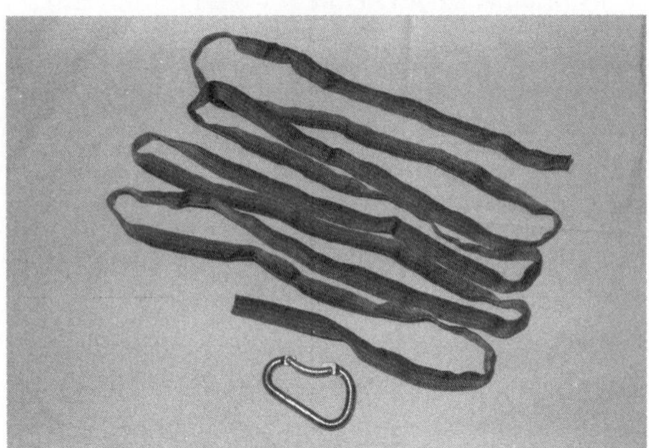

Fig. 26.2 5 metre nylon tape, 'webbing'.
Photos: Bob Timms

In addition to the 2.4 metre (8 foot) sewn sling discussed in Chapter 14 it is useful to have a selection of lengths of tubular nylon tape, '*webbing*'. These can be bought off the reel at any climbing shop. These can be cut in different lengths but for most purposes a couple of 5 metre (16 foot) lengths are most useful. Professional rescue teams use colour codes so that every member of the team knows how long a given colour of tape is. These are mostly used for linking a number of 'anchors' in order to create a strong point to attach a line to. (Fig. 26.2). The fact that these tapes are not 'pre-sewn' makes them slower to use but more versatile. The tape can be threaded through or passed around the anchor and then knotted to form a sling.

Knots for Tape

A simple overhand on the bight, (see Appendix B), is fast and easy to tie. This knot is strong but will allow the tape to creep about 4 cm under load; it is therefore essential to leave a long tail when tying the knot. If time isn't an issue the knot of choice is the tape knot, *'the water knot'*.

Like static ropes these items are not designed to absorb energy. If rescuers tie **directly** into a tape to protect themselves, they must do so in such a way that the tape is already in tension and the anchor or rescuer cannot be shock loaded. **A fall of only 1.2 metres, (4 feet), can snap a full weight static rope or tape.**

Prussik Loops

These are 1 to 1.5 metre, (three to four foot), lengths of 5 mm line tied with a 'Double Fisherman's' knot to form a sling. (Fig. 26.3). These prussik loops are wrapped around a rope in such a way that a combination of friction and a camming action grip a tensioned rope. This means that ropes or slings can be attached to a rope without the use of knots.

Larger and smaller diameters of line can be used but the following must be borne in mind:

1. Smaller diameter line grips better but is less strong and therefore could fail by breaking.
2. Larger diameter line is stronger but doesn't grip well and therefore could fail by slipping.

In certain conditions, such as where ropes are wet or icy, it is worth putting in an extra wrap or two more than usual, to compensate for the lack of friction.

Prussik knots should never be left unattended unless the rope they are securing is tied off with a knot or hitch as a safety back up.

'Prussik' Knots

There are a large number of different 'prussik' knots of which I will describe three. They have different characteristics which between them cover every situation we are likely to use them in.

The Three Wrap Prussik

This is the most reliable form of 'prussik' in that it cannot be released once it has gripped the rope unless it is slackened off. This makes it most suitable for use wherever it is essential that the knot doesn't release once it is under load. (See Fig. 26.3)

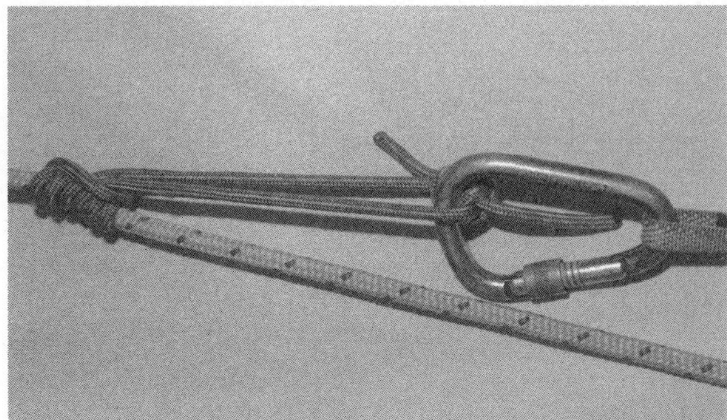

Fig. 26.3 Three wrap prussik knot.

The French Prussik

This knot grips the knot well when it is under tension and releases quickly and easily when it is not. It can be released even when it is under tension if pressure is applied on the end of

Fig. 26.4 French prussik, 'auto-block'.

the knot furthest from the anchor and pulling towards the anchor. (This is very useful in certain applications). The French prussik should not be used where it might be accidentally released, for example where a rope runs over an edge.

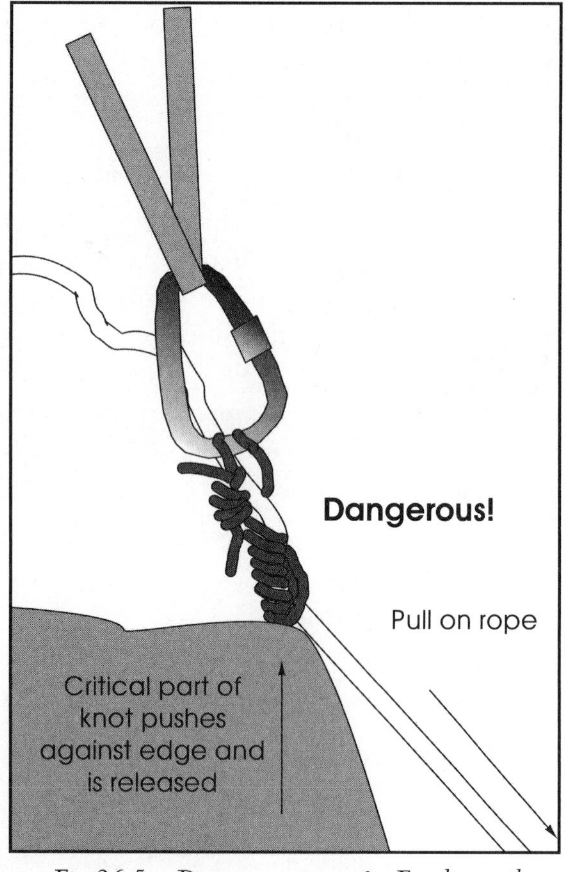

Fig. 26.5 Dangerous misuse of a French prussik.

The Klemheist Knot

The Klemheist is useful in that it cannot be released accidentally but frees off easier than a Prussik. It is also useful in that a tape sling can be used instead of prussik loops. (Fig. 26.6)

Mechanical Devices

There are a host of mechanical jamming and camming devices available to perform the same tasks as prussik loops. The problem is that they are all designed for fairly specific situations, uses and rope diameters. If you do use these, be sure to check that the use you are putting them to falls within the manufacturers' design specifications.

Prussik loops are lighter, cheaper and more versatile. For most recreational paddlers carrying a minimum of specialist equipment they are a far better bet.

Pulleys

Although it is possible to set up a pulley system using karabiners instead of pulleys, much of the mechanical advantage gained is lost because of the increased friction. Pulleys developed for industrial uses are too heavy and those designed for yachting are not designed to be used in rescue situations. The pulleys that are best suited for white water rescue or recovery are designed for caving or mountain rescue and made in aluminium, (*aluminum*).

Size

For most purposes 25 mm, (one inch) lightweight caving pulleys are fine. However, in situations where the pulley is going to bear high loads or where failure would be disastrous, it is better to use 50 mm (two inch) rescue pulleys. The latter are stronger, and because of the increased radius of the pulley, less prone to twisting which can in certain circumstances damage the rope.

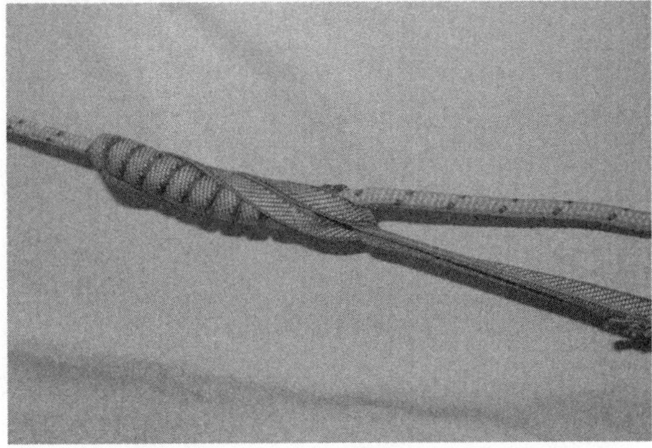

Fig. 26.6 Klemheist knot.

Swing or Fixed Cheek

Most pulleys designed for rescue and recovery purposes are swing cheeked, (fig. 26.7). This allows pulleys to be quickly clipped on to a line at any point, without the need to thread the whole length of the line through the pulley as would be the case with a fixed cheek pulley.

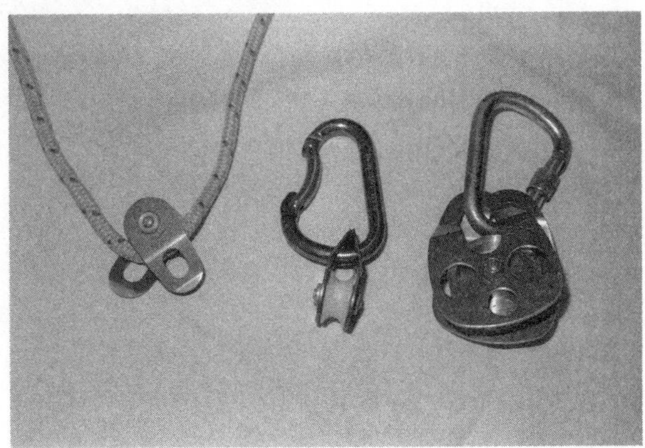

Fig. 26.7 Pulleys.

Karabiners

Most karabiners have a rating of between 2,200 and 2,500 kg. However, if they are loaded sideways instead of lengthways, their strength is reduced to about 500 kg.

This is also the case if the gate is open when they come under load. Therefore for any activity involving people suspended over drops it is best to use screwgate karabiners.

Chapter 27
Rope Dynamics

An understanding of what forces are involved when we load ropes and other items of equipment is essential if we are to work efficiently and avoid disasters. The various items of climbing, caving or rescue equipment we might use are manufactured to extremely high standards, and in Europe are covered by PPE (Personal Protective Equipment) laws. When we link items together they form a chain; these links in the chain are designed to be of similar strengths. Weak links in the chain usually occur through a poor understanding of the dynamics involved and a subsequent misuse of equipment.

Due to the nature of the topic being covered, it is essential that the reader consults the diagrams closely when reading this chapter.

Ropes

The difference between static and dynamic ropes has already been explained. Rope failures are rare.

Fig. 27.1 Rope damage on an edge. Photo: Bob Timms

Edges

Investigations into rope failures in both climbing and caving situations show that the most common cause is when ropes that are under tension rub on a sharp or angular edge, (fig. 27.1). The ideal is to set up the rope system so that the rope doesn't run over an edge in the first place. If this is not possible then one of the following methods can be used to protect the rope:

- Pad the rope
- Pad the edge
- Improvise a roller
- Use a pulley to change the direction in which the rope travels

Pad the Rope

A rope that is not being hoisted or lowered can still move enough to damage the rope. However, if the rope is limited in its movement it may be easier to pad the rope than the edge. Professional rescue teams carry 'rope protectors' made of strips of heavy duty material.

A simple and effective alternative is to protect the rope by wrapping a few layers of repair tape around the area that needs protecting.

Fig 27.2 Padding an edge with spare clothing.

Edge Padding

A spare article of clothing, (preferably a cheap one as it is going to get trashed), or a dry bag, can be draped over the offending edge and tied in place using any old pieces of rope. (Fig. 27.2).

Rescue teams carry 'edge protectors' which can be made cheaply by using old carpet squares or short sections of old fire hose.

Fig. 27.3 Driftwood used as an edge roller.
Photos: Bob Timms

Improvised Rollers

Although padding an edge prevents rope damage it also increases the friction and therefore the effort required when tensioning or hoisting a rope. Rescue teams sometimes use edge rollers to allow a rope to be run over an edge without causing damage or increasing the amount of friction.

We can improvise by tying a smooth driftwood log in position. (Fig. 27.3).

Knots and Hitches

A hitch can only be tied around another object, such as a karabiner. If you remove the karabiner the hitch unravels on its own. A knot is free standing; this means that a knot can be tied with just a piece of rope.

To retain one hundred percent of its original strength a rope must not be made to curve through an arc of a diameter of less than four times its own diameter. Most knots will therefore create a link in the chain that is weaker than the rope itself.

The rope is also weakened where the rope is passed around a karabiner which is only 9-10 mm in diameter. If a 12 mm static rope, with a breaking strain of 4,000 kg, is tied around a karabiner with a breaking strain of 2,200 kg, it doesn't really matter if the rope loses twenty percent of its original strength as it will still be as strong as the karabiner. If, however, we are using a 9.5 mm canyoning rope its breaking strain is 1,950 kg. Reduced by twenty percent it becomes 1560 kg. Whilst this is still more than strong enough for most situations, there are some situations where creating such a weakness in the chain would be undesirable. An example would be when rigging a high line Tyrolean, (see Chapter 29).

The No Knot

When making the end of a rope fast to a large tree, the rope can be simply wrapped around the tree several times until the friction is so great that the rope is as securely tied as if a knot were used. Because the diameter of the tree is far more than four times the diameter of the rope there is no loss of strength. The other advantage is that it can, if necessary, be released even when the rope is under tension by simply unwrapping the rope and reducing the amount of friction.

Fig .27.4 The no knot.

Other Knots

I have deliberately kept the number of knots used in this book to an absolute minimum. (See Appendix B). This is to keep things simple, quick and easier to get right in a stressful situation. Although the knots I suggest will always be suitable, there will be situations where an ideal, even better knot could be used in its place. Those who have a good working knowledge of knots should feel free to use their judgment and use any appropriate knot that they are familiar with.

Karabiners

Karabiners should be used as the link between ropes and tapes and not clipped to each other. If a twisting action is induced when a system is loaded, karabiners can be levered one against the other. The effect is similar to loading a karabiner sideways and the chain is massively weakened.

Anchors

An anchor is a strong point to which a rope is made fast. These can be strong points on a boat or raft, or trees or rocks on the bank.

Anchor Selection

When selecting an anchor the following points should be borne in mind:

- Strength of the anchor
- Direction of pull

Strength

Never take it for granted that an anchor is strong enough. There are three ways to inspect an anchor:

1. We can look at it. If it is a tree, is it big; is it healthy; has the root system been exposed by erosion? If it's a rock, is it large and heavy enough; does it slope in such a way that a rope would roll over it rather than stay put; has it got any sharp edges?
2. We can listen to it. If we thump it does it sound hollow?
3. We can physically test it. Push it for all you are worth! This can produce real surprises; sometimes rocks that looked 'bomb proof' can turn out to be precariously balanced. Boulders that appeared to be jammed solid can be moved with ease.

Direction of Pull

It is vital that we don't lose sight of the whole picture. The strongest anchor in the world is of no use if it doesn't allow us to exert force in the required

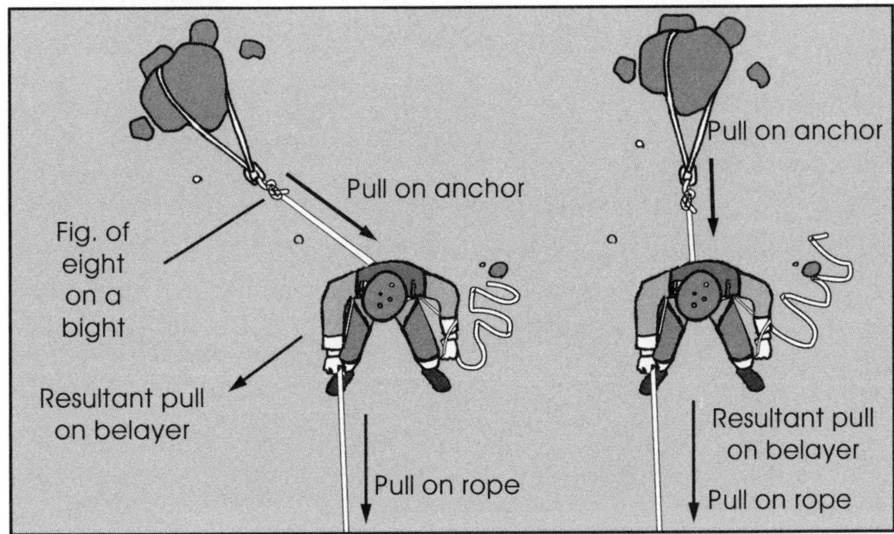

Fig. 27.5 Anchor, belayer and direction of pull should form a straight line.

direction. When using an anchor to safeguard a belayer, the system should be set up so that the anchor, belayer and swimmer form a straight line. (See fig. 27.5). If this is not done, when a load is applied, the belayer will be dragged along the bank until he is in line and may get hurt or let go of the rope he is holding on to.

Single Point Anchors

Single point anchors are simple and quick to set up. The disadvantage is that 'all your eggs are in one basket'. An anchor that is going to be used on its own must be one hundred percent reliable, such as a large healthy tree or a massive rock.

Multiple Anchors

If there is the slightest doubt about the reliability of an anchor, two or more anchors should be linked together. The aim is to spread the load between the anchors.

Angles

Anchors should ideally be close enough together that the angle formed between the anchors and centralised anchor point is less than 60°. Once the angle reaches 120°, the load is the same as if only one anchor was used. (See fig. 27.6). Once the angle reaches 160°, the leverage caused by what is known as a 'vector pull' is such that the force on each of the anchor points is nearly **four times** the force pulling on the centralised anchor point.

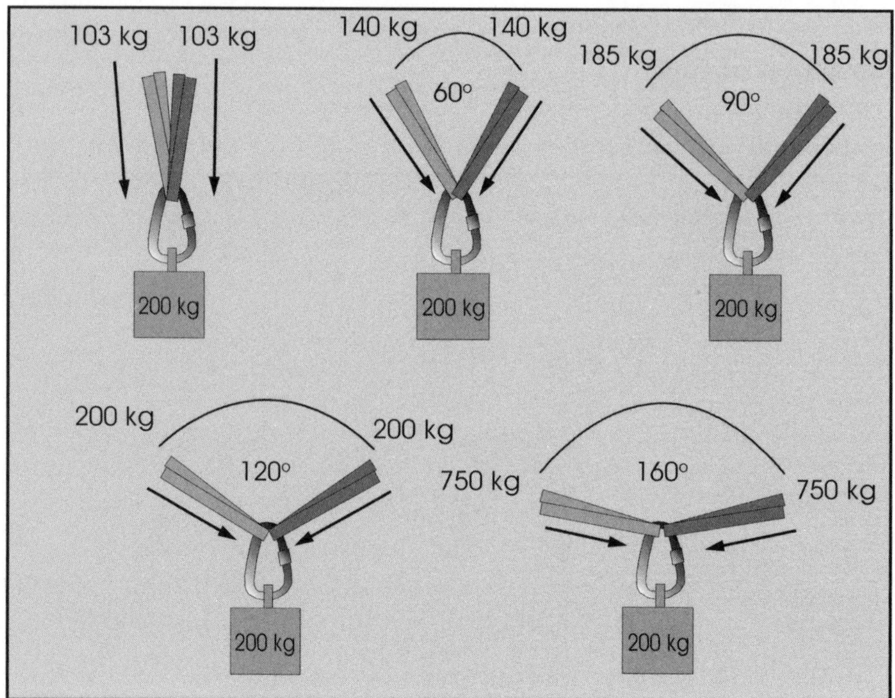

Fig. 27.6 The effects of angles on forces.

Linking Anchors

There are two approaches to linking anchors; each is suited to different situations.

Self Equalising Anchors

The aim here is that **the load on the anchors is evenly spread even if the angle of pull varies.** See fig. 27.7.

Pros

This system is great when used in a situation such as hauling a wrapped boat. Here, should anything in the anchor system fail, the slack introduced would ensure that the forces on the other anchors would **decrease** as the boat settles back on to the rock.

Cons

This system should not normally be used in any situation where **gravity** is involved, such as: raising, lowering, high line Tyrolean, abseiling or belay ropes. This is because, should an anchor fail and slack be introduced into the system, the remaining anchor/s will be shock loaded. The resulting forces would be far in excess of the original load.

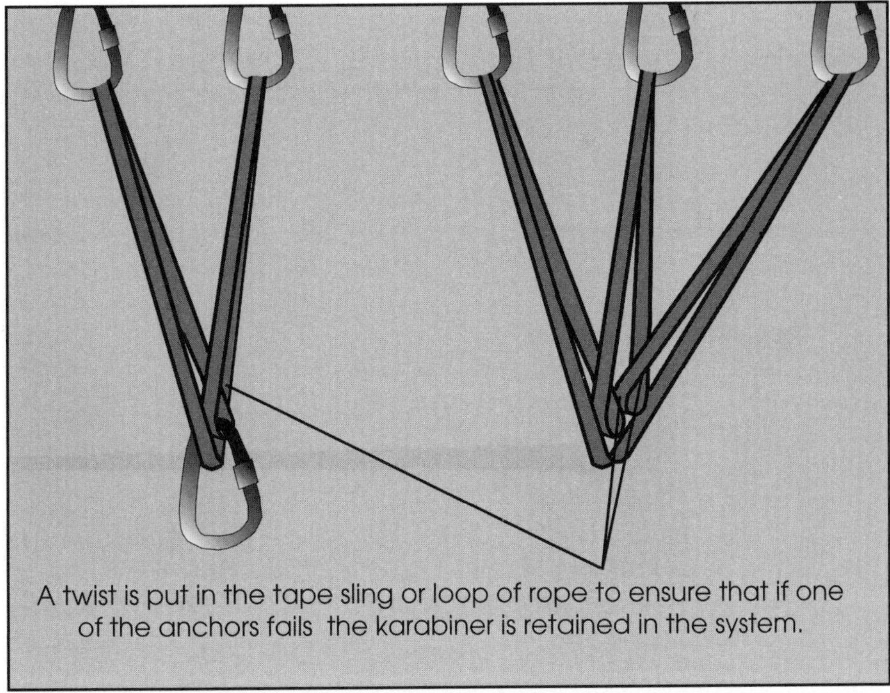

Fig. 27.7 2 and 3 point self equalizing anchors using a closed loop of tape, 'webbing'. There are no knots, so when the direction of the pull changes the tape slides around and self equalizes.

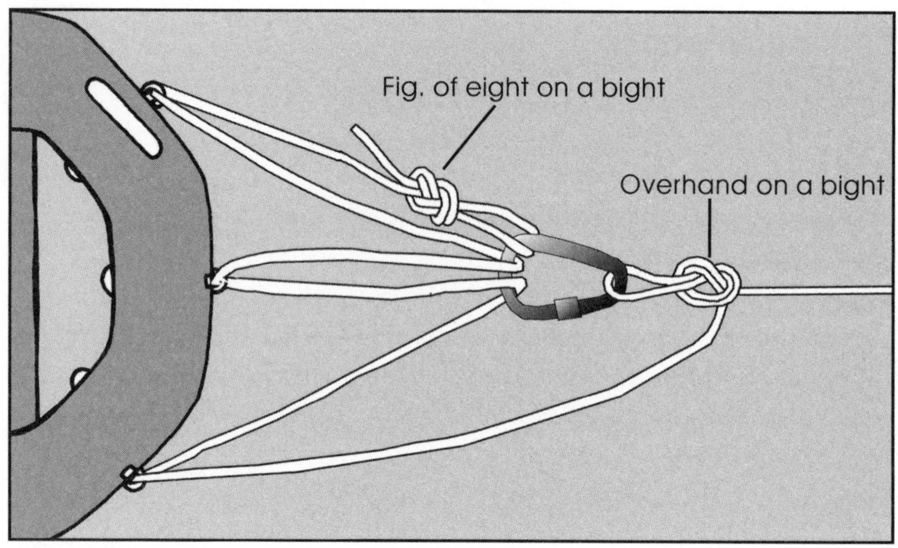

Fig, 27.8 Multi-point self equalizing anchor made by threading a rope through raft strong points. More could be added.

Linked Independent Anchors

The aim here is that **the load is evenly spread and each anchor is entirely independent.** Therefore should any anchor fail the others would not be shock loaded. See fig. 27.9.

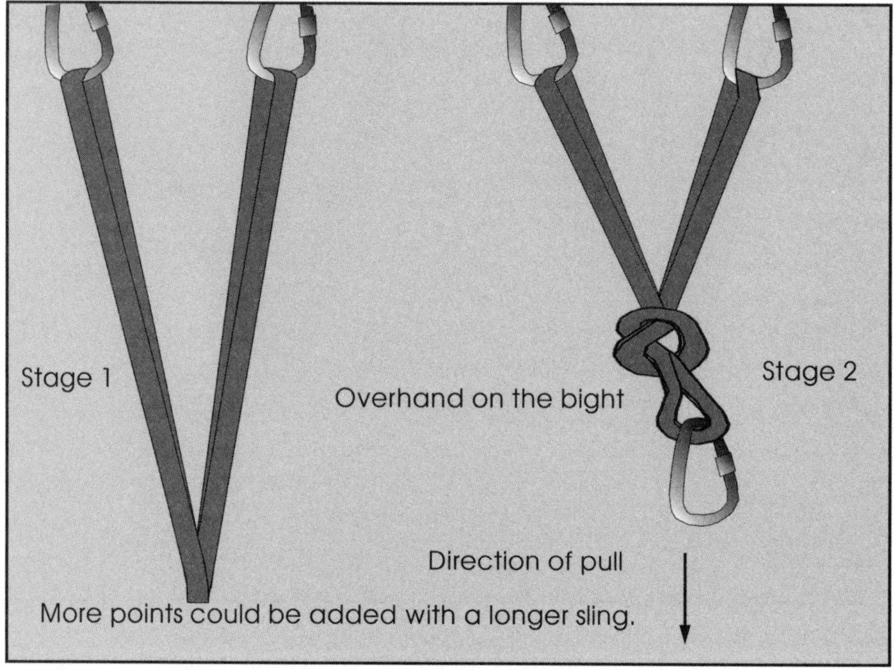

Fig. 27.9 2 point linked independent anchors using tape slings.

Cons

If the direction of pull changes, the load will come on to one anchor. Therefore if there is no way to avoid the direction of pull changing, it may be better to use a self equalising belay even in situations involving gravity.

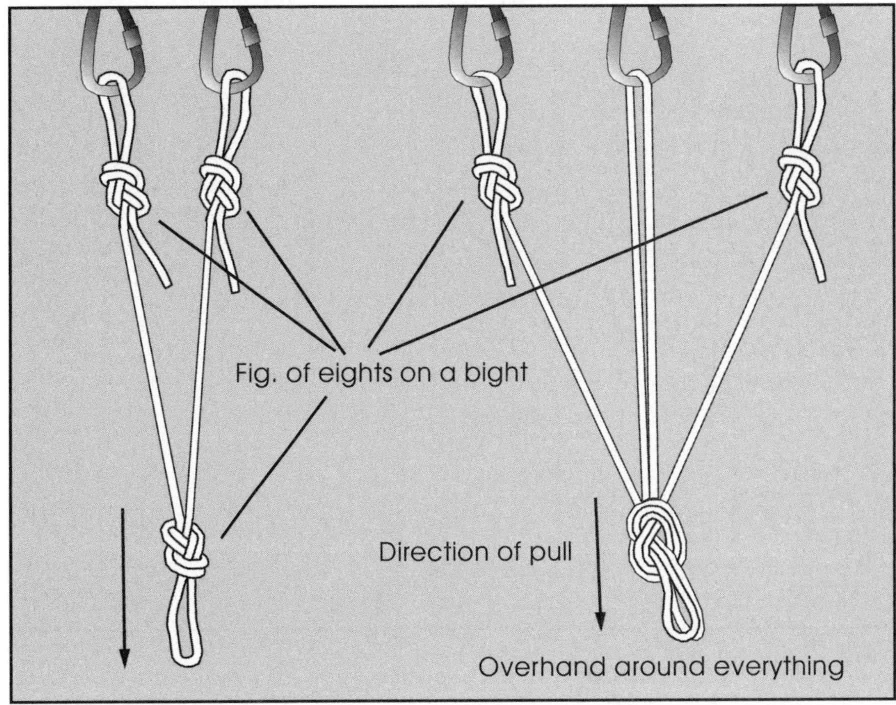

Fig. 27.10 Spare rope used to link independent anchors.

The Italian Hitch

The Italian or Munter hitch is a friction hitch which can be used in any situation where a rope needs to be taken in or let out under control. It requires only a pear shaped karabiner, which should be a screwgate, and is remarkably easy to tie. It creates so much friction that one person can easily hold as much force as the system can cope with. (Fig. 27.11).

Locking Off

By simply holding on tight to the dead end of the rope, the Italian hitch locks and will not allow any movement until the operator allows rope to feed through. It can be locked off by using a bight of the dead rope to tie two half hitches around the live rope. This frees the operator to perform other tasks .

As it can be easily released without losing control, a locked off Italian hitch is an excellent way to make fast a rope that may need to be released later or in an emergency.

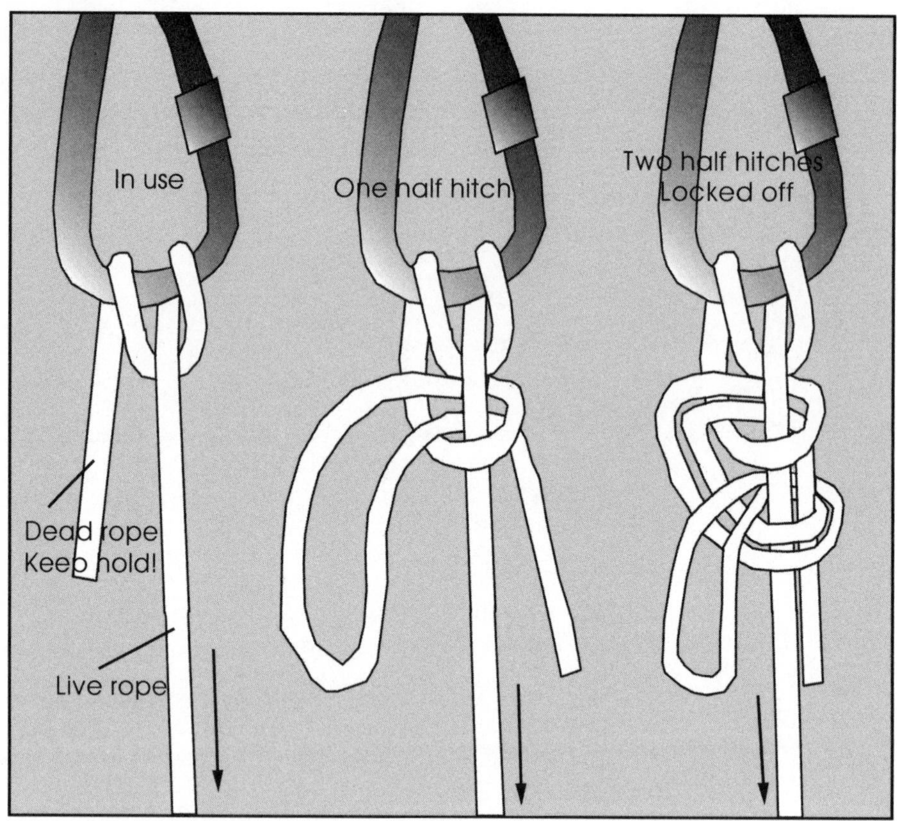

Fig. 27.11 The Italian hitch

Mechanical Advantage

Mechanical advantage allows us to increase the amount of force that we can exert for a given amount of muscle power. However, as will become clear, there is a price to pay for these gains.

No Advantage 1:1

If a 100 kg weight is to be pulled a distance of 10 metres **a force of 100 kg** will have to be applied and 10 metres of rope will pass through the rescuer's hands. (Fig. 27.12A).

2:1 Pulley System

If a 100 kg weight is to be pulled a distance of 10 metres **a force of 50 kg** will have to be applied **but 20 metres** of rope will pass through the rescuer's hands. (Fig. 27.12C).

Note that in a 2:1 pulley system the end of the rope is tied to the anchor and the pulley is tied to the object to be moved. If the system is rigged the other way around the pulley simply changes the direction of pull. (Fig. 27.12B)

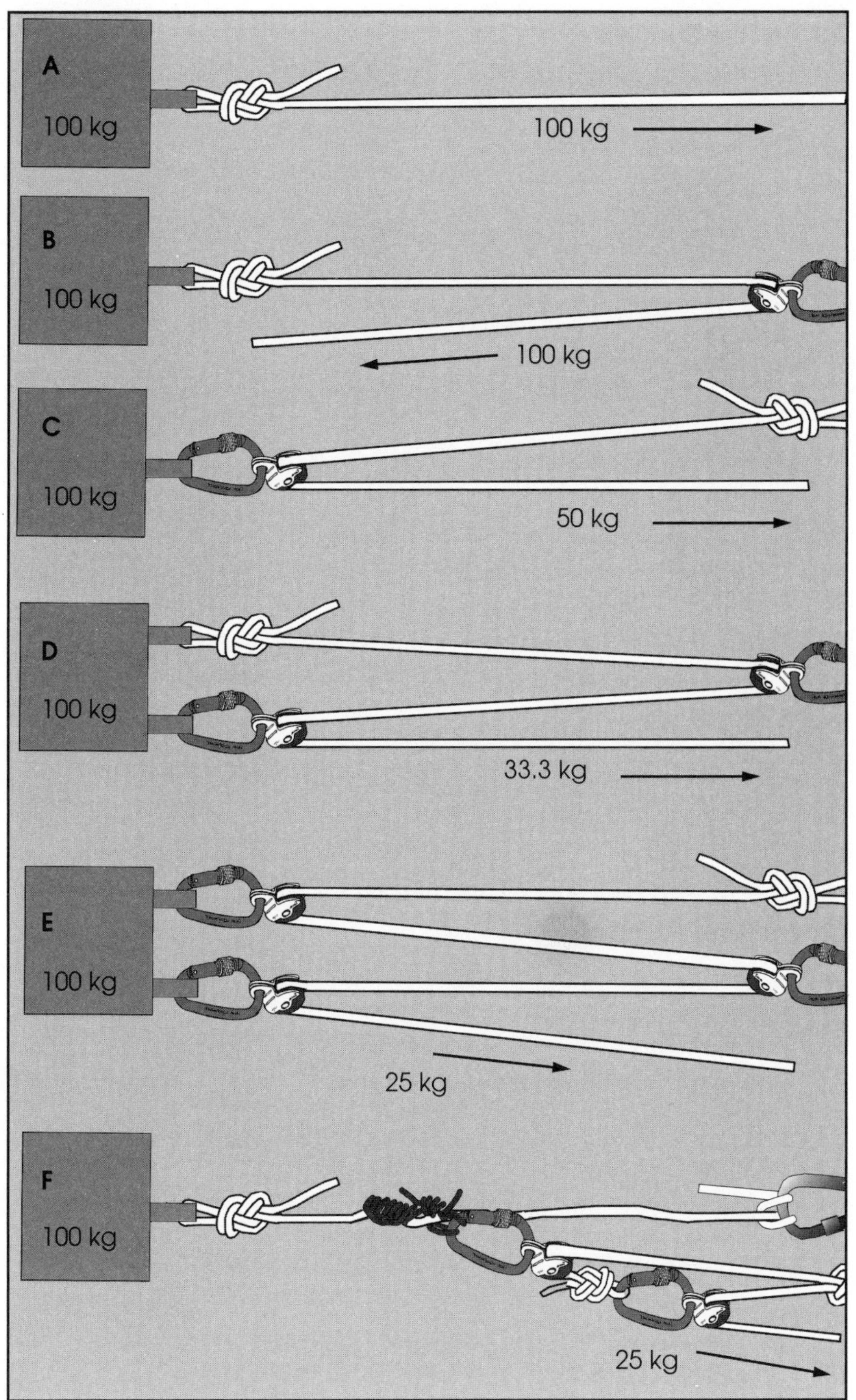

Fig. 27.12 Mechanical advantage

3:1 Pulley System

If a 100 kg weight is to be pulled a distance of 10 metres **a force of 33.3 kg** will have to be applied **but 30 metres** of rope will pass through the rescuer's hands. (Fig. 27.12D).

4:1 Pulley System

There are two ways to create a 4:1 pulley system. One involves using three pulleys, (fig. 27.12E), the other needs only two pulleys and works by multiplying one 2:1 system by another. (Fig. 27.12F).

Key Points:

1. If the rope that is being pulled on is tied off at the object being moved, the mechanical advantage is uneven, e.g. 1:1, 3:1.
2. If the rope that is being pulled on is tied off at the anchor, the mechanical advantage is even, e.g. 2:1, 4:1.
3. If a pulley system **divides** the **force** required by a factor of 3, it also **multiplies** the amount of pulling needed by a factor of 3. If you choose to use a 3:1 pulley system where you could have managed without, allowing for the extra time it takes to rig, it will probably take five times as long to get the job done.

Friction

To simplify the figures used to explain how pulley systems work, we have conveniently ignored friction. In fact, even with pulleys, we lose a little of the advantage gained. If we use karabiners instead of pulleys, a 3:1 system will in fact only have the same effect as a 2:1 system that uses a pulley.

Diminishing Returns

Although adding extra pulleys increases the theoretical mechanical advantage, the percentage of the gain that is lost to friction also increases. If you construct a pulley system using karabiners instead of pulleys, more force is lost than gained if a system involving more than two pulleys is used.

Chapter 28
Recoveries

Many recovery situations are made far more difficult than they need be. It is important to remember that we are no longer in a rescue situation. We can afford to take as much time as is necessary over planning our actions. What is more, we should do so, for reasons of safety as well as efficiency.

In a rescue situation we need to find the fastest solution that is within acceptable limits of risk. In a recovery situation, speed is not an issue. The solution we use must be the one that offers the least risk to those attempting the recovery.

Planning a Recovery

Once the leader has gathered the team and ensured that everyone is safe, the team will have to carry out the following tasks:

1. Assess the situation.
2. Work out which way the stuck object will have to be pushed or pulled.
3. Work out how the object will be brought to shore once it is free of the obstacle.
4. Work out how to attach lines and/or place rescuers.
5. Decide if and how any downstream hazards need to be covered.
6. Decide whether an upstream look out is needed to warn other paddlers about lines and other hazards.

Incident Management

All the points covered in Chapter 19, Incident Management apply. The plan must be communicated to the team. Each member of the team must be clear as to who their boss is and what their job is. Most importantly of all, it is essential that the leader does not get physically involved, and stays detached, so as to keep the whole picture in view.

If the team is very small this may not be possible. In this case leaders should allocate themselves the least involving job, with the clearest view of the whole situation.

Attaching a Line

This is the part of the operation that potentially involves the most risk to rescuers. If it is possible for a rescuer to quickly paddle, wade or swim to a point where he can easily attach a line at no risk to himself, then he should do so. However, if this involves any real risk to the rescuer another way must be found. If a safe way cannot be found, the gear should be abandoned and a fresh attempt made when water levels have dropped, and/or more specialist equipment and knowledge can be brought to bear. Alternative methods of accessing difficult locations are examined in Chapter 29.

Lines can often be attached remotely using one of the following methods:

Paddle Hooks

Paddle hooks can either be improvised as shown in Chapter 14, or commercial ones used. Improvising a hook, using a karabiner, has the advantage of ensuring the line stays attached even if the tension is temporarily released. The commercially available models are literally just hooks. They are easier to attach but, once attached the line must be kept tensioned or it will drop off.

These 'hooks' don't have to be attached to a paddle. By using a canoe pole or a piece of driftwood we can extend our reach even further.

Drift Lines

A line is floated down the current in such a way that the middle of the line is caught against the object. The free end of the line is then recovered and, by pulling on both ends of the line simultaneously, the object can be moved.

Weighted Line

As above except that the end of the line is weighted so that the line goes under the object concerned.

Single Line Cinch

After either a drift line or a weighted line has been deployed, instead of pulling on both lines simultaneously, the bag end of the rope is clipped to the other end of the line. This is then pulled tight till the object involved is effectively 'lassoed'.

Two Line Cinch

This is the same system that is described in Chapter 17 for use in foot entrapments. It is particularly useful for recovering paddles that are snagged in mid stream.

Using the Force

In this case, the forces we are concerned with are either the power of the current or gravity. If we find a way to work with, rather than against these forces we are far more likely to be successful. More often than not, if a boat can't be moved, it is because the rescuers are pulling or pushing in the wrong direction.

Exercise involving a tethered raft on a high line Tyrolean. Note that they are using a 2:1 pulley system rather than a 1:1 as in fig. 29.5. This requires very long ropes. Note also the stern lines to prevent the raft being pulled into the stopper. Lower Oertz, Austria.
Photos: Paul O'Sullivan

All else being equal, it will be necessary to relieve some of the pressure between the boat and the rock, as well as pull the boat towards the bank. A good rule of thumb is to pull at an angle of 45° to the flow of the current. (Fig. 28.1).

Off Centre Broach

More often than not, a boat will broach in such a way that the current exerts more pressure on one side of the boat than on the other, (fig. 28.1). In the case illustrated it will obviously be easier to pull the boat off to river left. Some teams might be tempted to pull in the other direction because the right bank is conveniently close. This would be a mistake.

Less obvious is the exact direction in which the rescuers need to pull to get it to move. Some experimentation may be necessary, but taking the time to try and work it out in the first place will save a good deal of time and effort.

Centre Broach

If the current has broached a boat or raft in such a way that the pressure is exerted equally on both sides, there are a number of possible solutions:

Weak Current

If the current is weak, it may be possible to pull it off in either direction. In which case it makes sense to choose the side that is easiest to get to.

Rafts

With rafts it is possible to deliberately relieve the pressure on one side of the raft by deflating the appropriate air tubes. The advantage here is that we can choose on which side the current will exert the most pressure. This means that we can sometimes choose which bank to work on.

Two Point Broach

These situations can usually be dealt with in much the same way as a one point broach. On some occasions it so happens that the easiest solution is to lift one end of the boat over one of the two objects on which it is stuck. This operation may be so simple that one rescuer can stand on the obstacle and heave the boat off.

On the other hand it may require running a line through a pulley attached to a tree branch to change the direction of pull. A second line is also attached so that, once the end of the boat is lifted clear, the first line is let go so that the second line can be used to bring the boat into the side.

Top: Simple handrail used effectively to safeguard the paddler on a steep, slippery grass slope while he inspects a waterfall in Iceland. Photo: George Woods/Palm

Bottom: With grade V above and grade V below this is a committing gorge where extra ropes are a good idea. This was in fact a Search and Rescue reconnaissance mission. Leven Canyon, Tasmania, Australia. Photo: Chris Sladden

Vertical Pins

A vertical pin usually occurs because the bow of a kayak is trapped behind a small projection in a ledge. Usually all that is required is for the boat to be pulled back a short distance and then released. Once again it may be better to attach a second rope with which to recover the boat.

Practical Pulley Systems

Direct

It is only possible to attach a pulley system directly to a boat if the distance involved is very short. With a 20 metre line, a 2:1 system would have to be attached to an anchor less than 10 metres away. (Fig. 28.1).

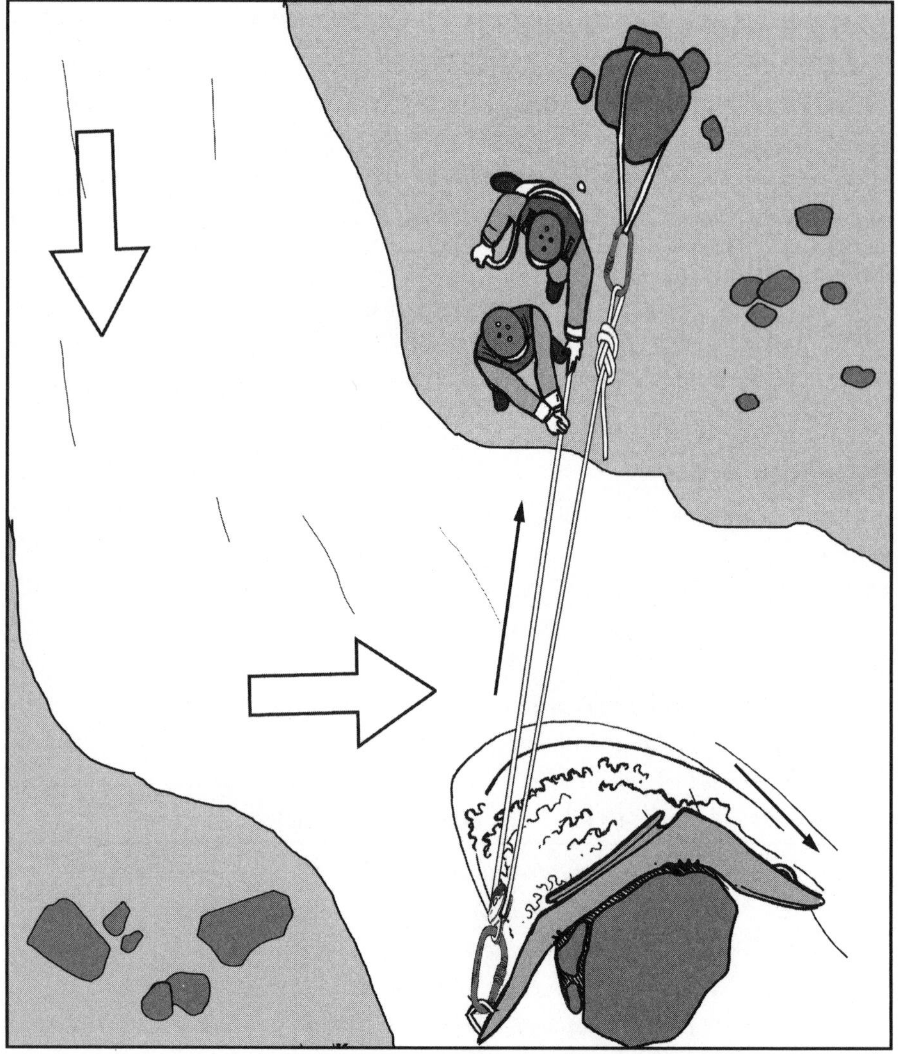

'Z' Drag

A 'Z' drag, (fig. 28.2), allows all but the last few metres of a rope to be used. Two prussik loops are used.

1. Prussik A is used to attach the second pulley to the rope that is being pulled.
2. Once the rope has been pulled as far as it will go, the rope is let out a few centimetres until the French prussik (B) takes the strain on the 'live' rope. (Prussik B is pushed against the pulley and releases automatically when the rope is pulled in).

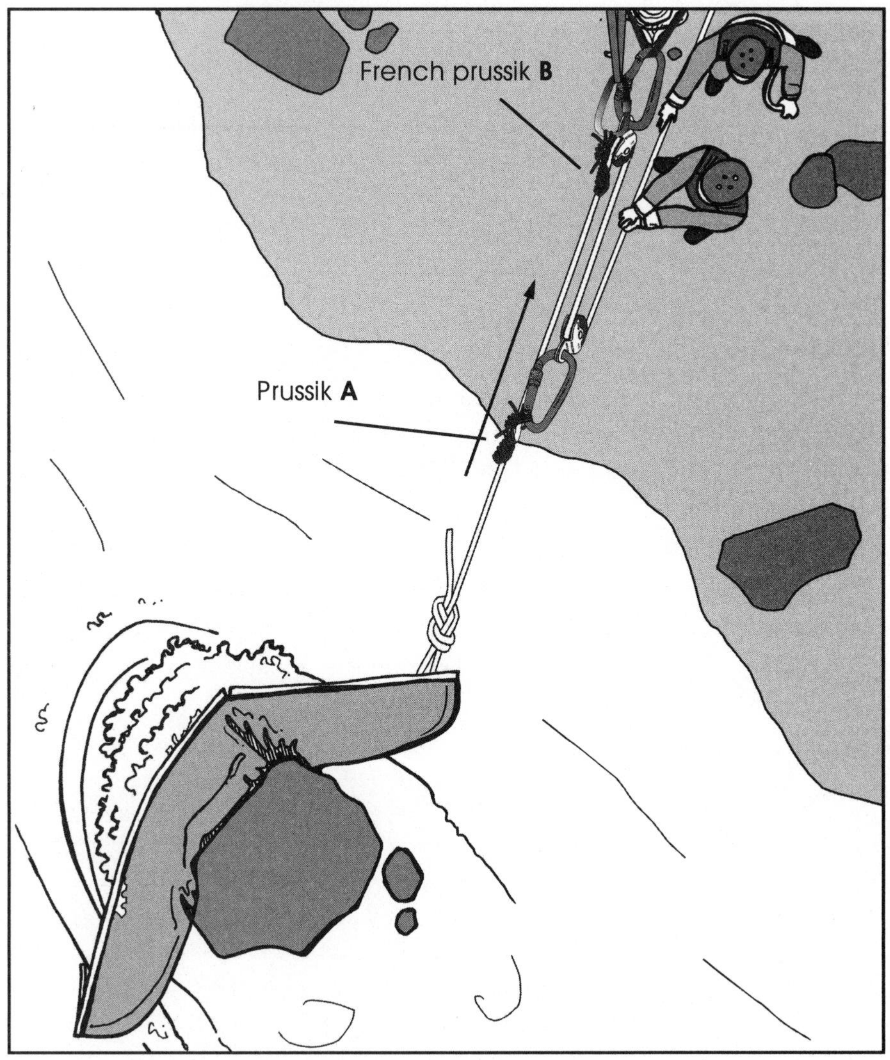

Fig. 28.2 'Z' drag.

Fig. 28.1 2:1 Pulley tied direct to kayak, using the force of the current.

3. Prussik A is then shunted back along the live rope and the procedure started again.

Piggy Back Rig (Pig Rig)

A piggy back system allows a full rope length, or even two or more ropes tied together, to be used. It can even be used to tension one rope and then be transferred to a second rope as in fig. 28.3.

1. A rope is tied to the boat and either 'no knotted' around a tree or attached to a karabiner with an Italian hitch.
2. A separate pulley system is then attached to the rope using a prussik loop, (A). Fig. 28.3 shows a 4:1 system in use, but if the force needed is less, a 3:1 or 2:1 would be more appropriate).
3. As the pulley system hauls the rope, the slack created is taken in by feeding the rope around the tree or by operating the Italian hitch.
4. When the pulley system can go no further the strain is taken by the 'no knot' or by locking off the Italian hitch.
5. Prussik A is then shunted back along the live rope and the procedure started again.

Passing a Knot

With a piggy back rig, passing a knot, that has been tied to join two ropes, through the system, doesn't present a problem. When the knot comes up against prussik A the strain is taken by the Italian hitch, allowing the prussik to be released and re-tied on the other side of the knot.

When the knot reaches the karabiner of the Italian hitch, the strain is taken by the piggy back rig and the Italian hitch is released and re-tied on the other side of the knot. Note that if the ropes have been joined using an overhand knot, (See: Appendix B), the knot can be worked through the karabiner without having to untie and re tie the Italian hitch.

Vector Pulls

When a rope has been tensioned in an unsuccessful attempt to pull a boat off a rock and then locked off, a vector pull can be used to good effect. (Fig. 28.3). It gives two major advantages:

1. The force already being exerted on the line is multiplied by a factor of 3-4.
2. A small but significant change in the direction of pull is achieved.

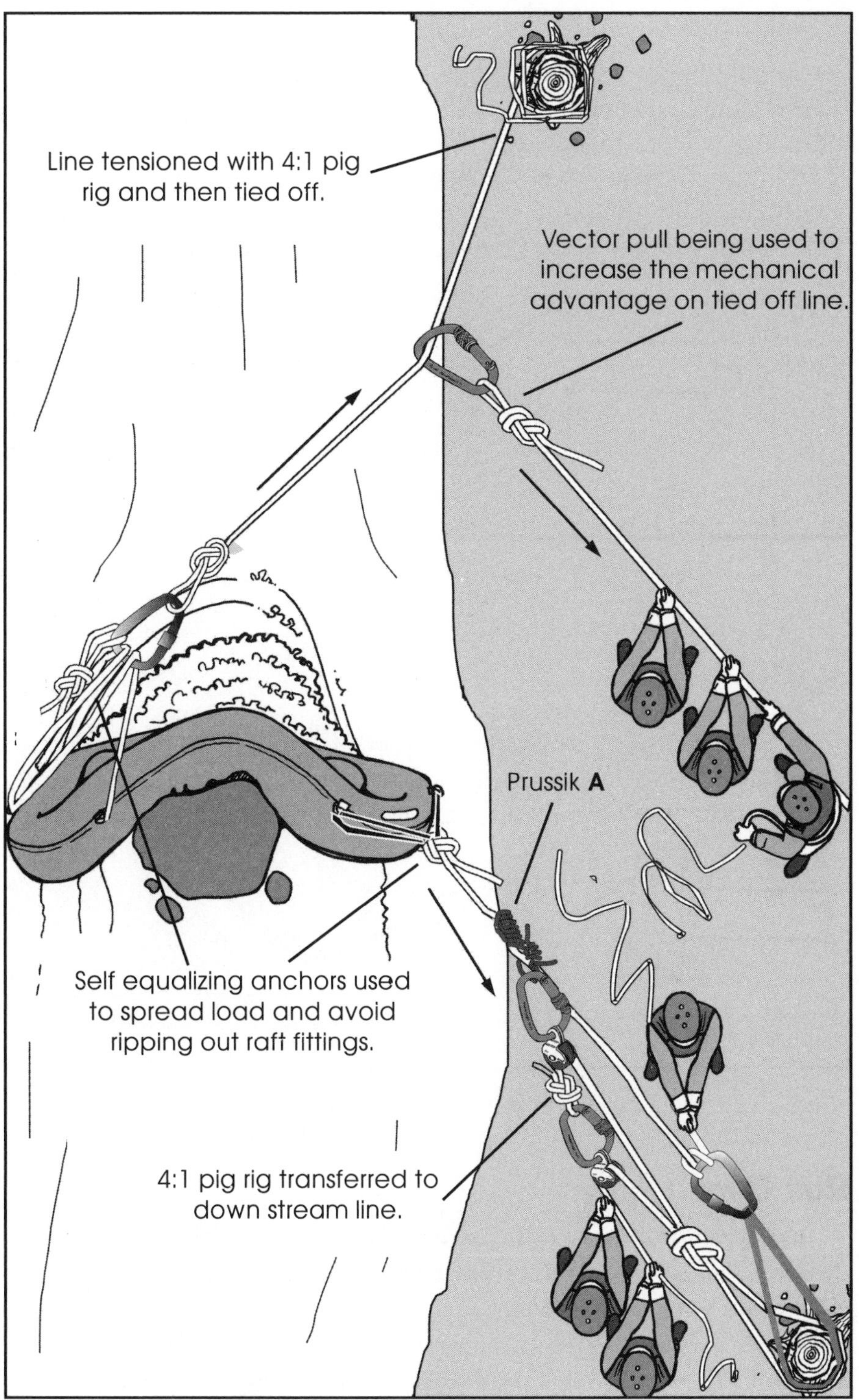

Fig. 28.3 Multiple techniques used because of the forces involved when a raft is badly wrapped.

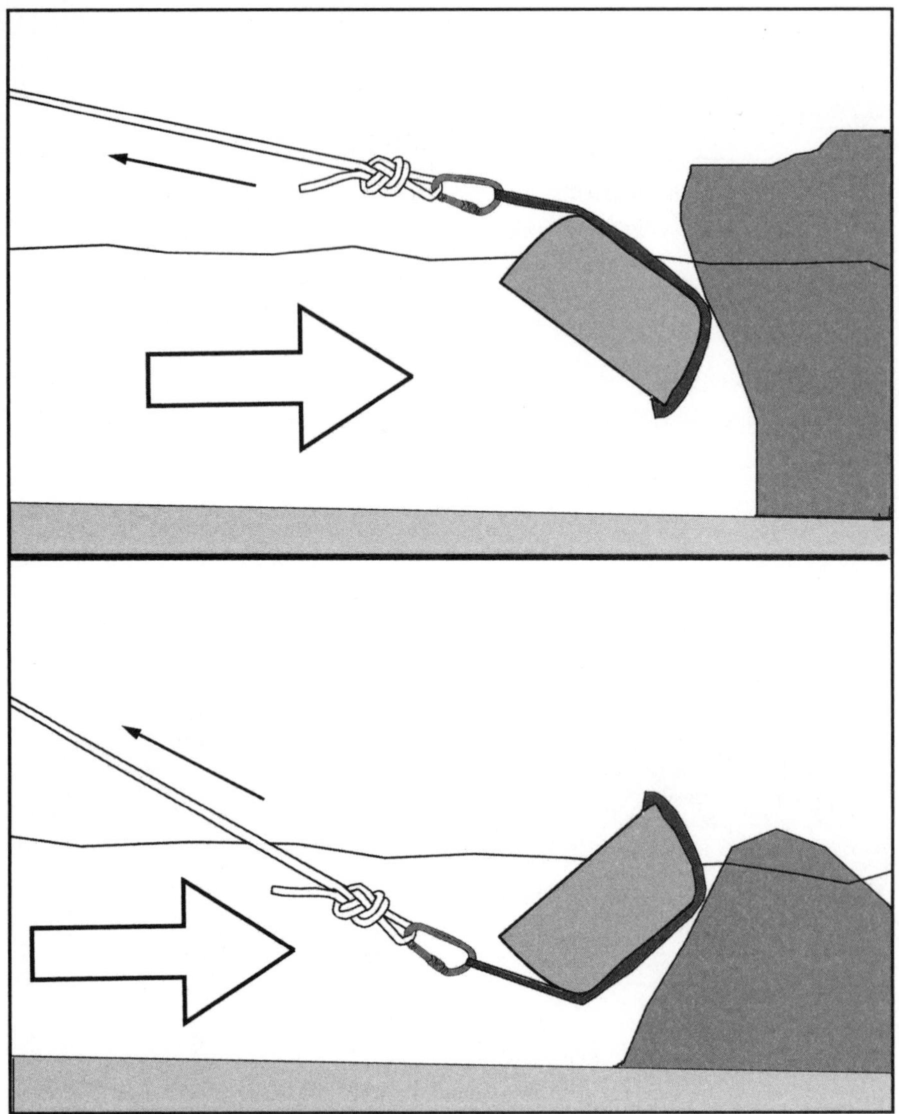

Fig. 28.4 Roll over technique used on a canoe.

Roll Over

In wrap situations, rafts and open boats offer a huge surface to the power of the water. This is particularly the case if the inside of the hull is facing upstream, trapping the power of the water.

If a line is attached as shown in fig. 28.4, the boat can be rolled over, (a roller is in itself a form of mechanical advantage), so that the bottom of the boat faces the current. When this line is pulled on, it acts as a 2:1 pulley, (see Chapter 28

Rope Dynamics), further increasing the mechanical advantage. Which way the boat is rolled depends on the shape of the rock that it is up against.

Attaching the Line

Due to the fact that nylon tapes sink, they are much easier to use than floating rope when it comes to setting up the roll over. One end of the tape can be attached to a thwart so that it can slide up or down as required. The other end can then be thrown in on the upstream side so that the current feeds it under the boat.

Chapter 29
Other Access Techniques

In this chapter we will look at some techniques that might be used to gain access to a location. This may be because other, more usual (for paddlers), methods won't work or that these methods are quicker or safer.

Water Based Access

Wading

If the current is not too powerful and is no more than knee deep, wading is an option. It is worth remembering that the heavier a person is, the less likely it is that the current will sweep him off his feet. There are a number of methods that can be used to improve the chances of success and to move groups of people in this way.

Pole

A pole can be used to gain stability. The wader faces upstream and leans forward on to the pole so that a kind of tripod is formed. Only one 'leg' of the tripod is moved at a time. (Fig. 29.1).

Three Man Tripod

Three people face inwards with arms firmly linked, heads together and feet apart. The heaviest person faces upstream and the other two are upstream of him, side on to the current. One person moves at a time so that the others can support him.

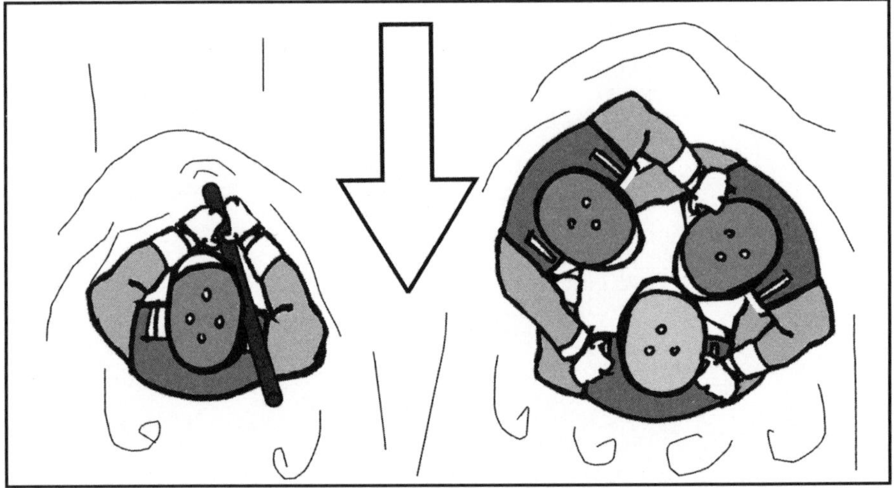

Fig. 29.1 Wading techniques.

Line Astern

The heaviest person in the group uses a pole and stands at the upstream end of the line. The others get in line behind him, hold the shoulder straps of the person in front of them and lean forward so as to hold the front person firmly on the river bed. (Fig. 29.2).

The Wedge

Useful for larger groups. Once again the heaviest person stands at the upstream end and leans on the pole. This time the remainder of the group form a wedge formation. (Fig. 29.2). Once again everyone leans onto the person in front of them to help give them a firm footing. Heaviest people at the front, lightest at the rear.

Note that by adapting it a little, the wedge can be used to ferry a stretcher across shallows. The victim **must** be wearing a buoyancy aid *(PFD)* and a helmet and **must not** be strapped into the stretcher.

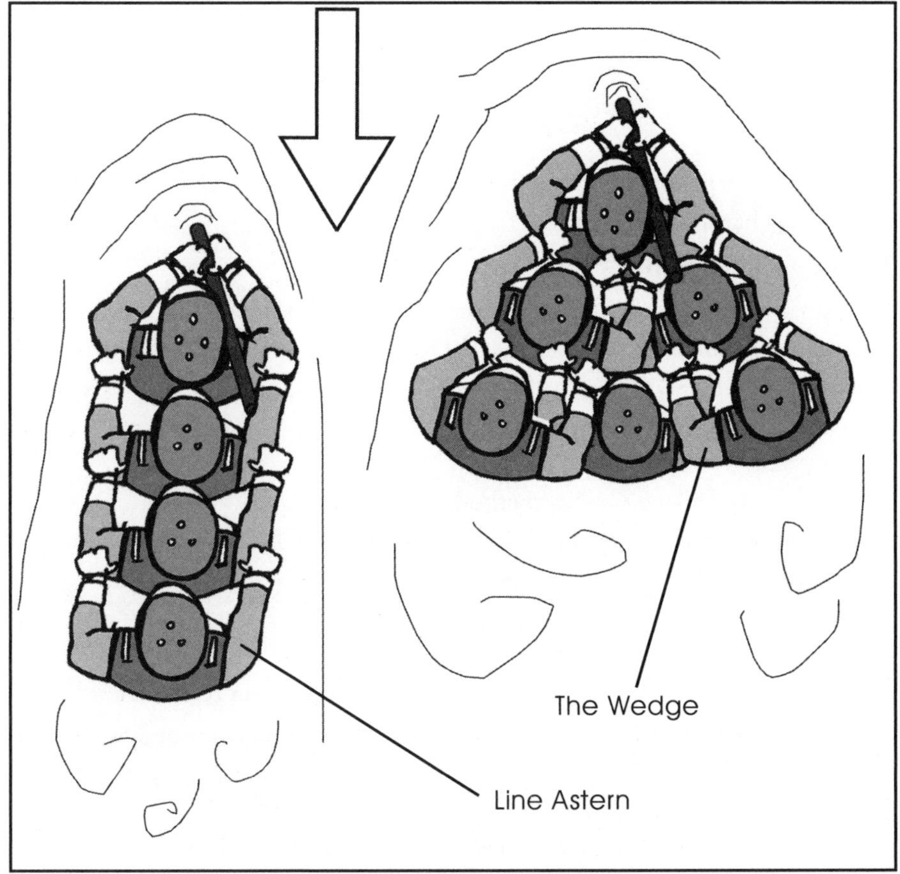

Fig. 29.2 Group wading techniques.

There is a good rule of thumb when deciding to use the above group techniques, which leaves a margin for error. Assume that if the heaviest person in the group can't wade across on his own, it is too risky.

Rope Assisted

I have deliberately omitted a number of roped river crossing techniques from this section. This is because I believe them to be unnecessarily risky. As paddlers we can always find another way. The two methods suggested here are useful and relatively safe.

Pendulum Traverse

A line is rigged as for a hand rail, see: Chapter 15, and the wader uses it for support to wade out into the current. If he loses his footing he will be swung back into the side.

Points to note:

1. The longer the hand rail the smaller the angle formed and the more support is provided.
2. The wader must not be tied into the system other than with a releasable chest harness.

Tensioned Diagonal

A line is tensioned so that it is out of the water but low enough to be easily reached by a swimmer. The angle that the rope forms in relation to the main flow must be 45 ° or less. (Fig. 29.3). Note that the diagonal can only be used to move across in one direction, downstream. To cross back again a second rope has to be rigged.

People cross by one of four methods, (fig. 29.3):

1. The swimmer lies in the water on his front and, holding on with both hands, shuffles down the line allowing his body to 'stream' in the current.
2. A tape sling is clipped to the line with a karabiner and the swimmer lies on his back and allows the current to ferry glide him to the far side. If the swimmer holds on with the hand nearest his start point and uses his other hand to point towards where he is going, his body will assume a better ferry angle.
3. The cow's tail of a chest harness is clipped on to the rope and the rescuer surfs on his back as he ferry glides across.

4. A raft or a catamaran made by lashing two canoes together is clipped to the rope and used to ferry people across. If canoes are used they should be attached with bridles. (Fig. 29.4).

Note that if there is enough person power available, only the upstream end of the rope need be tied off. The team can then tension the rope by hauling 'tug of war' fashion. When there is a lack of convenient anchors, this makes it easier to position a rope accurately enough to get a rescuer to a precise location.

Fig. 29.3 Tensioned diagonal.

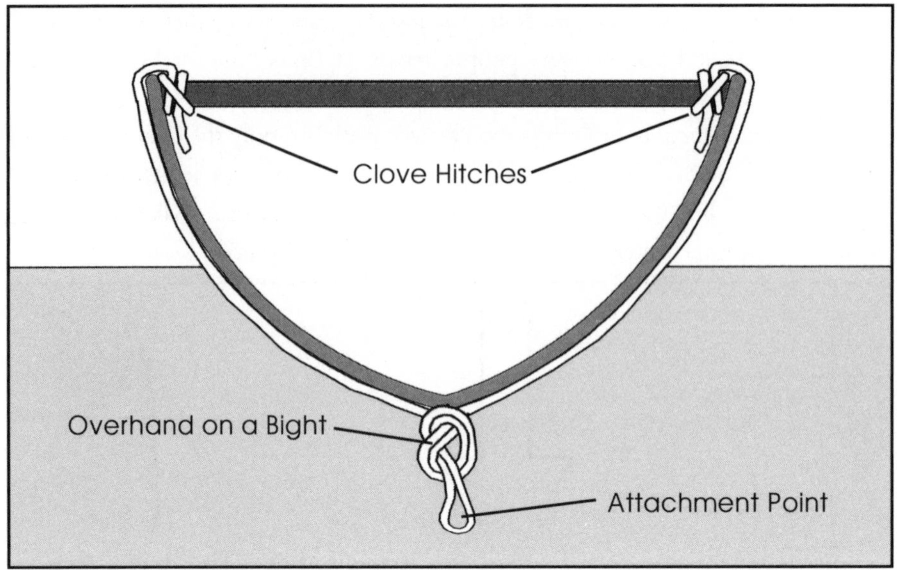

Fig. 29.4 Bridle tied so that the pulling point on a canoe is low and stable.

It is not a good idea to set a tensioned diagonal up on a bend, unless you have a good eye for how the angle of the main flow changes as it goes around the bend. The angle to the flow of the current will vary and the person crossing may find himself stuck in midstream.

Swimming Aids

If swimming is one of the options you are prepared to consider then it makes sense to increase efficiency.

Webs

These are simply neoprene gloves with webbed fingers. Play boaters sometimes use them as 'hand paddles'.

Fins

Small fins as used by surfers can be used. Anyone planning to carry them should become well practised in their use on a 'safe' rapid before using them in a real rescue.

River Boards

These are small boards, similar to but more buoyant than the belly boards used in surf. Rafters who are not accompanied by safety kayakers should consider these for access purposes. Inflatable versions are sometimes used. People using these need fins and once again should become proficient in their use before using them in a rescue or recovery situation.

High Line Tyrolean with Tethered Raft

This is more complicated and time consuming to set up than two or four point tethered raft systems. However it does provide a great deal more control and unlike the others can be used on more technically difficult and complex rapids. (Fig. 29.5). Points to note:

1. The crew must keep their weight well back so that the bow rides high and the water flows under the raft.
2. If this technique is used in a stopper rescue, two lines will have to be used to stop the raft being sucked in by the undertow. (See photo, opposite page 257).
3. The crew can use a guide's paddle to help fine tune the positioning of the raft.
4. Organisation and communication are the key to success.

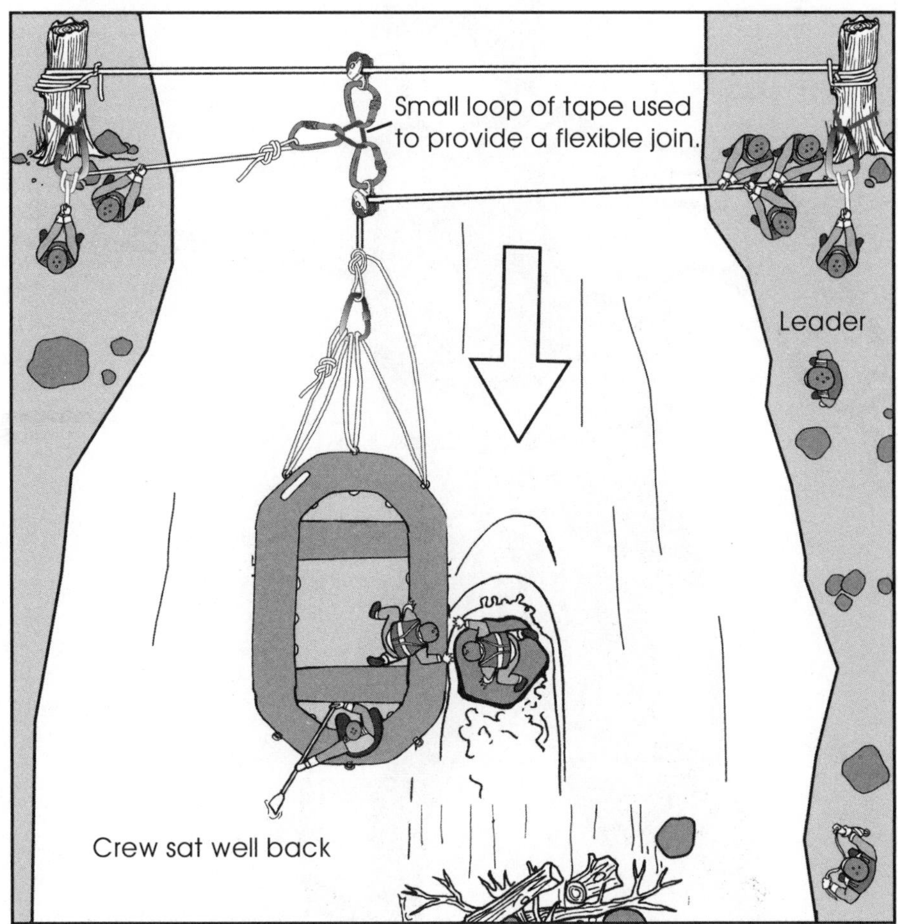

Fig. 29.5 High line tyrolean with tethered raft.

Vertical Access

I strongly recommend that if you do not have a climbing or caving background, you organise a training session supervised by someone who does, before attempting these techniques. Practice sessions should take place only a short distance above the ground so that if mistakes are made nobody gets hurt.

With all of these techniques it is good practice to provide a safety back up by belaying the person/s being lowered or hoisted with a separate line and an Italian hitch.

Sit Harness

Fig. 29.6 Improvised sit harness.

Handrail Line

When access involves descending or ascending a steep slippery bank, all that may be required is a 'fixed' rope to hold on to and steady oneself, so that a slip does not become a fall. (See photo, opposite page 256).

Improvised Harness

Fig. 29.6 shows how to make an improvised sit harness, fig. 29.7, an improvised chest harness and how to link the two to make a full body harness. The latter is particularly useful if an injured person needs raising or lowering. This is because it provides more support and helps the victim remain upright.

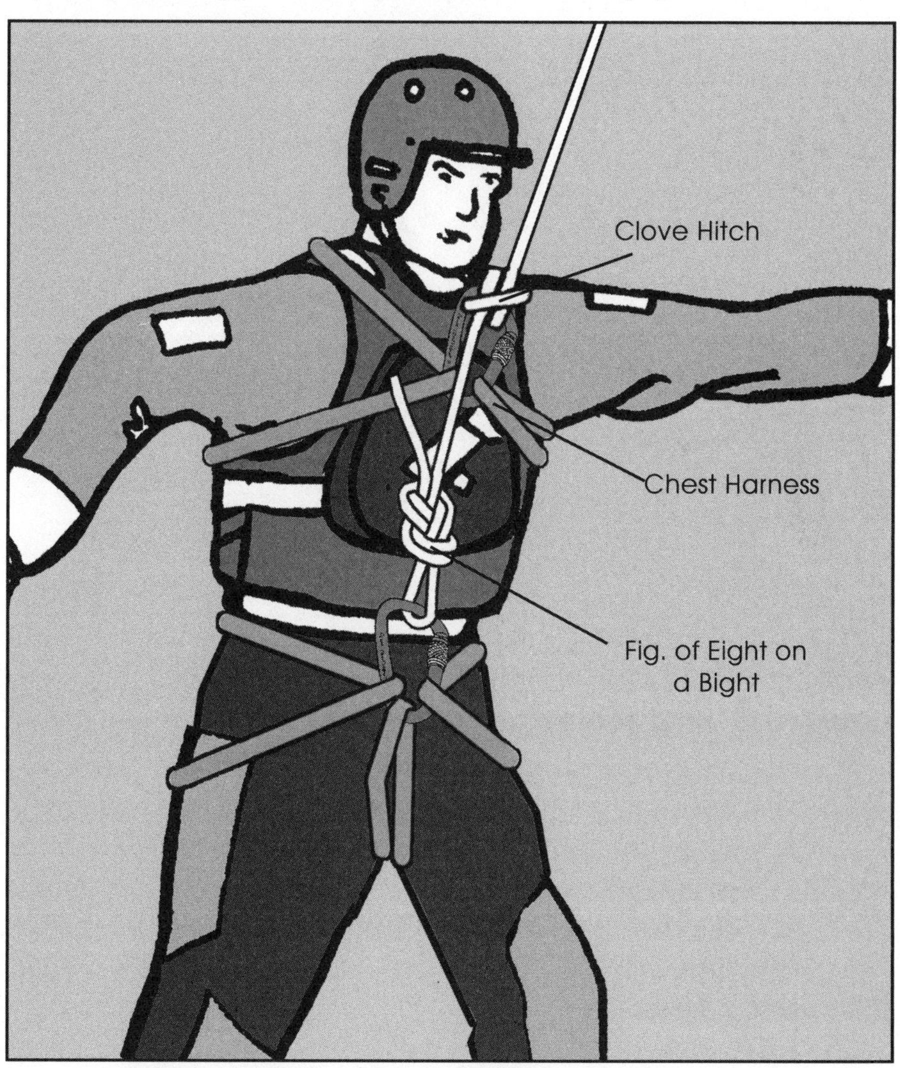

Fig. 29.7 Improvised chest and sit harnesses linked to make a full body harness.

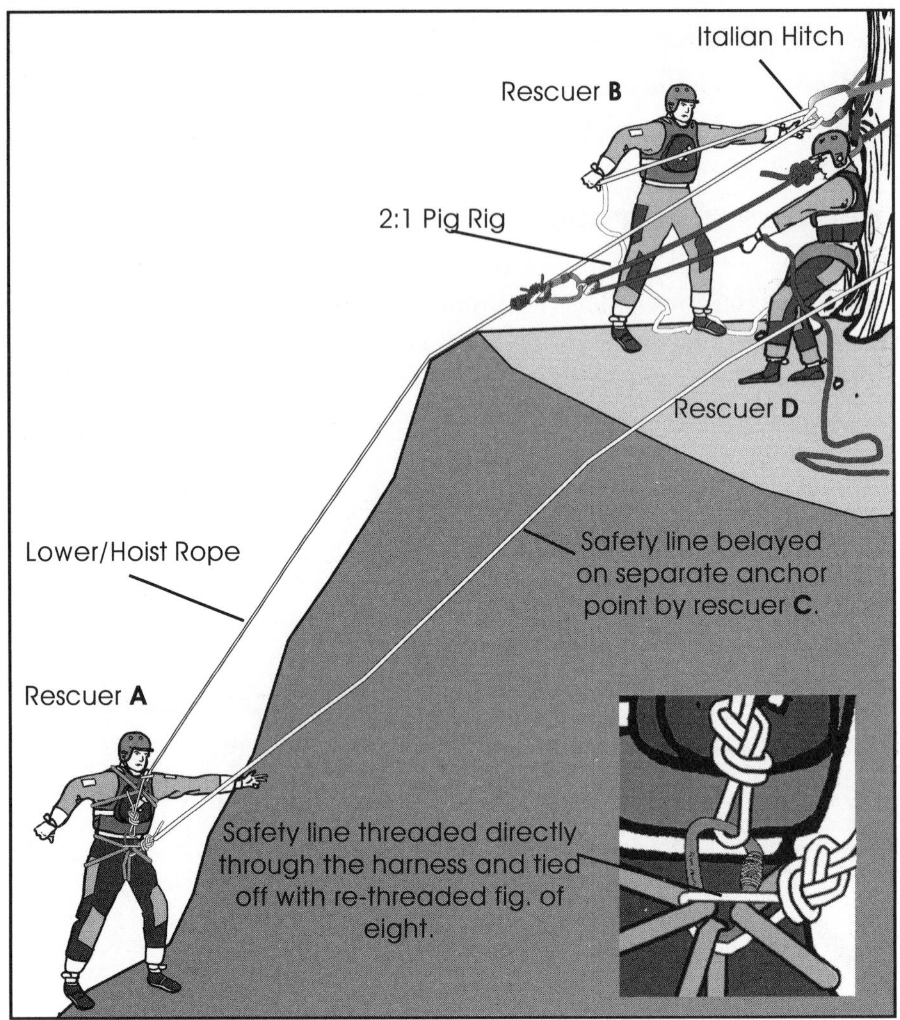

Fig. 29.8 Lower and hoist using 2:1 pig rig and an Italian hitch.

Lowering and Hoisting

If a rescuer needs to get to a place where vertical access is required there are a number of advantages in being lowered and hoisted by other team members:

1. The techniques involved are ones that even non climbers will be familiar with from recovery situations.
2. The rescuer on the end of the rope has his hands free and can concentrate on the task.

2:1 Lower / Hoist

This system is simple, quick and has the advantage of changing from a lower to a hoist with no change of the system or tying and untying of knots. The disadvantage is that it can only be used if the distance is half the length of the rope or less.

1. Rescuer A is lowered by other rescuers B using the same pulley system as shown in Fig. 28. 1. At the same time rescuer C safeguards his descent using an Italian hitch on a safety belay line.
2. When rescuer A is ready the other rescuers simply hoist him back up. Once again he is safeguarded by rescuer C.

Lower / Pig Rig

In this system, (Fig. 29.8), rescuer A is tied to the end of a rope and lowered using an Italian hitch by rescuer B. When rescuer A is in place the Italian hitch is locked off and a piggy back rig is attached to the line with a prussik. This is then used by rescuer D to hoist him back up.

Pros: Can work over more than one rope length.

Cons: Needs at least two people to operate it.

Lower / Z Rig

Rescuer A is tied to the end of a rope and lowered using an Italian hitch by rescuer B. When rescuer A is in place the Italian hitch is locked off and a French prussik is attached to the line with a separate karabiner. When the prussik has secured the live rope, a Z rig set up and, when the haulers are ready, the Italian hitch is removed. The 'Z' rig is then used to hoist him back up.

Pros: Can be operated by one person.

Cons: Can only be used for a few metres short of one rope length.

'Y' Hang

If an injured person is being hoisted, a Y hang, (fig. 29.9), allows a rescuer to travel up with him and support him.

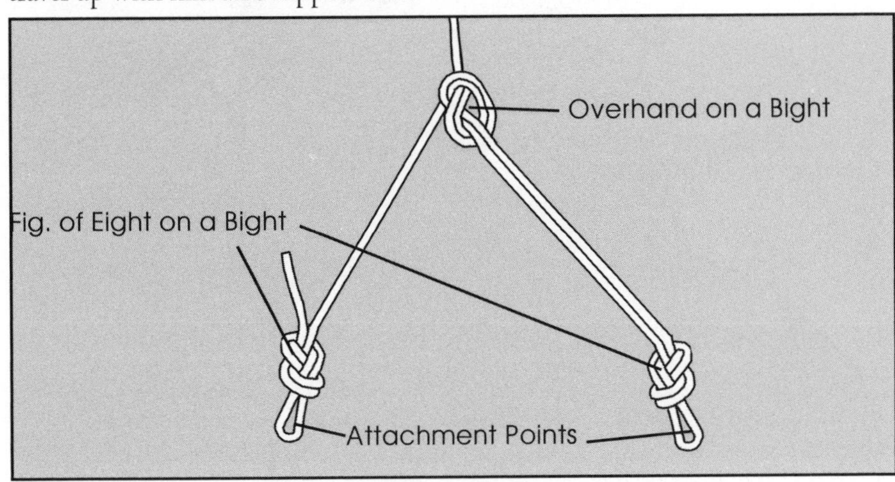

Fig. 29.9 A 'Y' Hang.

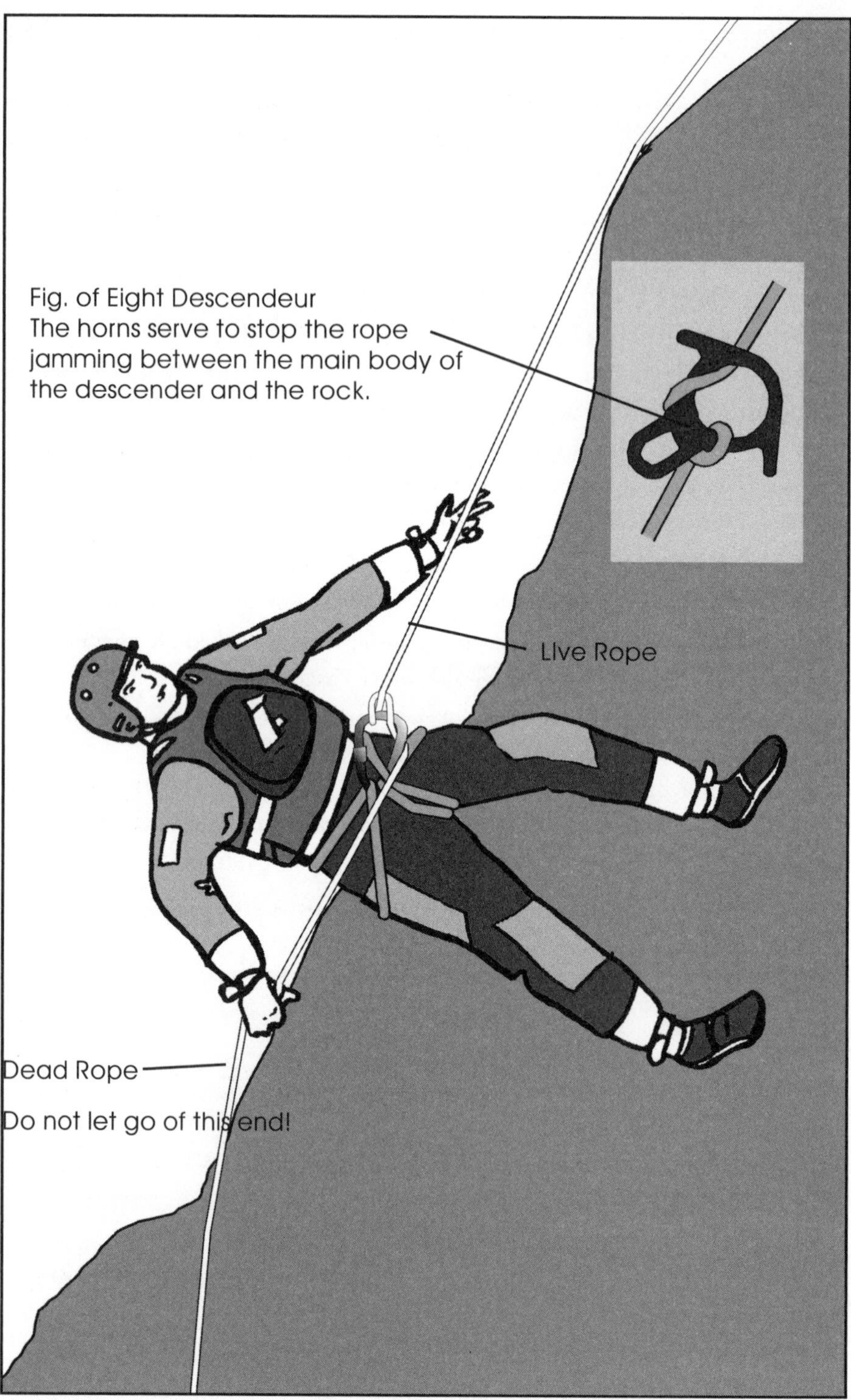

Fig. 29.10 Abseiling, 'rappelling'.

Single Rope Technique

Single rope techniques are the only methods that allow a rescuer to operate solo in a vertical access situation.

If you envisage using these techniques and do not have a climbing or caving background, I strongly advise that you get some expert tuition. All your eggs are in one basket and a single mistake can be fatal.

Descending

Abseiling, *(rappelling)*, involves the rescuer lowering himself down a fixed rope and controlling his rate of descent by means of the friction provided by an Italian hitch, or a figure of eight descender, (fig. 29.10).

1. The upper hand is held loosely around the 'live' rope for balance.
2. The lower hand holds on to the 'dead' rope and controls the rate of descent by tightening or loosening its grip. Whatever happens, the abseiler **must not let go with the lower hand.**
3. The abseiler's feet are kept flat against the rock and more than shoulder width apart so that he doesn't overbalance.
4. The descent should be made as smoothly as possible, avoiding any jumping or sudden movements that might shock load the system.

Ascending

Ascending involves the rescuer using two prussik loops or mechanical ascenders to ascend a fixed rope. (Fig. 29.11). A klemheist or prussik knot is used for the knot that is attached to the harness because they do not release under load. A French prussik can be used for the stirrup, as in this case the ease of movement is an advantage.

1. The ascender stands up in the stirrup, loosens the harness prussik and slides it as far up the rope as it will go.
2. He bends his knee so that the weight comes slowly on to the harness, ensuring that the harness prussik is holding before committing his weight to it.
3. While sitting in the harness he lifts his stirrup leg and slides the stirrup prussik up the rope as far as it will go.
4. Stages 1-3 are repeated as often as is required.

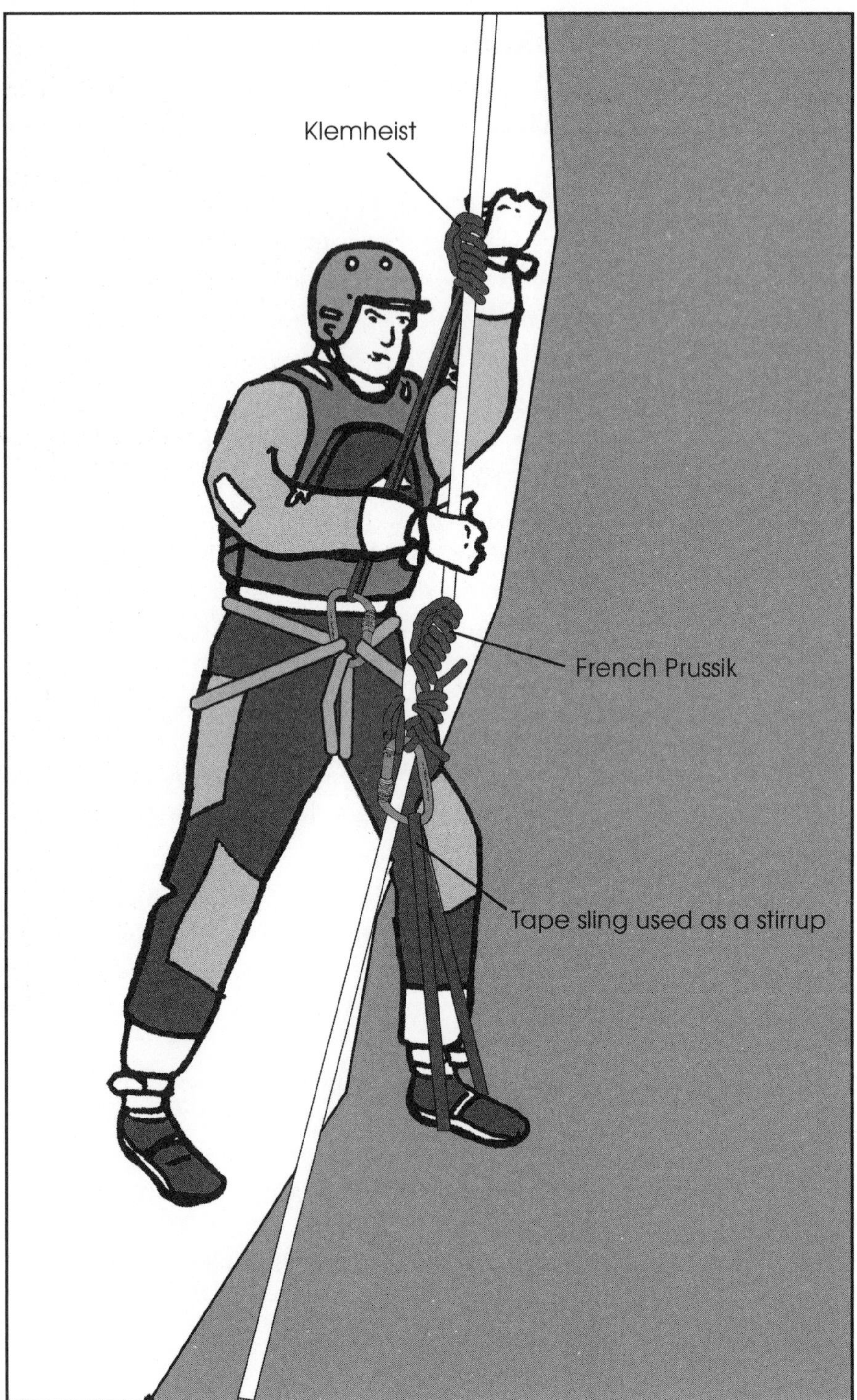

Fig. 29.11 Ascending, stage 1.

APPENDICES

Appendix A
Glossary of Terms

Air Bag A bag that is inflated with air through a valve so that it fills all the unused spaces in a kayak or canoe, and provides buoyancy in the event of a swamping.

Bight A loop of rope.

Bow The front end of a boat.

Broach When a boat is held sideways on against an obstruction by the force of the current.

Break In *'Eddy Out'* To paddle out of an eddy and into the main current.

Break Out *'Eddy In'* To paddle out of the main current and into an eddy.

CI A closed deck one person canoe. (The paddler uses a single bladed paddle and is kneeling).

Cow's Tail A short length of nylon tape, *'webbing'*, that extends from the chest harness attachment point on the back of a paddler's buoyancy aid, *'PFD'*,to the front, making it easier for the paddler to attach himself to a line.

Ferry Glide/Angle To paddle at an angle of 45° to the current so as not to lose ground whilst crossing a stretch of river.

Deep recirculating stopper. English for *'hydraulic'*.

Eddy Line or Fence The border between the calm or upstream flowing water in an eddy and the fast downstream flowing water in the main flow of the river.

End Grab or Loop A strong point on the end of a boat that can be used as a handle, or an attachment point for a recovery line.

Float Boat Any canoe or kayak that is not a squirt boat.

Gaffer Tape Strong, wide, 5 cm (2 inches) or more sticking tape, like carpet tape. Used by paddlers for all sorts of emergency repairs.

Gunwale The rim of an open canoe. Where the sides stop and the top or deck would start, if it had one.

'Hair Boater' Extreme white water paddler.

'Hole' American English for a surface stopper.

'Hydraulic' American English for a deep recirculating stopper.

Hypothermia Literally, too little heat. Cold injury sometimes referred to as 'exposure'.

Hyperthermia Literally, too much heat. Heat exhaustion and heat stroke.

Line Any piece of 'line', from the thinnest twine or string to the thickest rope.

Loom The shaft or handle of a paddle.

'Low Head Dam' American English for weir.

OCI A specialist white water open canoe, fitted out with a saddle and full length buoyancy bags and paddled by one person.

Outflow ***'Outwash'*** The water flowing out of a stopper.

Painter A length of line that is attached to the bow or stern of a boat. Traditionally used to tie the boat to the bank.

Play Hole A 'friendly' surface stopper, safe enough to play in.

Play Wave A well shape standing wave on which to hone one's surfing skills.

Portage To carry a boat around a rapid or obstacle.

Rope Thick line. For the purposes of this book, any line with a diameter of 8 mm or more.

Setting In To paddle into an eddy by reverse ferry gliding rather than forward paddling.

Squirt Boat Extremely low volume kayak or CI. There is so little buoyancy that the craft barely float, and spend as much time under the water as they do on the surface.

Thwart On an open canoe it is a length of wood or metal that spans the gap between the gunwales and strengthens the boat by keeping the sides apart. Though not specifically designed as such they can be used as seats. On a raft a thwart is an inflated tube that runs across the width of the raft and does the same job.

Towback ***'Backwash'*** The water that is flowing back into a stopper.

Siphon aka Sump Where the water has worn a pothole right through the bedrock and flows through this hole.

Stern The back end of a boat.

Stopper A vertically recirculating wave that can hold a boat or swimmer.

Strainer Any obstruction that has holes through which the current can flow but a swimmer can't. Strainers act like nets and are extremely dangerous.

Surface Stopper Standard English for *'hole'*.

Transom A flat square cut stern, as opposed to a 'canoe' or pointed stern.

Weir The Queen's English for *'low head dam'*.

Wrap Term used to describe what happens in a bad broach when a boat is 'wrapped' around the obstacle by the force of the water, often resulting in considerable damage.

Appendix B
Knots and Hitches

All knots or hitches that are tied on the end of a rope must have at least 30 cm of 'tail' left over. This is because, as knots are pulled tight, there is some slippage. A short tail could work its way through and the knot come undone.

All photos are by Bob Timms.

Figure of Eight on a Bight

This knot is used to create a loop or 'bight' on the end of a rope. It is the strongest knot that can be used for this job and is easier to untie after use than an overhand on a bight.

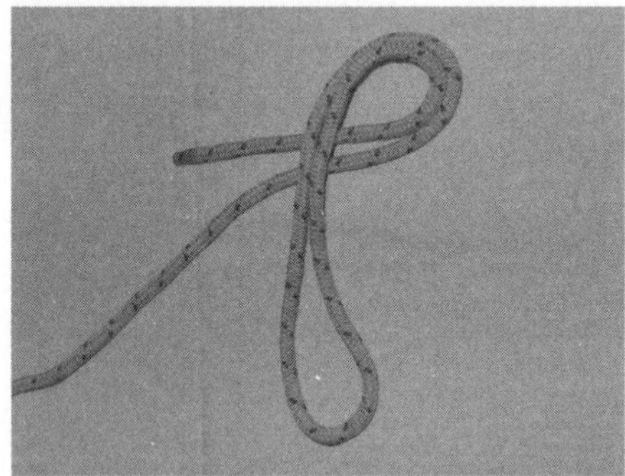

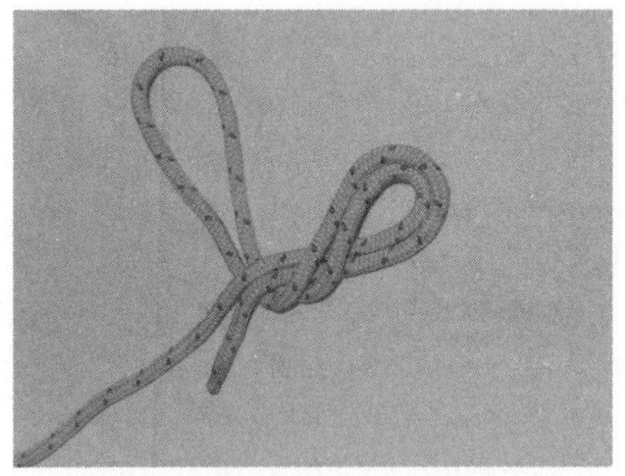

Overhand on a Bight

This knot is used to tie a loop away from the ends of a rope, where there may be a pull on both ends of the rope. A figure of eight tends to be pulled apart and weakened by this.

Other, more specialist knots that could be used are the in line figure of eight or the Alpine butterfly.

Re-Threaded Figure of Eight

This is simply a different way of tying a figure of eight on a bight so that it can be threaded through something, rather than be clipped in via a karabiner.

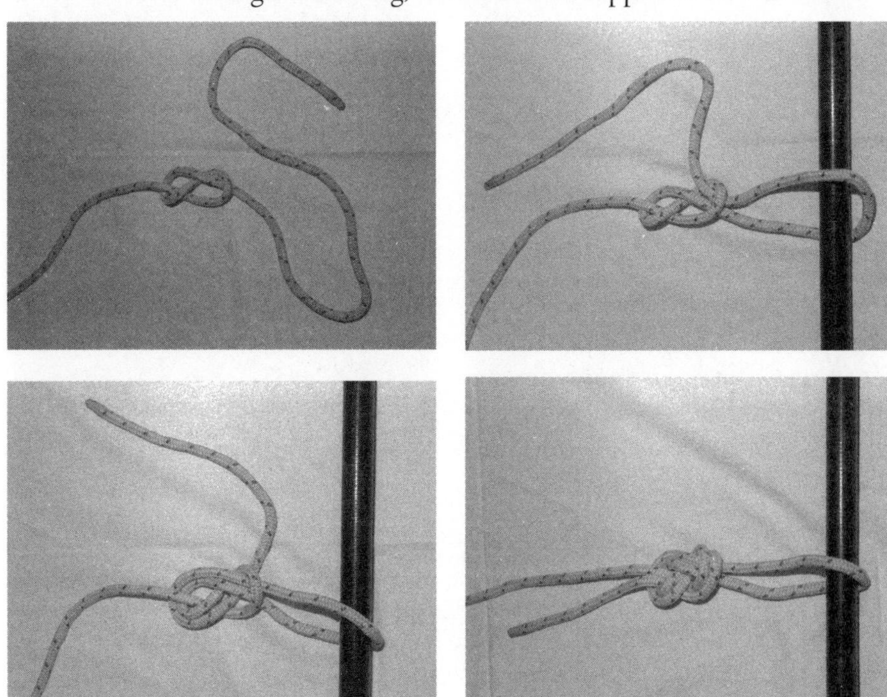

Overhand on a Double Rope

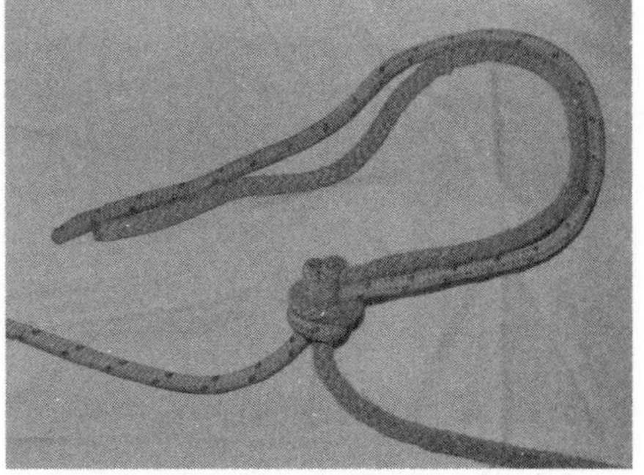

This is a fast and simple way to tie two ropes together. It also produces a knot that is easier to pass around or through karabiners and other obstructions than others. The only proviso is that at least 60 cm of tail must be left to prevent slippage.

An alternative is a double fisherman's knot.

Clove Hitch

A clove hitch can be adjusted without the need to take it out of the karabiner. It also encourages 'clean line' as hitches collapse as soon as they are removed from a karabiner.

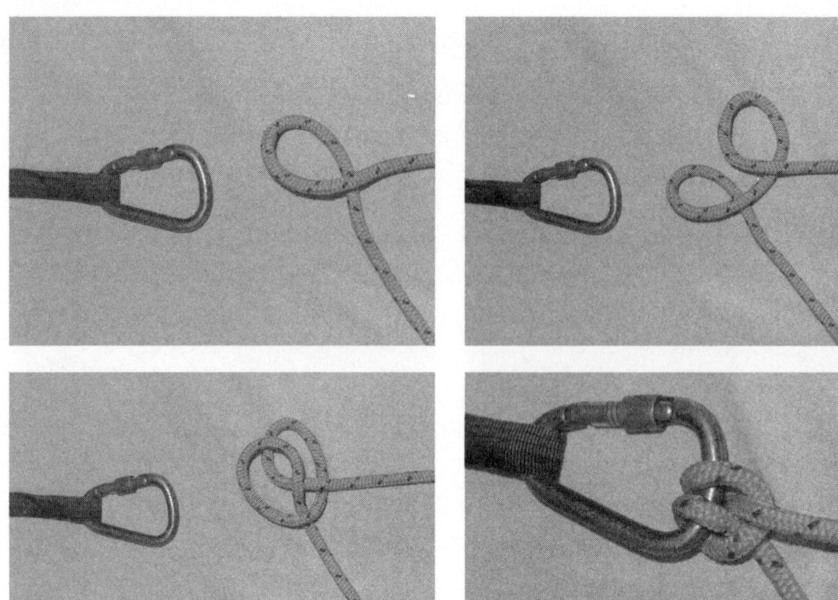

Italian or Munter Hitch

The Italian hitch is used for belaying, lowering, and abseiling, ('rappelling'). See also pages: 251-252.

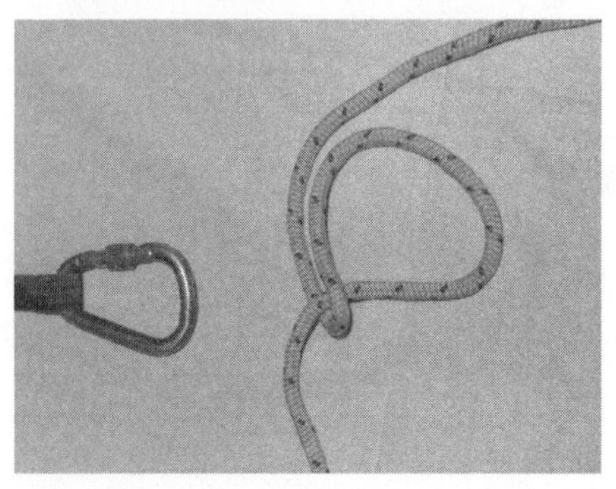

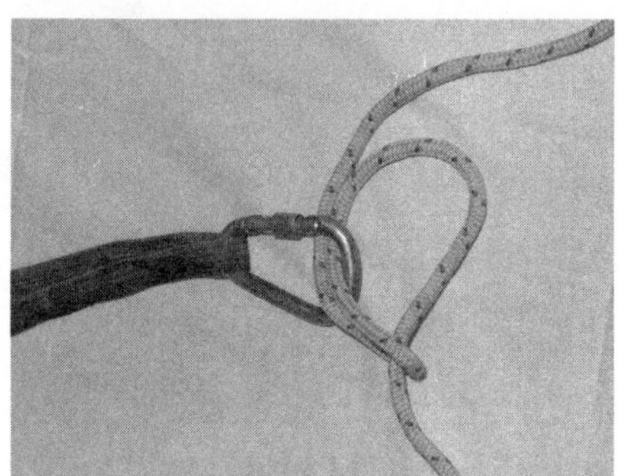

French Prussik

Simplicity itself! The prussik loop is wrapped around the rope 4-6 times depending on conditions and the ends of the loop are clipped together with a karabiner.

See also: pages 240-243.

Three Wrap Prussik

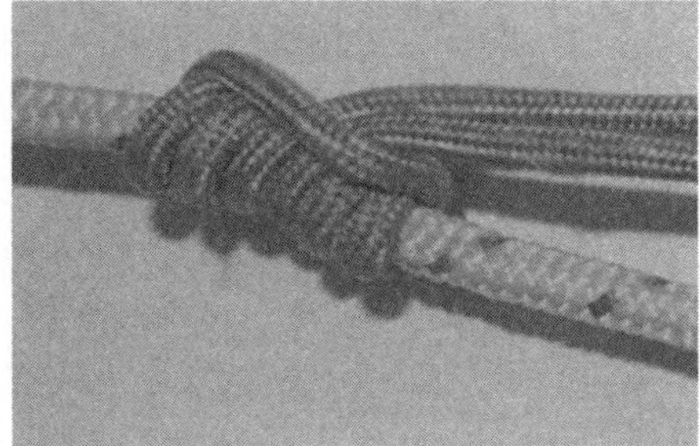

Klemheist

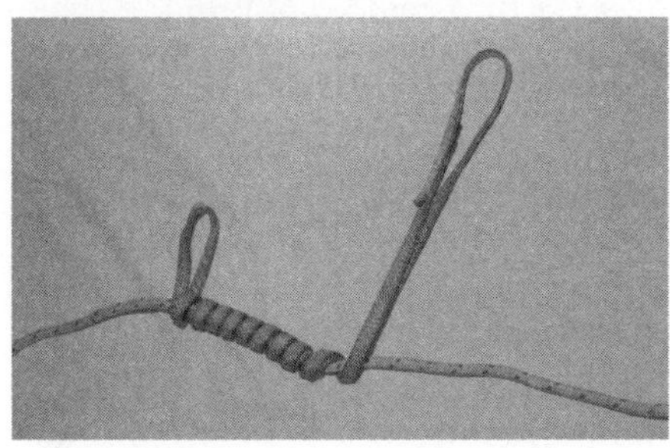
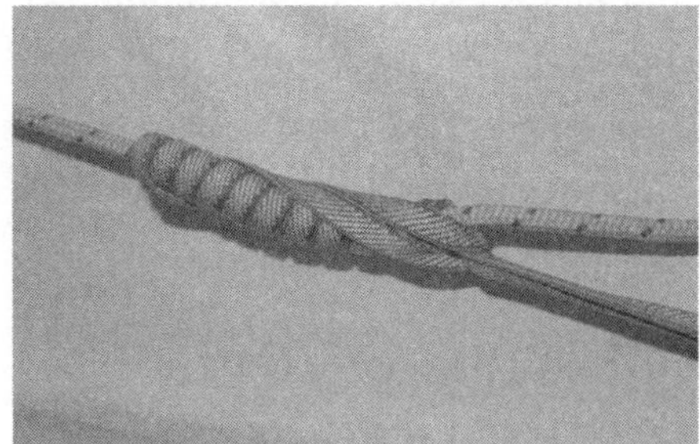

Tape Knot or Waterman's Knot

Leave at least 5 cm (2 inches) of tail and pull the knot as tight as you can after tying it. Check periodically to ensure that the knot doesn't work loose.

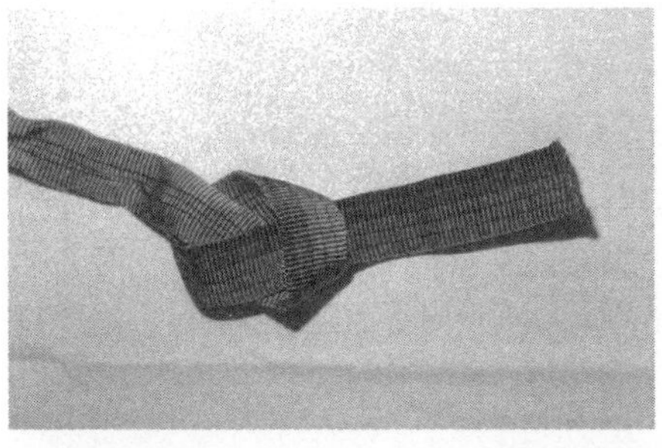

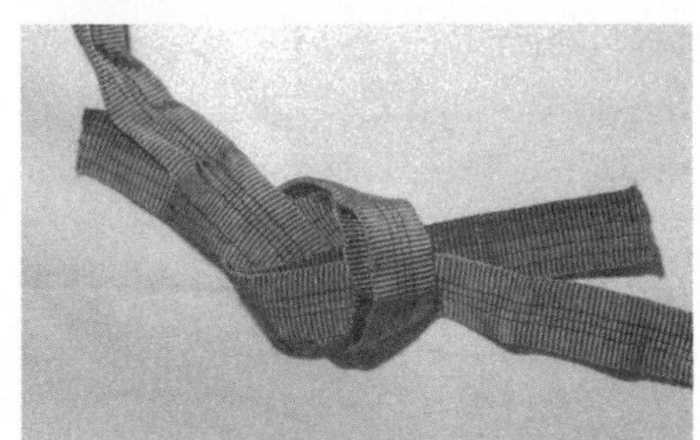

Appendix C
Briefing a Raft Crew

By Bob Timms

The key to a safe rafting trip is a cohesive disciplined and responsive crew. A guide has a very short space of time to knock a crew into shape. The initial briefing is critical. To help get it right the following mnemonic may help:

Safety-Have you given all the appropriate safety information for the intended trip and all the likely incidents (and not so likely) that may occur?

Atmosphere-Have you set the right atmosphere? You need to gain the crew's trust and respect. Give them an idea of what it's going to be like, but don't scare them so much with horror tales of what can go wrong that they are rigid with fear, and become excess baggage in the raft. Have a look at chapter 5 on mental preparation!

Techniques-Give them all the basic building blocks for paddling techniques; more complicated manoeuvres can be introduced on the water. Don't overload them too early with a vast array of manoeuvres and calls or they won't remember any of them.

Different Rigs

In an oar rig the guide does most of the work, and the crew are moving ballast used to trim the raft and keep it upright. The brief is likely to involve safe movement in the raft, bracing, dealing with swimmers, being a swimmer and flip drills.

A paddle raft involves a lot more crew participation and thus a lot more information.

The Briefing

The following is an outline brief for a paddle raft. Elsewhere in this book there is information on certain skills and techniques included in the brief. Any unique situations are discussed at the end of this section.

Introductions

1. Introduce yourself and your role. Ask about non swimmers and medical problems.
2. Introduce the raft, its safety features, different compartments and construction, hand lines, foot straps if appropriate and the dangers of

getting limbs trapped in the straps, drain gutters, under thwarts and hand lines.

Positions

Show how to sit correctly on the side tubes, not the thwarts, and how to brace one's self in the raft compartment. Then distribute the crew in the raft.

Paddles

Give the crew their paddles and explain the potential dangers of a 'T' grip without a hand on it. The hand makes a softer fleshy cover over the top of a very hard hammer-like weapon. Always keep the 'T' grip covered with the top hand because:

a. It is covered and does less damage if it does collide with someone.
b. With your hand on it, you are more aware of where it is and it won't be flailing around and liable to hit someone.

Basic Brace Position

Top hand holds 'T' grip, outside hand holds the hand line; lean in against the tension of the hand line towards the middle of the raft. Use a command word like 'Brace' or 'Hold on' and practice many times.

Paddling

1. Teach basic forward paddling. The two bow paddlers synchronise strokes by watching one another and everybody else follows the lead of the person in front of them.
2. Teach basic backwards paddling.
3. If the crew are coordinated enough introduce spinning the raft using their paddle power. One side paddle forward while the other paddles back. Get them to reach out away from the raft in a sweep stroke. Use the commands: 'Right back, Left forward'; i.e. everyone on the right, (facing the bow), paddle backwards and everyone on the left paddle backwards, and vice versa.

Crew first, direction second. The crew know which side of the raft they are on, and they will be listening for their side first. Practise this many times.

The crew now have the basic techniques to power the raft so go on to the trimming, bracing and safety techniques they need.

Enhanced Brace Positions

Practice the basic position again, now add tucking the chin in to the chest and bring the top 'T' grip hand down so that the forearm is across the stomach. This position is essential for stoppers or head on collisions. In the event of a violent jolt forward, the paddle shaft is out of the way to prevent face butting and the face is prevented from hitting the back of the helmet or person in front!

The ultimate brace is where the crew drop from their positions on the side tubes onto the floor of the raft between the thwarts facing forwards, chins tucked down, holding the hand lines with 'T' grip across the body. A must for stoppers which are steep and like a brick wall when you hit them.

It will take the crew time to return to their position afterwards, so it may not be the most practical thing to do in continuous powerful water where keeping the power on is more important!

High Sides

When a raft is in danger of broaching or flipping you need to move the weight of the crew to the high side of the raft to weight it and avoid a worse incident. (Chapter 3).

In practise it is best to shout 'high side' followed by 'left' or 'right' to avoid confusion and disorientation amongst the crew. Crew on the 'high side' throw their bodies over the tube as far as they can, grabbing the hand lines with the outside hand and wrapping the 'T' grip arm across the stomach. Crew on the 'low side' hurl themselves onto the high side tube into the gap in front of their opposite crew member, wrapping the 'T' grip arm across the stomach and the other hand grabbing the hand lines.

It is imperative that the 'T' grips remain held with normal hand as during the chaos of a high side it is very easy to 'chin' someone with an uncovered 'T' grip.

High sides should be practised many times until fast and slick.

High side bow is occasionally required where a steep backed stopper may pose the risk of a backwards flip. You might have to run such a stopper backwards; this requires the crew to turn around facing in and then backwards in the raft and hurling themselves to the rear of the raft on top of the guide who should be way over the rear tube.

Crew Overboard

Stress that, by listening and bracing when told, they will avoid being in the water, but that occasionally it can still happen.

Demonstrate the safe swimming position; (see Chapter 15), but with these raft specific points:

1. Emphasise a positive attitude, blowing out hard and shaking one's head on reaching the surface. Tell them to try to keep the paddle, but to ditch it if it is hindering them.
2. If close to the raft, they should grab a hand line, and a crew member or the guide will recover them. (Chapter 15).
3. If out of reach of the raft, either crew or swimmer reach out with a 'T' grip and pull them into the raft. If the swimmer is still out of reach,

both swimmer and rescuer can hook their 'T' grips together and pull the swimmer back to the raft. (Fig 15.4).

4. Introduce what to do when receiving a line from a rescuer.
5. The swimmer may be washed up onto a rock or into an eddy. He should stay there and not jump back in to get to the raft.
6. Ultimately every situation is different. Look to the guide to see and hear his directions. There may be a raft within the flotilla better positioned to effect a rescue. The swimmer may be about to be washed into a safe eddy or he may have to prepare for a longish but safe swim whilst the raft chases him.
7. Finally re-emphasise the importance of not standing up.

Guide Overboard

Explain what to do if the guide falls out; if he is having trouble getting in grab the bottom of the buoyancy aid, 'PFD', (not arms or shoulders) and drag him into the raft.

Flips

Explain what to do in the event of a flip. See Chapter 15.

Review and Rehearse

Re-run all the paddling, bracing, high siding exercises etc.

You may or may not have some easy water to warm up on. If you do then practise everything until it is slick. If it is warm enough and it won't compromise safety even rescuing swimmers can be practised!!

Down to You

Above all, make sure that the crew are as relaxed as possible and that you are approachable.

It is better for a crew member to tell you he is scared, then you can deal with it. If the crew don't perform don't yell abuse at them; it's more likely to be your fault than theirs!!

Communication On The Move.

The noise of the river and sometimes the squeals of the crew can mask the guide's commands. You must project your voice all the way to the front. The rest of the crew copy the bow paddlers, so if they don't respond, no one will.

Time your commands so that you give them when you are facing forward, not when you are finishing a sweep facing backwards. Where possible, eddy out above a rapid and pre-empt the commands by telling the crew what is likely to happen!!

Front Cover
Rob Hind gets a helping hand after a nasty swim on the Chimbu River, Papua New Guinea.
Photo: Waghi Kayak Expedition
Rear Cover
Top: OC1 running the Big Sandy Falls, West Virginia, USA.
Photo: John Moxham
Middle: Kayaker on the 'racecourse' section of the Ubaye, French Alps.
Bottom: Rafters on the Ubaye.
Photos: Bob Timms